Principles of Classroom Management

A Professional Decision-Making Model

Third Edition

James Levin

Pennsylvania State University

James F. Nolan

Pennsylvania State University

Allyn and Bacon

Boston • London • Toronto • Sydney • Tokyo • Singapore

Vice President, Editor in Chief, Education: Paul A. Smith
Editorial Assistant: Jill Jeffrey
Director of Education Programs: Ellen Mann Dolberg
Marketing Manager: Brad Parkins
Editorial-Production Administrator: Annette Joseph
Editorial-Production Coordinator: Holly Crawford
Editorial-Production Service: Karen Mason
Composition Buyer: Linda Cox
Manufacturing Buyer: Megan Cochran
Cover Administrator: Jenny Hart
Cover Designer: Brian Gogolin

Copyright © 2000, 1996, 1991 by Allyn & Bacon
A Pearson Education Company
160 Gould Street
Needham Heights, MA 02494
Internet: www.abacon.com

Between the time Website information is gathered and then published, it is not unusual for
some sites to have closed. Also, the transcription of URLs can result in unintended typograph-
ical errors. The publisher would appreciate notification where these occur so that they may be
corrected in subsequent editions. Thank you.

Library of Congress Cataloging-in-Publication Data
Levin, James
    Principles of classroom management : a professional decision-making model /
James Levin, James F. Nolan. — 3rd ed.
    p. cm.
    Includes bibliographical references and index.
    ISBN 0-205-28862-6
    1. Classroom management—United States—Problems, exercises, etc.
2. Teaching—United States—Problems, exercises, etc. I. Nolan, James F.
II. Title.
LB3013 .L475 2000
371.102'4—dc21   99-12693
                                              CIP

Printed in the United States of America
10 9 8 7 6   04 03 02

Photo Credits: Brian Smith: pp. 3, 27, 107; Will Hart: pp. 9, 22, 33, 65, 82, 85, 130, 156; Will
Faller: pp. 32, 42, 62; Stephen Marks: pp. 63, 153, 160.

**To
Sylvia and Herman Levin,
Jim and Mary Nolan,
Rocky and Andy**
*for their support,
encouragement,
and understanding*

Contents

SECTION III • *Managing Common Misbehavior Problems*

SECTION IV • *Managing Chronic Behavior Problems*

9 *Classroom Interventions for Chronic Problems* • **185**

10 *Seeking Outside Assistance* • **214**

Preface to the Third Edition

In the first edition of this text, we identified the two essential principles that provide the underpinnings for many of the concepts related to classroom management and positive classroom learning environments found here. The first principle states that learning is the responsibility of both the teacher and the student. The second principle states that to increase the likelihood of bringing about a change in student behavior, the teacher must first be willing to examine and change his or her own behavior. In the second edition of the text, we emphasized the success/failure ratio. Students who experience chronic behavior problems in schools are often unsuccessful in many other aspects of their lives. Because these students need to feel successful, they need a classroom learning environment in which all students experience genuine success. Recognizing that classroom behavior does not occur in a vacuum, our third principle states that if students are successful and enjoy positive relationships with adults, they are generally more interested in school, engaged in learning activities, and interact with their peers and teachers. These three principles—joint responsibility for behavior, the necessity of teacher behavior change in order to influence student behavior, and the importance of experiencing success—are the foundation for this third edition.

Relationship Building as the Foundation of Management

This edition of the text goes beyond the first two in its conviction that relationship building is a critical factor in managing student behavior and establishing classroom learning environments in which students can thrive. Too often classroom management is viewed as a purely technical matter. New teachers, and sometimes veteran teachers, are led to believe that there is some finite set of magical techniques that, when used properly, will turn the most disastrous classroom into a wonderful, high-powered learning environment. Although there are many management techniques that are powerful when used appropriately, there are no silver bullets. The creation of positive classroom learning environments is hard work and requires professional knowledge, thoughtfulness, patience, and consistency over time. At the heart of any classroom management system are the relationships that are established among the members of the classroom learning community.

As this edition of the text points out, relationship building is particularly important in dealing with students who exhibit chronic behavior problems. And yet, these students who are in the most need of positive relationships with their teachers are often the ones to whom, because of their behavior, teachers are least attracted. For many problem students, a positive relationship with a teacher may be the single positive relationship with an adult role model in their entire lives. When students perceive the classroom as a place where they are cared about and are physically and psychologically safe, they are likely to be cooperative, prosocial, and successful. However, these learning environments do not arise spontaneously. They result from the persistent hard work of teachers who have deep professional knowledge about human learning and behavior and who put that knowledge into practice. In our experience, the majority of chronically disruptive secondary students who choose to change their behavior do so because of the intervention of a single teacher who establishes a positive relationship with the student.

As you read this text and attempt to understand and apply the concepts you encounter, we hope that you will remember that one of the most powerful tools you possess for creating positive learning environments is your ability to establish supportive, personal relationships with your students.

We would like to thank the following reviewers for their helpful suggestions: Ralph Shibley of the University of Rio Grande and Brent L. Wendling of the University of Central Oklahoma.

Changes to the Third Edition

Accompanying the new emphasis on relationship building are a number of changes in the text of this edition. The five major revisions include:

1. An attempt to clarify the distinction between discipline problems and nondiscipline problems. We have provided multiple scenarios that help the reader to differentiate between the two. This distinction is important in deciding how to respond to problems in the classroom.
2. Updated statistics. We have updated the statistics on discipline problems in the schools, on the impact of discipline problems on teaching, and on societal problems that impact on schools, school violence, and classroom behavior.
3. A new section in Chapter 4 on student-directed management theories. In contrast to the old theories of student direction that were drawn from counseling and psychology, there is now a growing literature surrounding practical classroom strategies that can be used to provide students with more choice and direction in the learning environment. We have also changed the names of the theories of management from noninterventionist to student-directed, from interactionalist to collaborative, and from interventionist to teacher-directed. We believe these new labels portray the theories more accurately.
4. More information on cultural alienation and cultural resistance. We have attempted to convey how important it is for minority students to feel that their culture is valued and represented within the school, the curriculum, and the classroom.

5. We have reconceptualized Chapter 9. In addition to the three techniques for managing chronic behavior problems that were presented in Chapter 9 of the second edition, we are now offering two long-term strategies— relationship building and breaking the cycle of discouragement—for solving chronic behavior problems.

This edition also offers updated references, new case studies, and additional end-of-chapter exercises that support the use of this text in the classroom.

Preface to the Second Edition

In the preface to the first edition we recounted a first-year teaching experience of one of the authors that led him to two insights. First, learning is the responsibility of both the teacher and the student. Second, if a teacher wants a student's behavior to change, the teacher must first examine his or her own behaviors and be willing to change them to increase the likelihood that the student's behavior will change. These insights served as the foundation of the first edition and also served as the foundation of the second edition.

Success/Failure Ratio

An additional concept that we want readers to be mindful of as they study *Principles of Classroom Management: A Professional Decision-Making Model* is the success/failure ratio. Although first proposed over one hundred years ago (James, 1890), it remains somewhat obscure. The authors have recently realized its value in understanding disruptive students in order to work effectively with them, especially now at the end of the twentieth century when our schools are being called on to work with an ever-increasing number of disruptive, violent, and at-risk students.

The success/failure ratio is a theoretical construct equal to the algebraic sum of a student's perceived successes divided by the algebraic sum of his or her perceived failures. While this cannot be precisely calculated for any given student, it is a useful way to conceptualize how a student views himself or herself in a school setting. It is hypothesized that for the appropriately behaved child the success/failure ratio is greater than one; that is, the child perceives many more successes than failures. On the other hand, as Dr. Benson Gever, a colleague and a clinical child psychologist, said at a recent workshop, "Show me a disruptive child and I'll show you a child with a success/failure ratio less than one." In other words, it is hypothesized that the most disruptive students perceive many more failures than successes.

Traditional classroom management interventions such as detentions, public reprimands, removed privileges, suspensions, calls to parents, and failing grades seem to do little to motivate disruptive students toward appropriate behavior. In fact, these interventions seem to be viewed as additional failures by disruptive students, therefore decreasing the success/failure ratio even further. This second edition offers teachers a comprehensive approach to classroom management that does not rely on these types of interventions. We hope the reader is continually cognizant of the success/failure ratio for each of their students when putting the professional decision-making hierarchy of interventions into practice.

Changes to the Second Edition

Along with this newly suggested conceptualization, additions have been made to the book's content itself. These additions reflect recently published statistics, the latest research, and new ideas on classroom management that have been formulated since the publication of the first edition in 1991. The six major additions are the following:

1. Recent statistics demonstrate renewed public and teacher concern over the increased number of school discipline problems. These statistics indicate that violence, once rare in schools, now occurs with alarming frequency.
2. The findings of the American Psychological Association's study and review of fifty years of research on media violence and its influence on children's behavior are detailed.
3. The components of self-esteem are examined in order to provide teachers with a new understanding of students' internal motivations for both prosocial and disruptive behavior.
4. The content on effective teaching methodology has been expanded with the emphasis less on direct teacher instruction and more on students' engagement with higher-level cognitive tasks. The teacher is viewed as the "scaffold," coach, and guide while the students are placed in the role of constructors of knowledge. Methodologies discussed include teaching for understanding, using authentic learning tasks, teaching thinking and problem-solving skills, developing learning communities, teaching toward multiple intelligences, and using cognitive motivational theory.
5. Techniques have been added for creating group norms supporting student academic engagement and achievement with consideration for the many cultural backgrounds found in most of today's classrooms.
6. Five implementation guidelines are offered to assist teachers in choosing the most appropriate intervention from the decision-making hierarchy. Commonly used ineffective communication patterns are analyzed. Finally, a number of effective techniques that teachers can use to deliver logical consequences through a process of student choice are explained.

This second edition also offers more case studies and additional end-of-chapter exercises to assist the reader in understanding the concepts in the book.

Acknowledgments

The authors wish to acknowledge the contributions of many people who have helped with the completion of this book: Dr. Andrea Commaker, of Penn State's Multicultural Resource Center, for her excellent critical feedback, editing, and encouragement throughout the development of the book; Dr. Benson Gever, psychologist, whose years of working with children provided significant contributions to the final chapter; and Dr. Robert Shrigley, Professor of Education, Penn State University, for introducing us to the systematic study of classroom management.

We would also like to thank the following reviewers for their suggestions: Leo Anglin, Berry College; Cindy Kelley, West Virginia University—Parkersburg; and Doug Stanwyck, Kent State University.

As always, our thanks go to Rocky, Geoff, Daniel, Andy, Heidi, and Sarah for their understanding, interest, and encouragement. Finally, thanks to all the teachers, student teachers, and the many disruptive students who provided the real examples used throughout the text.

Reference

James, W. (1890). *Principles of Psychology* (2 vols.). New York: H. Holt and Company.

Preface to the First Edition

It was a warm sunny day in early June as I accepted my baccalaureate degree in engineering with a certificate to teach mathematics in the state's secondary public schools. The next day I was interviewed at the school administration building of a very large urban school district. Within a few days I was notified that, starting in September, I was to be a junior high school mathematics teacher.

The following week I met with the principal of the inner city school. The principal informed me that the school was the largest junior high in the city and one of the largest in the nation, with an enrollment of approximately 3,500 students. It served a blue-collar community, with an ethnic background equally divided among whites, blacks, and Hispanics. Classes were large, averaging approximately 35 students, but absenteeism was prevalent. The principal warned me that many of the students were low achievers and that the school had more than its share of discipline problems. He stressed that the school needed dedicated teachers and assigned me to teach four classes of eighth-grade general math and one class of ninth-grade algebra.

Over the summer I thought about what teaching would be like. How could I not do a good job? After all I graduated from the same urban district. I was tough and felt that I could handle teenagers. Also, my engineering degree provided me with the knowledge to relate mathematics to the students' lives; something I learned was necessary for effective teaching in my educational psychology class.

I arrived early the first day of classes and was met by the assistant principal. After welcoming me to the staff, she informed me that throughout the year she would observe my classes and work closely with me to help improve my teaching. With seating charts, a list of rules, and a lesson plan that contained activities that I knew would capture my students' attention, I was ready to become a teacher.

As soon as school was in session, the vice-principal visited at least one of my classes every week. The visits were always followed by an after-school conference, during which we discussed the observations that she made and plans for future classes. She was quite observant in noting both my and the students' behaviors in class, many of which I was unaware of. She continually stressed that teachers must not only be aware of their behavior, but how their behaviors affected students' behaviors.

One result of these conferences was that I began to watch other teachers, and particularly the vice-principal, as they interacted with students. I noticed that she commanded the students' respect as no one else in the school.

As November arrived I was quite pleased with all my classes except my fifth-period eighth-grade general math class. Students were constantly unprepared, out of their seats, calling out, and disturbing others. In other words, this class was out of control. I tried talking to them and reasoning with them. Then I began to scream, give detentions, and exclude students from class; but nothing seemed to work. This class began to ruin my day. It made me nervous, frustrated, and doubtful about my effectiveness as a teacher.

On numerous occasions the vice-principal visited this class, noted how disruptive the students were, and continually asked how I planned on handling the situation. Finally, around Thanksgiving, during one of our conferences, I reluctantly confessed to her that I needed help with my fifth-period class. She said that she was waiting for me to realize that the class was not improving. Using her notes from past observations, we began to discuss my own and the students' behaviors in the class.

She pointed out that I began class when the bell rang no matter what the students were doing. After a few moments I would reprimand a few students and demand that they sit. This resulted in only a few additional minutes of quiet before the next disruption exploded. She also pointed out that I always reminded them, "I have material to cover, and I can't cover it if you don't stop fooling around!" She stressed that I was continually competing with my students and appeared to feel totally responsible for their learning. She asked if I was willing to begin to change my teaching behavior. I eagerly answered, "Yes!"

She suggested that I go to class prepared to teach as usual and when the bell rang start the lesson. She further suggested that as soon as the class interfered with my ability to teach, stop, and not saying a word, sit down at my desk. With a smile on my face, I told her that this would play right into the students' hands because this would allow them to engage in disruptive behavior during the entire class without any teacher reprimands. She reassured me by pointing out that what I had been doing wasn't working, so it was time for new approaches. She asked that I try it, and report back to her with the results.

The next day I employed these new techniques. I taught for only five minutes when the class became disruptive. As I had predicted, when I stopped teaching the students proceeded to walk around the room talking and kidding with each other for the rest of the forty-five-minute period.

Upon hearing this, the vice-principal asked me to please use the same strategy the next day. I did, and as on the previous day, within five to ten minutes I was sitting at my desk. However, by the end of class a significant change took place. A student came up to my desk and said, "Aren't you going to teach us any math?" I replied, "Yes. I'm ready to teach, but I can't when the class behaves the way it does." When I reported this event to her she was very pleased and told me that she felt the technique was beginning to have an effect. She requested that I continue to employ the same strategy.

The next day, I was able to teach for about 20 minutes before I had to sit down. But unlike the previous days, by the last ten minutes of class, the students were ending their conversations and most of the class was in their seats. When I observed this, I began to teach again. To my surprise, the next day I had to stop my teaching for only five minutes in the middle of the period.

Throughout the year, my fifth-period class continued to be my most troublesome, but the class never returned to the way it was earlier in the year. Whenever their behavior reached a point that disrupted either my teaching or the students' learning, I stopped teaching and without my having to say a word, within minutes the disruption ceased.

This early experience in teaching taught me two important lessons. First, don't compete with your students or assume the full responsibility for their learning. Learning is a dual responsibility of both student and teacher. Second, if teachers want students' behaviors to change, they must first examine their own behavior and be willing to change any inappropriate or ineffective ones. These lessons have stayed with me throughout my teaching career and have assisted me in shaping my philosophy of classroom management. It is these two concepts that serve as the foundation of this book.

Throughout this book case studies have been used extensively to illustrate classroom management principles and techniques. Each of these cases is drawn from actual classroom experiences of the authors, who have combined experiences of over seventeen years of classroom teaching in rural, suburban, and urban schools and over eighteen years supervising hundreds of in-service and preservice teachers in hundreds of different classrooms. This book is a practical, eclectic approach to classroom management based on both theory and practice.

The Basics

The Basics
Conceptualizing the Process of Teaching • Understanding Classroom Management
Principles • Understanding the Professional Decision-Making Hierarchical Approach

Principles of Classroom Management

1. The single most important factor in determining the learning environment is teacher behavior. Intentionally or unintentionally, teachers' verbal and nonverbal behaviors influence student behaviors.
2. Teachers have the professional responsibility for assuming the role of instructional leader, which involves employing techniques that maximize student on-task behavior.
3. Teachers who have clearly developed ideas of: (a) the relationship between teaching and discipline; (b) the factors motivating student behavior; (c) their own personal expectations for student behavior; and (d) a systematic plan to manage misbehavior have classrooms characterized by a high percentage of on-task student behavior.
4. A preplanned decision-making hierarchy of management strategies increases the likelihood of appropriate student behavior.

Introduction

Many years ago we both had the opportunity to take a graduate class on classroom management. It was our first formalized instruction in this area. At that time not much research had been conducted on the subject of classroom management. Even with this limitation the instructor did an excellent job of organizing what was available into a systematic approach for managing disruptive behavior.

Throughout the course, however, students continually asked the instructor to define teaching and explain how teaching and classroom management were related. Unfortunately, the instructor was never able to give a satisfactory answer, which disturbed many students. Questions about the relationship between teaching and classroom management continually arose: Should a teacher plan objectives for classroom management in her[1] lesson plan? How do various teaching strategies increase or reduce the likelihood of disruptive behavior? Should a student's grades be affected by misbehavior?

---

[1] To foster equality without being cumbersome, gender pronouns will be alternated by chapter. Chapter 1 will have female pronouns; Chapter 2, male; Chapter 3, female; and so forth.

The lack of a definition of teaching not only plagued this class but also several other education courses. Even today many books on classroom management and many teachers who use various management techniques lack a clear definition of teaching. This is most unfortunate because teaching and classroom management cannot exist independently of each other.

Therefore we begin by setting forth a definition of teaching and explaining how classroom management is part of the teaching process. The rest of this chapter presents a structural overview of the book. First, we present the principles of management that form the book's foundation. Second, we provide an explanation of the decision-making hierarchical approach to management. Last, we offer a flowchart of the knowledge, skills, and techniques that make up a management hierarchy and result in successful classrooms in which teachers are free to teach and students are free to learn.

Defining the Process of Teaching

Each year colleges and universities educate and graduate thousands of students who then enter the teaching profession. All of these new teachers have accumulated many credit hours of coursework in their chosen area of specialization, in professional knowledge, in methodology, and in practical experiences. Armed with this background, they enter classrooms and teach for an average of almost 20 years (National Education Association, 1997).

Even with this background, however, many teachers, seasoned professionals as well as recent graduates, are unable to provide an adequate operational definition of teaching. Some argue that a formal definition is not necessary because they have been teaching for years and whatever they do seems to work. For those of us who consider teaching a professionally sophisticated endeavor, however, experience, although invaluable in many teaching situations, is not the only thing that should be used to develop and plan instruction. Furthermore, this "gut-reaction" approach is sorely limited when the old "proven methods" seem not to work and there is a need for modifying or developing new instructional or management strategies. Others, when asked, define teaching as the delivery, transference, or giving of knowledge or information. Definitions like these give no clue to how knowledge is transferred and what strategies are used to deliver it. They limit teaching to only the cognitive domain, thus fail to recognize the extraordinary level of competence needed for making hundreds of daily content and pedagogical knowledge-based decisions in complex and dynamic classroom environments.

Teaching always has emphasized the cognitive domain. However, when teaching is viewed as concerned solely with cognitive development, teachers limit their effectiveness in managing students who exhibit disruptive behavior. Disruptive students often need growth and development in the affective domain, such as cooperating with others, valuing others' viewpoints, volunteering, and developing motivation and interest, as well as in cognitive areas. Teachers who understand the critical nature of the affective domain are in a much better position to work with disruptive students.

Through careful lesson planning, teachers can design strategies that have an increased probability of gaining students' interests and preventing discipline problems.

Indeed, many exceptional teachers actually approach their work with the attitude that the reason students need teachers is because there are behaviors that seriously interfere with teaching and learning (Haberman, 1995). Teachers with this attitude are better prepared to work effectively with disruptive students. They do not get as frustrated or feel as if they are wasting their time because they understand that teaching is helping students to mature not only cognitively but also affectively.

When teaching is defined, teachers have a clearer perception of what behaviors constitute the practice of their profession. Before we present our formal definition, however, we must consider an important assumption that underlies it. One of the major tenets of Adlerian psychology is that each individual makes a conscious choice to behave in certain ways, either desirable or undesirable (Sweeney, 1981). Building on this tenet, we believe that individuals cannot be forced to change their behavior; they must choose to do so. Therefore, individuals cannot be forced to learn or to exhibit appropriate behavior. In other words, teachers do not control student behavior. Students control their own behaviors. If this idea is accepted, it follows that a teacher changes student behavior only by *influencing* the change through changes in her own behavior, which is the only behavior over which she has total control. In the classroom, then, a teacher is continually involved in a process in which student behavior is monitored and compared with the teacher's idea of appropriate behavior for any given instructional activity. When actual student behavior differs from appropriate student behavior, the teacher attempts to influence a change in student behavior by changing her own behavior. The behavior the teacher decides to employ should be one that maximizes the likelihood that student behavior will change in the appropriate way. The probability of choosing the most effective behavior increases when teachers have a professional knowledge of instructional techniques, cognitive psychology, and child development and use it to guide the modification of their own behavior (Brophy, 1988).

With this background, we can define teaching as *the use of preplanned behaviors, founded in learning principles and child development theory and directed toward both instructional delivery and classroom management, that increase the probability of affecting a positive change in student behavior.* The significance of this definition in trying to change any student's behavior is threefold. First, teaching is concerned with what the teacher controls, her own behavior, and this behavior is preplanned. Teaching is not a capricious activity. Second, the preplanned behaviors are determined by the teacher's professional knowledge. This knowledge guides the teacher in selecting appropriate behaviors. It is the application of this specialized body of professional knowledge and knowing why it works that makes teaching a profession (Tauber and Mester, 1994). Third, many teaching behaviors are well founded in professional knowledge. The teacher's challenge is to select those behaviors that increase the probability that a corresponding behavioral change will take place in the student. For this to occur, the teacher not only must know the students' initial behaviors but also have a clear picture of desired student behaviors for any given instructional activity.

The emphasis on the use of professional knowledge to inform teacher behavior is critical. The public should expect no less from teachers than it does from physicians, engineers, or other professionals. When a physician is asked why she performed a certain procedure, we expect her answer to be more scientifically based than "It seemed like a good thing to do at the time" or "It worked before." If teaching is a profession, teachers must understand and be able to explain the research and philosophies that lie behind their teaching decisions. If a teacher is asked why she interacted with a student in a particular manner or why she used a particular instructional strategy, her response should be based in pedagogical or psychological research, theory, or methodology.

CASE 1.1 • *Getting Students to Respond*

Ms. Kelly believes that students must actively participate in class activities for learning to take place. She prides herself on her ability to design questions from all levels of the cognitive domain; she believes that students benefit and enjoy working with questions that require analysis, synthesis, and evaluation. However, she is sorely disappointed because very few students have been volunteering to answer questions and those that have have given very brief answers.

Observation of Ms. Kelly's class indicates a fairly regular pattern of behaviors during questioning. Standing in front of the class, she asks the first question: "Students, we have been studying the westward movement of pioneers during the 1800s. Why do you think so many thousands of people picked up and moved thousands of miles to a strange land knowing that they would face incredible hardship and suffering during the long trip?" Two hands shoot up. Ms. Kelly immediately calls on Judy. "Judy, why do you think they went?" "They wanted new opportunities," she answers. Ms. Kelly immediately replies "Great answer. Things where they lived must have been so bad that they decided

that it was worth the hardships that they would face. In a new land they would have a new beginning, a chance to start over. Another thing might be that some of the pioneers might not have realized how difficult the trip would be. Do you think that the hardships continued even after the pioneers arrived in Oregon and California? Ted."

After discussion, Ms. Kelly realizes how her behaviors are affecting student behavior. Instead of increasing participation, they actually hinder participation. After further discussions and reading about questioning strategies, Ms. Kelly decides to change her questioning behavior. She begins to ask questions from different locations throughout the room. She also waits three to five seconds before calling on any student. After a student answers, she again waits at least three seconds and then points out the salient parts of the response, rephrases another question using the student's response, and directs this question to the class.

As before, her behaviors affect student behavior. However, this time more students volunteer initially, responses are longer, and additional students are willing to expand on initial answers.

Case 1.1 illustrates the application of the definition of teaching to instructional delivery. Ms. Kelly was aware of the present student behavior and had a clear picture of what she wanted the behavior to become during questioning. To effect this change she analyzed her behaviors and how they affected her students. Because changes in teacher behavior influence changes in student behavior, the former is often termed "affecting behavior" and the sought-after student behavior is termed "target behavior" (Boyan and Copeland, 1978). Using her professional knowledge, Ms. Kelly modified her behavior to improve her practice of teaching and bring about the target behavior. The behaviors she chose to employ were well founded in the educational literature on questioning methodology (see Chapter 5). Ms. Kelly performed as a professional.

CASE 1.2 • *"Why Study? We Don't Get Enough Time for the Test Anyway!"*

Mr. Fox has a rule that test papers will not be passed out until all students are quiet and in their seats with all materials, except a pencil, under the desk. He explains this to the class before every test. Without fail he has to wait five to ten minutes before everyone in the class is ready. Typically, some students complain: "Why do we have less time just because a few other kids take their good old time?" Sometimes students will get visibly angry, saying, "This isn't fair," "This is stupid," or "Why study? We don't get enough time for the test anyway!" Mr. Fox dreads test days.

During a discussion of this situation with another teacher, Mr. Fox is introduced to the concept of logical consequences; in other words, allowing students to experience a logically related consequence of their behavior. Employing this concept, Mr. Fox announces to the class that he will pass out tests on an individual basis. "Once you are ready, you receive a test." He walks down the aisles giving students who are ready a test paper and passing by without comment those who are not. As a result of his changed behavior, student behavior changes. Complaining stops, and in a few minutes, more students are ready to take the test.

Case 1.2 illustrates the relationship between teacher behavior and targeted student behavior in classroom management.

Like Ms. Kelly, Mr. Fox changed his behavior to one that reflected a well-accepted educational practice. With this change came corresponding changes in student behavior.

How do teachers become aware of the methodology and theory to support their behaviors and from where do the methodology and theory come? The methodology and theory is generated by research, often conducted by educational psychologists in controlled laboratory settings. Their findings are then applied to classroom situations, where they may or may not be applied properly and may or may not result in expected outcomes. Research about teaching moved into the modern era only within the last 35 years. When reliable, replicable studies began to be conducted in actual classrooms with real teachers (Berliner, 1984), research developed rapidly. Indeed, research now shows that a set of teacher behaviors, referred to as effective teaching or effective instruction, is present in many classrooms in which noteworthy gains in achievement are made by students. Teachers need to incorporate these behaviors into their daily instruction. They may do so by becoming thoroughly familiar with the professional literature that synthesizes and summarizes the research (see also Chapter 5). Some teachers may prefer a more experiential approach. These individuals may wish to participate in many of the formalized workshops that use the research to develop effective teaching practices, such as Madeline Hunter's "Essential Elements of Instruction," Phi Delta Kappa's "Teacher Expectations/Student Achievement Program," and the Association for Supervision and Curriculum Development's "Dimensions of Learning" and "Multiple Intelligences," to name a few.

Although not as plentiful, there now is a body of knowledge concerning effective classroom management (Emmer et al., 1997; Evertson et al., 1997; Kounin, 1970; Redl and Wineman, 1952). As stressed throughout this book, effective classroom management is inseparable from effective instruction. Without effective instructional practices, teachers are unlikely to be able to maintain successfully appropriate student behavior. However, although effective instruction is absolutely necessary, it is not in itself sufficient to guarantee that classrooms are free from disruptive behavior. Even the best teachers experience some disruptive behavior.

Principles of Classroom Management

As a result of the research on classroom management, a number of well-accepted principles governing teacher behavior to prevent and manage disruptive behavior have emerged. Some of these principles are quite specific to a particular philosophical underpinning (see Chapter 4), whereas others are philosophically generic. This book presents 38 generic principles of classroom management developed through years of experience, research, and study. Each of the remaining nine chapters emphasizes some of these principles and discusses in detail how they may be incorporated by the teacher into effective management practices.

The following paragraphs summarize the contents of each chapter and its relevant principles. These paragraphs are followed by an explanation of the decision-making hierarchical approach to managing classroom behavior. Just as it is good classroom practice to provide the learner with an anticipatory set before in-depth instruction, these sections provide the reader with the scope, sequence, and structure of this textbook.

Chapter 2 discusses the nature of the discipline problem. First, there is a review of the limitations of current definitions of what behaviors constitute a discipline problem. These limitations are rectified by offering a new operational definition of the term *discipline problem.* This definition is then used to classify common classroom behaviors. Second, misbehavior is analyzed historically by frequency and type to determine what schools are like today. Finally, research concerning the effect of disruptive behavior on both teachers and students is presented.

The related principles of classroom management are the following:

A discipline problem exists whenever a behavior interferes with the teaching act, interferes with the rights of others to learn, is psychologically or physically unsafe, or destroys property.

For effective teaching to take place, teachers must be competent in managing student misbehavior so as to maximize the time spent on learning.

Teachers who manage their classrooms effectively enjoy teaching more and have greater confidence in their ability to affect student achievement.

Chapter 3 explores the underlying complex causes of misbehavior and provides multiple reasons for why children misbehave. Societal changes have created an environment vastly different from that in which children of previous generations grew up. How these out-of-school changes have influenced children's attitudes and behaviors is examined first.

Like adults, children have strong personal, social, and academic needs. At the same time, they undergo rapid cognitive and moral development. The chapter goes on to describe typical behaviors associated with children's attempts to meet their needs as well as normal developmental behaviors. Behaviors that may appear when the home or school fails to recognize and respond to these needs and developmental changes are detailed.

We emphasize that the teacher has little control over many of the changes that occur in society and in children. However, she does have total control over her instructional competence. Excellent instruction is a significant way to lessen the effects of uncontrollable factors and to prevent misbehavior.

The following principles may be found in Chapter 3:

An awareness of the causes of misbehavior enables teachers to use positive control techniques rather than negative techniques, which stem from erroneously viewing misbehavior as a personal affront.

Basic human needs such as food, safety, belonging, and security are prerequisites for appropriate classroom behavior.

The need for a sense of significance, competence, virtue, and power influences student behavior.

Societal changes beyond the schools' control greatly influence student behavior.

Cognitive and moral developmental changes result in normal student behavior that often is disruptive in learning environments.

Instructional competence can lessen the effects of negative outside influences as well as prevent the misbehavior that occurs as a result of poor instruction.

Chapter 4 describes three theoretical models of classroom management. A series of nine questions help the teacher to define her beliefs about classroom management. These questions are then used to analyze, compare, and contrast the three models. It is the teacher's underlying beliefs concerning how children learn and develop and who has the primary responsibility for controlling a child's behavior that determine which model provides the best fit.

Different management strategies are presented as either compatible or incompatible with certain schools of thought. When teachers employ behaviors that are inconsistent with their beliefs about children, they feel emotionally uncomfortable and usually do not see the desired change in student behavior.

Teachers exert influence through the use of five different social power bases. In this chapter, each power base is placed along a continuum, which begins with those power bases most likely to engender students' control over their own behavior and proceeds to those bases that foster increasing teacher management over student behavior. The chapter concludes with a discussion of teacher behaviors that are congruent with the various power bases.

Many teachers keep up to date on the latest techniques by attending professional development workshops.

The principles of classroom management contained in Chapter 4 are the following:

Theoretical approaches to classroom management are useful to teachers because they offer a basis for analyzing, understanding, and managing student and teacher behavior.

As social agents, teachers have access to a variety of power bases that can be used to influence student behavior.

The techniques a teacher employs to manage student behavior should be consistent with the teacher's beliefs about how students learn and develop.

Chapter 5 explores the effective instructional techniques used by the professional teacher. Effective teaching prevents most discipline problems. The discussion of effective teaching is divided into two parts. The first part, The Basics of Effective Teaching, describes the knowledge gained from research on teacher effects. This research focuses on teacher behaviors that facilitate student achievement on lower-level cognitive tasks as measured by paper and pencil tests. The second section of the chapter, Beyond the Basics, describes more recent conceptualizations of teaching and learning, which focus on student cognition and higher-order cognitive learning tasks.

Chapter 5 emphasizes the following two principles:

Student learning and on-task behavior are maximized when teaching strategies are based on what educators know about student development, how people learn, and what constitutes effective teaching.

Understanding and using the research on effective teaching enhance the teacher's instructional competence and help to prevent classroom management problems.

Chapter 6 details how to structure the environment to minimize disruptive behavior. Many classroom management problems arise because students are either unaware of or unclear about what types of behaviors are expected of them or why certain procedures must be followed in the classroom. This lack of awareness usually occurs when the teacher herself is unclear about how and why she wants her students to behave. Thus, developing meaningful classroom guidelines is extremely necessary.

The procedures for designing classroom guidelines are presented, with emphasis on the importance of having both a rationale and stated consequences for each rule. Techniques to communicate guidelines to students in a way that maximizes understanding and acceptance are offered.

This chapter also discusses the influence of cultural background on both teacher and student values, norms, and expectations for appropriate behavior. In addition, the chapter advocates the use of cooperative learning activities and the teaching of social skills as techniques for creating classroom group norms that are supportive of prosocial behavior and student engagement in learning activities.

The principles of Chapter 6 include the following:

When environmental conditions are appropriate for learning, the likelihood of disruptive behavior is minimized.

Students are more likely to follow classroom guidelines if the teacher models appropriate behavior and explains the relationship of the guidelines to learning, mutual student–teacher respect, and protection and safety of property and individuals.

Clearly communicating guidelines to students and obtaining their commitment to following them enhances appropriate classroom behavior.

Enforcing teacher expectations by using natural and logical consequences helps students to learn that they are responsible for the consequences of their behavior and thus are responsible for controlling their own behavior.

When classroom guidelines and rules match the culture of students' homes and communities, the likelihood that students will behave appropriately is increased.

When the teacher creates group norms that are supportive of engagement in learning activities, the likelihood that students will behave appropriately is increased.

Chapters 7 and 8 explore the management of common misbehaviors through the use of a three-tiered hierarchical decision-making model of nonverbal and verbal behaviors called coping skills.

Research reviewed in Chapter 7 reveals that the majority of misbehaviors are verbal interruptions, off-task behavior, and disruptive physical movements. The frequency of these surface disruptions can be greatly reduced with proper planning, instructional strategies, environmental structure, and verbal and nonverbal teacher behaviors.

Chapter 7 covers the first tier of the decision-making hierarchy. It discusses the appropriate use and limitations of four nonverbal coping skills: planned ignoring, signal interference, proximity interference, and touch interference. The chapter includes an intervention decision-making model that hierarchically orders nonverbal behaviors teachers can use to manage student behavior. The hierarchy begins with those nonintrusive techniques that give students the greatest opportunity to control their own behaviors and proceeds to intrusive strategies in which the teacher assumes more responsibility for managing student behavior. Five implementation guidelines are also presented.

Chapter 7 covers the following principles:

Classroom management techniques need to be consistent with the goal of helping students to become self-directing individuals.

Use of a preplanned hierarchy of remedial interventions improves the teacher's ability to manage misbehavior.

The use of a hierarchy that starts with nonintrusive, nonverbal teacher behaviors gives students the opportunity to exercise self-control, minimizes disruption to the teaching/learning process, reduces the likelihood of student confrontation, protects students' safety, and maximizes the teacher's management alternatives.

Chapter 8 discusses in detail the second and third tiers of the decision-making hierarchy, verbal intervention and the application of logical consequences. Twelve verbal intervention techniques are presented along with nine guidelines for their appropriate use as well as their limitations. Once again these techniques are ordered along a continuum that ranges from nonintrusive student control to intrusive teacher management of behavior. The use of verbal intervention is founded on the assumption that teachers do have effective alternatives to angry, personal, sarcastic confrontations with students. Such alternatives typically defuse rather than escalate misbehavior.

The third tier of the decision-making hierarchy, the use of logical consequences, is a powerful technique in managing student behavior. The concept of logical consequences is explained in detail along with the guidelines teachers use to develop effective logical consequences for a wide range of misbehavior. The assertive delivery of logical consequences is also discussed.

These are the principles dealt with in Chapter 8:

When nonverbal teacher intervention does not lead to appropriate student behavior, the teacher should employ verbal intervention to deal with the misbehavior.

Some forms of verbal intervention defuse confrontation and reduce misbehavior; other forms of verbal intervention escalate misbehavior and confrontation.

When verbal intervention does not lead to appropriate student behavior, the teacher needs to apply logical consequences to the student's misconduct.

Chapter 9 looks at classroom interventions for students with chronic problems. Two long-term problem-solving strategies—relationship building and disrupting the cycle of discouragement—are presented along with three techniques for managing behavior. Most strategies used with chronic behavior problems involve referral outside the classroom. However, there are three effective field-tested, in-classroom techniques: self-monitoring, behavior contracting, and anecdotal record keeping. The effective use of these three techniques assumes that the teacher's classroom behaviors have met the prerequisites discussed in previous chapters and reviewed here. The step-by-step implementation of these techniques is explained specifically, and a detailed discussion of the critical communication skills that can make the difference in successful management of chronic misbehavior is presented. Lastly, teacher-controlled exclusion from the classroom, an interim step between in-classroom management and outside referral, is explained.

The following principles are a part of Chapter 9:

When dealing with students who pose chronic behavior problems, teachers should employ strategies to resolve the problems within the classroom before seeking outside assistance.

Finding positive qualities in students who have chronic behavior problems and building positive relationships with them increase the possibility that the problems can be resolved within the classroom.

Breaking the cycle of discouragement in which most students with chronic behavior problems are trapped increases the likelihood that the problems can be resolved within the classroom.

When teachers conduct private conferences and use effective communication skills with students who have chronic behavior problems, the likelihood that the problems can be resolved within the classroom increases.

Interventions that require students to recognize their inappropriate behavior and its impact on others increase the likelihood that the problems can be resolved within the classroom.

Interventions that require students with chronic behavior problems to be accountable for trying to control their behavior on a daily basis increase the likelihood that the problems can be resolved within the classroom.

Interventions that call for gradual but consistent improvement in behavior increase the likelihood that chronic problems can be resolved within the classroom.

The final chapter offers advice on seeking assistance. When in-classroom techniques have been exhausted and have not resulted in appropriate student behavior, it is necessary to seek outside assistance. Teachers are offered guidelines to follow when deciding whether or not outside consultation is warranted. The concept of a success/failure ratio is explained along with a discussion of how this ratio contributes to persisting misbehavior.

Other students may need outside referral even though they do not display any forms of chronic misbehavior. These students may exhibit signs of emotional stress or family dysfunction. The chapter discusses six warning signs of these problems. A referral process that stresses multidisciplinary team consultation is offered as an effective means of working with these students. The roles of the counselor, parents, administrator, and school psychologist are presented along with the legal issues that must be considered when making outside referrals.

Parental support and cooperation with the school is critical when working with students who misbehave chronically. The chapter outlines specific guidelines that teachers can use to decide when parents need to be contacted. Techniques on how to conduct parent conferences to facilitate and enhance parental support and cooperation are discussed.

The classroom management principles in Chapter 10 are these:

Professional teachers recognize that some chronic misbehavior problems are not responsive to treatment within the classroom or are beyond their expertise and necessitate specialized outside assistance.

When outside assistance must be sought to manage a chronic misbehavior problem adequately and appropriately, the use of a multidisciplinary team is the most effective approach.

Parental support and cooperation with the school is critical when attempting to manage a student who chronically misbehaves. Careful planning and skilled conferencing techniques are essential in developing a positive home–school working relationship.

Professional Decision-Making Hierarchy

Professionals, regardless of their fields, use the specialized body of knowledge they possess to make decisions in their area of expertise. For example, engineers rely on their knowledge of science and mathematics to make engineering decisions, and physicians rely on their knowledge of biology and medical science to arrive at medical decisions. Educators who make hundreds of instructional and management decisions on a daily basis do so after considering their specialized knowledge in pedagogy, cognitive psychology, and child development.

In these professions and in others, hierarchies, taxonomies, and classification systems are used to organize vast amounts of isolated bits of data into manageable, comprehensible bodies of knowledge. Some common examples of classification systems to organize scientific information are the periodic table of elements in chemistry, the taxonomy of the plant and animal kingdoms in biology, and the electromagnetic spectrum in physics. In the social sciences there are the taxonomies of cognitive, affective, and psychomotor abilities in education and stages of cognitive and moral development in psychology, as well as many more.

Hierarchies may be used for more than just organizing information. They may also be used to guide professional decisions. Scientists, who use the scientific method to guide their inquiries, and doctors, who diagnose and treat patients by using a step-by-step approach, are using hierarchical approaches. The advantage of using a hierarchical approach is twofold: (1) it allows for the systematic implementation of the knowledge that informs the practice of a given profession, and (2) it provides the practitioner with a variety of approaches rather than a limited few. Thus, the hierarchical approach increases the likelihood that successful outcomes will result. The hierarchical strategies are based on professional knowledge, and if early strategies are ineffective, there are numerous other strategies that may produce positive results.

Applying a hierarchical approach to classroom management decisions allows teachers to employ knowledge effectively in order to understand, prevent, and manage student behavior. When such an approach is not used, a teacher may find herself with few alternatives for managing student behavior. Consider, for example, Case 1.3.

CASE 1.3 • *The Vice-Principal Wants to See Whom?*

Ms. King decides one way to maintain discipline in her eighth-grade class is, from the beginning of the school year, to be firm and consistent with the enforcement of classroom rules and procedures. One of her rules is that students must raise their hands to be called on before answering questions. She explains this rule to the class: "By eighth grade I'm sure you all understand that everyone has an equal chance to participate. For this to happen everyone must raise her hand to be called on. I hope I will have to tell you this only once."

During the year's first question-and-answer session, Jill calls out the answer. Ms. King reminds her, "Jill, you must raise your hand if you want to answer. I do not expect this to happen again." However, it isn't much longer until Jill calls out again. This time Ms. King says, "Jill, please leave the room and stand in the hallway. When you feel that you can raise your hand, come back and join us."

In a few minutes Jill returns to class and as before calls out an answer. This time Ms. King says, "Go to the office and speak with the vice-principal." Within minutes Jill is sent back to class. Later that day Ms. King receives a message in her mailbox requesting her to set up a meeting with the vice-principal to discuss the matter.

Needless to say, Ms. King's approach to managing a common student behavior was a gross overreaction. It not only led to an administrator-initiated meeting but also would probably result in increased student misbehavior as students recognize the discrepancy between the minimal student behavior and maximum teacher response. Furthermore, Ms. King's approach left her with few if any alternatives in managing other students who called out answers in the future. It is highly unlikely that this approach would be supported by parents, students, administrators, or other teachers. The technique of exclusion from class is usually reserved for use after many less intrusive strategies have been attempted. In other words, classroom management is best accomplished when the teacher employs management strategies in a hierarchical order.

When teachers use a professional body of knowledge to make decisions, the decisions are usually professionally acceptable, defendable, and result in desired changes in students' behaviors. When teachers make "gut" or emotional decisions, sometimes called reactions, the decisions more often than not result in unexpected and undesirable student behaviors. The principles of classroom management and the decision-making hierarchy of coping skills presented in this book have served many educators well in making effective decisions concerning the management of student behavior.

Two hierarchies are presented in this book. The first is a summary of how classroom management should be viewed. This hierarchy is represented by the four sections into which the chapters are grouped. The first section, Chapters 1 through 4, presents the foundational knowledge base. The second section, Chapters 5 and 6, addresses the prevention of management problems. The third section, Chapters 7 and 8, deals with the management of common misbehavior problems. The fourth and final section, Chapters 9 and 10, addresses managing chronic misbehavior problems.

The second hierarchy concerns the implementation of management strategies. This hierarchy is a decision-making model that uses specific techniques called *coping skills*. Entering the decision-making model, the teacher finds a variety of nonintrusive coping skills that provide the student with the opportunity to manage her own behavior while at the same time curbing the common forms of classroom misbehavior efficiently and effectively (Shrigley, 1985). As the teacher moves through the coping skills, the techniques become more and more intrusive, with the teacher playing an increasingly larger role in managing student behavior. The overall hierarchy of the book is shown in Figure 1.1. In addition, each chapter begins with a flowchart depicting those parts of the hierarchy that have been covered in previous chapters and the specific parts of the hierarchy that are now to be discussed. We hope this arrangement will provide a systematic, step-by-step approach to building a comprehensive management system.

Summary

This chapter first discussed a critical premise concerning successful classroom management that the reader should clearly understand before continuing. Teaching—which is defined as *the use of preplanned behaviors, founded in learning principles*

FIGURE 1.1 *A Hierarchical Approach to Successful Classroom Management*

Section I   Foundations *(Chapters 1–4)*
Conceptualizing the process of teaching
Understanding classroom management
    principles
Understanding the decision-making
    hierarchical approach
Defining a discipline problem
Understanding the extent of discipline
    problems in today's schools
Understanding how discipline problems
    affect teaching and learning
Understanding societal change and its
    influence on children's behaviors
Recognizing student needs
Understanding developmental changes
    and accompanying behaviors
Recognizing the importance of
    instructional competence
Understanding and employing different
    power bases of teachers
    Referent
    Expert
    Legitimate
    Reward/Coercive
Understanding theories of classroom
    management
    Student-directed
    Collaborative
    Teacher-directed

Section 2   Prevention *(Chapters 5-6)*
Developing effective teaching strategies
    Lesson design
    Student motivation: Teacher variables
    Teacher expectations
    Classroom questioning
    Time-on-task
Teaching for understanding
Authentic instruction
Thinking and problem-solving skills
Creating learning communities
Teaching for multiple intelligences
Student motivation: Student cognition
Designing the physical environment
Establishing classroom guidelines
    Determining procedures
    Determining rules
    Determining consequences

    Natural • Logical • Contrived
    Communicating rules
    Obtaining commitments
    Teaching rules
Understanding cultural embeddedness of
    behavior
Creating positive group norms

**Section 3   Managing Common
Misbehavior Problems** *(Chapters 7–8)*
Using proactive coping skills
Using preplanned remedial nonverbal
    intervention
    Planned ignoring
    Signal interference
    Proximity control
    Touch control
Using preplanned verbal intervention
    Adjacent reinforcement
    Calling on the student
    Humor
    "I message"
    Direct appeal
    Positive phrasing
    "Are not for's"
    Reminder of rules
    Glasser's triplets
    Explicit redirection
    Canter's "broken record"
Applying logical consequences

**Section 4   Managing Chronic Behavior
Problems** *(Chapters 9–10)*
Relationship building
Disrupting the cycle of discouragement
Using self-monitoring
Using anecdotal record procedure
Using behavioral contracts
Understanding the nature of persisting
    misbehavior
Recognizing when outside assistance is
    needed
Making referrals
    Counselors
    Administrators
    School psychologists
Working with parents
Protecting student rights

and child development theory and directed toward both instructional delivery and classroom management, that increase the probability of affecting a positive change in student behavior—and classroom management are really the same process. Therefore, by deliberately changing her behavior the teacher can influence positive changes in students' behaviors.

Second, the principles and the decision-making hierarchical approach to management on which the entire book is based were explained. These serve as the foundation on which specific management techniques are developed throughout the rest of the book.

References

Berliner, D. (1984). The half-full glass: A review of research on teaching. In P. Hosford (Ed.), *Using What We Know, About Teaching.* Alexandria, VA: Association for Supervision and Curriculum Development.

Boyan, N. J., and Copeland, W. D. (1978). *Instructional Supervision Training Program.* Columbus, OH: Merrill.

Brophy, J. (1988). Research on teacher effects: Uses and abuses. *The Elementary School Journal, 89,* 1, 3–21.

Emmer, E. T., Evertson, C. M., Clements, B. S., and Worsham, M. E. (1997). *Classroom Management for Secondary Teachers,* 4th ed. Boston: Allyn and Bacon.

Evertson, C. M., Emmer, E. T., Clements, B. S., and Worsham, M. E. (1997). *Classroom Management for Elementary Teachers,* 4th ed. Boston: Allyn and Bacon.

Haberman, M. (1995). *Star Teachers of Children in Poverty.* West Lafayette, IN: Kappa Delta Pi.

Kounin, J. S. (1970). *Discipline and Group Management in Classrooms.* New York: Holt, Rinehart & Winston.

National Education Association. (1997). *Status of the American Public School Teacher, 1995–96.* West Haven, CT.

Redl, F., and Wineman, D. (1952). *Controls from Within: Techniques for Treatment of the Aggressive Child.* New York: Free Press.

Shrigley, R. L. (1985). Curbing student disruption in the classroom—Teachers need intervention skills. *National Association of Secondary School Principals Bulletin, 69,* 479, 26–32.

Sweeney, T. J. (1981). *Adlerian Counseling: Proven Concepts and Strategies,* 2nd ed. Muncie, IN: Accelerated Development.

Tauber, R. T., and Mester, C. S. (1994). *Acting Lesson for Teachers.* Westport, CT: Praeger.

Exercises

1. Many teachers define teaching as the delivery of knowledge or the giving of information. In your opinion are these definitions adequate? If so, explain why. If not, what are the limitations?

2. What problems may arise when teachers base most of their decisions on "gut reactions"? Give specific examples.

3. In recent years there has been much discussion over whether or not teaching is a profession. In your opinion is teaching a profession? If yes, explain why. If no, why not and what must occur to make it a profession?

4. Review the definition of teaching presented in this chapter. Do you agree with the definition or should it be modified? If you agree, explain why. If not, what should be changed?

5. The definition of teaching in this chapter focuses on the teacher changing her behavior to manage discipline problems because that is the only behavior over which she has control. Given this, how might you reply to a principal who believes that teachers should be able to control their students' behavior?

6. This chapter discusses how teacher behaviors (affecting) influence changes in student behavior (targeted). For each targeted behavior that follows, suggest an appropriate affecting behavior and explain why such a behavior would increase the likelihood of a positive change in the student's behavior.

Situation	Targeted Behavior	Affecting Behavior
calling out answers	raising hand	
not volunteering	volunteering	
daydreaming	on task	
forgetting textbook	prepared for class	
short answers to questions	expanded answers	
few students answer questions	more participation	
passing notes	on task	
walking around room	in seat	
noisy during first five minutes of class	on task from start of class	

7. Suggest some ways that a busy teacher can keep up with the latest research on effective teaching.

8. This book offers 38 principles of classroom management. Principles are usually quite broad statements. How can a teacher use these principles to guide her teaching practice and specific management techniques?

9. This book supports the use of a decision-making hierarchical approach to classroom management. Discuss the advantages as well as the disadvantages to such an approach.

2

Nature of the
Discipline Problem

The Basics

↓

Nature of the Discipline Problem
Defining a Discipline Problem • Understanding the Extent of
Discipline Problems in Today's Schools • Understanding How
Discipline Problems Affect Teaching and Learning

Principles of Classroom Management

1. A discipline problem exists whenever a behavior interferes with the teaching act, interferes with the rights of others to learn, is psychologically or physically unsafe, or destroys property.
2. For effective teaching to take place, teachers must be competent in managing student misbehavior so as to maximize the time spent on learning.
3. Teachers who manage their classrooms effectively enjoy teaching more and have greater confidence in their ability to affect student achievement.

Introduction

When educators, public officials, or parents with school-age children discuss schooling, the topic of classroom discipline inevitably arises. Discipline and classroom management are topics that have been widely discussed by both professionals and the public for a considerable period of time.

In these discussions it is generally assumed that everyone knows what is meant by a discipline problem and that discipline poses major problems for educators. However, when we have asked pre- or in-service teachers at workshops, "What is a discipline problem?" there has been no consensus whatsoever in their responses. Thus, contrary to popular belief, there does not seem to be a professional operational definition of what behaviors constitute a discipline problem. So what would seem to be the obvious starting point for effective classroom management, that is, the definition of a discipline problem, has yet to be adequately formulated.

A second common topic among educators, public officials, and parents is the magnitude of discipline problems in today's schools. Many think that our schools are plagued by crime, violence, and frequent disruptive classroom behavior, but is this true? Do today's schools differ greatly from those of 10 or 20 years ago? How does the lack of an agreed-upon definition of a discipline problem affect the gathering of statistics to assess the extent of disruptive behavior?

Finally, while almost everyone agrees that it is important for students to behave properly in a classroom, a survey of pre- and in-service teachers shows no agreement on why it is important. What are the actual effects of misbehavior on students and their learning and on teachers and their teaching?

In this chapter we will (1) develop a working definition of what constitutes a behavior problem in a classroom; (2) assess the magnitude of the discipline problem in today's schools; and (3) determine the effect of misbehavior on both students and teachers.

Defining a Discipline Problem

Teachers often describe students who have discipline problems as lazy, unmotivated, belligerent, aggressive, angry, or argumentative. These words at best are imprecise, judgmental, and descriptive of a wide range of behaviors. After all, a student can be lazy or angry and yet not be a disruptive factor in the classroom. Furthermore, attribution theory (Weiner, 1980) tells us that our thoughts guide our feelings, which in turn guide our behavior. Therefore, when teachers describe children using negative labels, they are much more likely to feel and behave negatively toward those children (Brendtro et al., 1990). Negative teacher behavior is ineffective in helping children learn appropriate behavior. Thus, for a definition of a discipline problem to be useful to a teacher, it must clearly differentiate student behavior that requires immediate corrective action from that which does not.

The amount of material that has been written on discipline and classroom management is staggering. Hundreds of books and articles on this subject have been produced for both the professional and the general public, the great majority of them appearing since the mid-1970s. They typically cover such areas as the types and frequency of behavior problems, the causes of student misbehavior, and the strategies that teachers can employ to improve classroom management. However, surprisingly, the most basic question, "What types of student behaviors constitute discipline problems?" has rarely been considered. Having a clear understanding of what behaviors constitute discipline problems is a prerequisite for effective classroom management; without this understanding, it is impossible for teachers to design and communicate to students rational and meaningful classroom guidelines, to recognize misbehavior when it occurs, or to employ management strategies effectively and consistently.

In developing an operational definition, it is helpful to examine some infrequent definitions found in the literature. Kindsvatter (1978) defines discipline in terms of student behavior in the classroom, or "classroom decorum." He uses terms such as *behavior problems* and *misbehavior* but never gives meanings or examples for them. However, he does associate discipline with student behavior (which we will see does not always have to be the case).

Feldhusen (1978) uses the term *disruptive behavior,* which he defines as a violation of school expectations interfering with the orderly conduct of teaching. This definition is significant because it states that misbehavior is any student behavior that interferes with teaching. In defining disruptive behavior in this manner, Feldhusen attempts to provide teachers with a guideline for monitoring student behavior: Any behavior that keeps the teacher from teaching is a disciplinary problem; any behavior that does not interrupt the teaching process is not a discipline problem.

Using this guideline, it seems relatively easy to identify discipline problems. Or is it? Let's test it by applying it to a number of common classroom behaviors: (1) a student continually calls out while the teacher is explaining material; (2) a student quietly scratches his name into his desk; and (3) a student quietly passes notes to his neighbor. According to Feldhusen's definition only the first student is exhibiting a discipline problem because his calling out interferes with the teacher's ability to teach. Unless a teacher were quite observant, the second and third behaviors could go unnoticed. Even if the teacher were aware of these behaviors, he could easily continue to teach. However, how many teachers would agree that scratching one's name on a desk and passing notes do not constitute discipline problems? Teachers realize inherently that such behaviors do constitute discipline problems and must be managed. Therefore, Feldhusen's definition is inadequate.

Emmer et at. (1989) offer a more comprehensive definition: "Student behavior is disruptive when it seriously interferes with the activities of the teacher or of several students for more than a brief time" (p. 187). Under this definition, disruptive behavior interferes not only with the teacher or teaching act but also with students or the learning act. This is an important enhancement because it recognizes the right of every student to learn (Bauer, 1985), and most of the time in a classroom the need of the group must override the need of an individual student (Curwin and Mendler, 1980).

Unfortunately the definition includes the terms *seriously, several,* and *brief time.* Although these terms are used to generalize to a wider range of situations, they allow room for disagreement and misinterpretation. First, a brief time or a serious interference for one teacher may not be a brief time or serious interruption for another. Second, is it only when several students are disrupted that a discipline problem exists? If we apply this definition to the three types of behaviors listed previously, the student who calls out and possibly the note passer would be identified. The student who is defacing the desk would not be covered.

By far one of the most comprehensive definitions has been offered by Shrigley (1979), who states that any behavior that disrupts the teaching act or is psychologically or physically unsafe constitutes a disruptive behavior. This definition includes behaviors that do not necessarily interfere with the teaching act but are definitely psychologically

When teachers are not prepared to start classes on time, discipline problems can result.

or physically unsafe, such as running in a science lab, unsafe use of tools or laboratory equipment, threats to other students, and constant teasing and harassing of classmates. However, the same problem is evident in this definition as in Feldhusen's: name-scratching and note-passing would not be considered discipline problems because they do not interfere with teaching and are not unsafe.

It should be clear from this discussion, that any definition of the term *discipline problem* must provide teachers with the means to determine instantly whether or not any given behavior is a discipline problem. Once this identification has been made, the teacher can then decide what specific teacher intervention should be employed.

Consider the following six scenarios. For each, ask yourself the following questions:

1. Is there a discipline problem?
2. If there is a discipline problem, who is exhibiting it?
3. Why is the behavior a discipline problem or why isn't the behavior a discipline problem?

Scenario 1: Marisa quietly enters the room and takes her seat. The teacher requests that students take out their homework. Marisa does not take out her homework but instead takes out a magazine and begins to flip quietly through the pages. The teacher ignores Marisa and involves the class in reviewing the homework.

Scenario 2: Marisa quietly enters the room and takes her seat. The teacher requests that students take out their homework. Marisa does not take out her homework but instead takes out a magazine and begins to flip quietly through the pages. The teacher publicly announces that there will be no review of the homework until Marisa puts away the magazine and takes out her homework.

Scenario 3: Marisa quietly enters the room and takes her seat. The teacher requests that students take out their homework. Marisa does not take out her homework but instead takes out a magazine and begins to flip quietly through the pages. The teacher begins to involve the class in reviewing the homework and at the same time moves closer to Marisa. The review continues with the teacher standing in close proximity to Marisa.

Scenario 4: Marisa quietly enters the room and takes her seat. The teacher requests that students take out their homework. Marisa does not take out her homework but instead takes out a magazine and begins to show the magazine to the students who sit next to her. The teacher ignores Marisa and begins to involve the class in the review of the homework. Marisa continues to show the magazine to her neighbors.

Scenario 5: Marisa quietly enters the room and takes her seat. The teacher requests that students take out their homework. Marisa does not take out her homework but instead takes out a magazine and begins to show the magazine to the students who sit next to her. The teacher does not begin the review and, in front of the class, loudly demands that Marisa put the magazine away and get out her homework. The teacher stares at Marisa for the two minutes that it takes her to put the magazine away and find her homework. Once Marisa finds her homework the teacher begins the review.

Scenario 6: Marisa quietly enters the room and takes her seat. The teacher requests that students take out their homework. Marisa does not take out her homework but instead takes out a magazine and begins to show the magazine to the students who sit next to her. The teacher begins the homework review and, at the same time, walks toward Marisa. While a student is answering a question the teacher, as privately as possible, assertively asks Marisa to take out her homework and put the magazine away.

If you are like many of the teachers to whom we have given these same six scenarios you probably have found answering the questions that preceded them difficult. Furthermore, if you have taken time to discuss your answers with others, you undoubtedly have discovered your answers differ from theirs.

Much of the difficulty in determining what constitutes a discipline problem can be avoided using the following definition, which recognizes that discipline problems are multifaceted: *A discipline problem is behavior that (1) interferes with the teaching act, (2) interferes with the rights of others to learn, (3) is psychologically or physically unsafe, or (4) destroys property.* This definition not only covers calling out, defacing property, or disturbing other students but also other common behaviors that teachers confront every day. Note, however, that the definition does not limit behavior to student behavior. This is very important, for it means the teacher must consider his own behavior as well as his students' behavior.

Using our new definition, review the six scenarios again and compare your analysis with ours. In Scenario 1 there are no discipline problems because neither Marisa's nor the teacher's behavior is interfering with the rights of others to learn. The teacher has decided to ignore Marisa for the time being and focus on involving the class with the homework review.

In Scenario 2 the teacher is a discipline problem because the teacher has interrupted the homework review to intervene with Marisa, who isn't interfering with any other students' learning. In this situation, it is the teacher who is interfering with the rights of the students to learn.

In Scenario 3 there is no evident discipline problem. Neither Marisa's nor the teacher's behavior is interfering with the other students' right to learn. The teacher has not decided to ignore Marisa but has wisely chosen an intervention strategy that allows the homework review to continue.

In Scenario 4 both Marisa and the teacher are discipline problems. Marisa is interfering with the other students' right to learn. Since Marisa is a discipline problem, by ignoring her, the teacher also interferes with the other students' right to learn.

In Scenario 5 Marisa and the teacher are again discipline problems. Marisa's sharing of the magazine is disruptive but the teacher's choice of intervention is also a problem. In fact, the teacher is interfering with the learning of more students than Marisa.

In Scenario 6 Marisa is still a discipline problem. However, the teacher is not because the intervention strategy allows him to work with the class and, at the same time, manage Marisa.

The guidelines provided by the definition make it far easier to determine whether or not a discipline problem exists, and if it does, who has the problem. Most nondiscipline problems can be managed at some later time, after the other students have begun their work, during a break, or before or after class. When a discipline problem is evi-

---

CASE 2.1 • *Can a Teacher Be a Discipline Problem?*

Usually when the bell rings, the students in Mr. Karis's ninth-grade social studies class have their books out and are quietly waiting to begin work. Today, when Mr. Karis finished taking roll and is asking a few questions to review the previous day's work, he notices that Tom is just starting to get his book out. Mr. Karis asks Tom why he isn't ready. Tom replies that he has a lot on his mind. Mr. Karis then reminds Tom in a strong tone that when the bell rings he is to be ready to start. Tom replies in a tone that makes it very certain that he is annoyed, "Look, you don't know what my morning's been like!" Mr. Karis tells Tom that he "is not to be spoken to in that tone of voice." The rest of the class members are now either talking among themselves or deeply involved in the outcome of the confrontation rather than in social studies. By the time Tom decides it probably is not in his best interest to continue the escalating conflict, at least five minutes of class time has elapsed and no teaching or learning has taken place.

dent, however, the teacher must intervene immediately, because by definition there exists a behavior that is interfering with other students' rights or safety. When a teacher inappropriately or ineffectively employs management strategies that result in interference with the learning of others, he, in fact, becomes the discipline problem.

Let's examine Case 2.1. Did Tom's late opening of his book interfere with teaching or his classmates' learning? Was it unsafe or did it destroy property? Wasn't it Mr. Karis's behavior that caused escalation of a minor problem that would have corrected itself? Using our definition, Mr. Karis was the discipline problem. It is doubtful that any teacher intervention was necessary at all. See Chapter 7 for a full discussion of when teacher intervention is appropriate. Note that under the terms of the definition, inappropriate or ill-timed classroom procedures, public address announcements, and school policies that tend to disrupt the teaching and/or learning process are discipline problems.

Problem Student Behavior Outside the Definition

By now some readers have probably thought of many student behaviors that are not covered by our definition; for example, students who refuse to turn in homework, who are not prepared for class, or who are daydreaming, as well as the occasional student who gives the teacher "dirty looks." A careful analysis of these behaviors will reveal that under the terms of the definition, they are not discipline problems. They may be motivational problems.

Motivational problems can occur because of low levels of self-confidence, low expectations for success, lack of interest in academics, lost feelings of autonomy, achievement anxieties, or fears of success or failure (Stipek, 1998). Thus, working with students who have motivational problems often involves long-term individualized intervention and/or referrals to professionals outside the classroom.

Although in-depth coverage of motivational problems is beyond the scope of this book, it must be recognized that some strategies used to manage these problems, which generally do not interfere with other students' learning, disturb the learning of others or reduce the time spent on learning. Therefore, it is best to work with students who have motivational problems individually *after* involving the rest of the class in the day's learning activities. Doing so allows the teacher to protect the class's right to learn and to maximize the time allocated for learning.

Even though the strategies presented later in this book are usually used to manage discipline problems, some of them, particularly coping skills and anecdotal record keeping, can be used quite successfully for motivational problems. It cannot be stressed enough, however, that motivational problems must be properly addressed, usually by focusing on the student's expectation of success and the value the student places on the learning activity, so that they do not develop into discipline problems (see Chapter 5). Case 2.2 illustrates how one teacher ensures that this does not occur.

Mr. Hill recognized that Bill's behavior did not interfere with the teaching and learning act and so did not need immediate action. He employed effective strategies that protected the class's right to learn. The strategies were the beginning of a long-

CASE 2.2 • *Solving a Motivational Problem*

Mr. Hill teaches fourth grade. One of his students, Bill, rarely participates in class and often is the last one to begin class-work. One day the class is assigned math problems for seat work. After a few minutes Mr. Hill notices that Bill has not started. He calmly walks over to Bill, kneels down beside his desk, and asks Bill if he needs any help. This is enough to get Bill to begin his math problems. Mr. Hill waits until three problems are completed; he then tells Bill that since Bill understood them so well, he should put them on the board. After the class has finished the assignment, Mr. Hill begins to review the answers, stressing the correct procedures Bill used to solve the problems and thanking Bill for his board work.

term effort to build up Bill's interest and confidence in mathematics and to have him become an active, participating member of the class. Probably many readers have witnessed similar situations in which the teacher unfortunately chose to deal with the student's behavior in ways that were disruptive to the entire class.

Extent of the Problem

According to all 29 annual Gallup polls of the "Public's Attitudes Toward the Public Schools" (Rose, Gallup, and Elam, 1997) discipline is one of the most serious problems facing public schools. From the poll's inception in 1969 until 1985, discipline was ranked as the primary problem facing public schools. From 1986 until 1991, it was ranked second to drug use. In 1992 and 1993, discipline was ranked third, behind school funding and drug use, while in 1994, 1995, and 1996 it ranked first in two out of the three years. In 1997, discipline was again ranked as the biggest problem facing public schools.

Teachers seem to share the public's concern. A 1980 survey of urban and suburban teachers in two schools in a Mideastern or Midatlantic metropolitan area revealed that 60 percent felt the public's alarm was warranted (Levin, 1980b). In a nationwide sampling of teachers in 1984, 95 percent believed that efforts to improve school discipline should have a higher priority than they then had (Harris, 1984). In a national poll that same year, 19 percent of the teachers surveyed felt that discipline was the most serious of the problems facing public schools. By 1988 this percentage had risen to 25 percent (Elam, 1989). By 1991, 44 percent of the teachers surveyed for a national poll were reporting that student misbehavior interfered substantially with their teaching (Mansfield, Alexander, and Farris, 1991).

The results of the most recent national poll, conducted in 1997, reported that 58 percent of all the teachers surveyed noted that behavior that disrupted the class occurred most of the time or fairly often in their schools (Langdon, 1997).

Daydreaming students are not interfering with teaching or the rights of others to learn. Therefore, the teacher should first involve the rest of the class in the learning activity before individually managing the daydreamer.

Students themselves are aware of the frequency of disruptive behavior. Nationwide in 1993, the majority of students in grades 8, 10, and 12 reported that student disruptions were fairly common occurrences in their classes. Sixteen percent of the eighth-graders and 11 percent of the tenth-graders surveyed reported that their teachers often interrupted instruction to manage disruptive student behavior (National Education Goals Panel, 1994). In 1996, 16 percent of the tenth-graders surveyed reported frequently interrupted instruction (National Education Goals Panel, 1997).

In attempting to assess the magnitude of the discipline problem in the past, Doyle (1978) has pointed out that serious historical investigation of student behavior is lacking and that the studies that are available use data that are typically incomplete and in some cases unreliable. Doyle has reviewed evidence from the few available sources and has found that crime (violence and vandalism) was not a serious concern among school officials during the late 1800s to the early 1900s. However, there is evidence that juvenile crime outside of school was a problem during this period. In the early 1900s, less than 50 percent of the school-age population was enrolled in school. Of this, only 40 percent finished eighth grade, and only approximately 10 percent graduated. Thus, the children most likely to commit crimes were not in school (Hawes, 1971; Mennell, 1973; Schlossman, 1977). It was the growing concern over juvenile street crime that initiated a movement for public education. Authorities argued that street crime could be lessened if those youths responsible for it were brought under the influence of the school (Doyle,

1978). Doyle therefore concluded that youth behavior in the 1970s was no worse than it was in the past, but what was once a street problem was now a school problem, the result of more students attending school for longer periods of time.

Since the early 1980s, researchers have made a concerted effort to distinguish between crime (violence and vandalism) and common misbehavior (off-task and disruptive classroom behaviors). Such a distinction is essential because crime and routine classroom misbehavior are inherently different problems that require different solutions administered by different professionals both in and outside the school. Whereas teachers are responsible for managing routine classroom misbehavior, crime often must come under the control of the school administration and outside law-enforcement agencies.

Once crime is separated from common misbehavior, what do the schools of the late 1980s and early 1990s look like? Data from the National Institute of Education reveal that by the early 1980s the number of incidents of crime in the schools had decreased (Moles, 1983). Teachers and principals also reported decreases in classroom misbehavior. In a 1983 National Education Association teacher opinion poll, 45 percent of the teachers surveyed felt that student misbehavior interfered to a "great" or "moderate extent" with their teaching. This was a decrease of nine percent from the 1980 survey (National Education Association, 1983). In 1986 a similar decrease in disruptive classroom behavior was reported by 66 percent of 900 secondary school principals nationwide (U.S. Department of Education, 1986).

As we have noted previously, such improvement did not go unnoticed by the public. In the 1986 "Gallup Poll of the Public's Attitudes Toward the Public Schools," a lack of discipline was listed for the first time in 15 years as the second most important problem facing public schools (Gallup, 1986). Replacing it as the most important problem was the use of drugs. This trend continued through the 1993 Gallup poll (Elam, Lowell, and Gallup, 1994).

By the mid-1980s, Wayson (1985) was able to state that "most schools never experience incidents of crime and those that do seldom experience them frequently or regularly" (p. 129), but disruptive behavior of "the kinds that have characterized school children for generations . . . continue to pose frequent and perplexing problems for teachers" (p. 127). After a thorough examination of studies since the 1977 Senate and National Institute of Education reports, Baker (1985) concluded that there had been improvement, but "the level of disruptive behavior in the classroom is a major problem for public education" (p. 486).

These conclusions were supported by numerous studies reporting that teachers and administrators consistently ranked common classroom misbehaviors (excessive talking, failure to do assignments, disrespect, lateness) as the most serious and frequent disturbances, whereas they ranked crime (vandalism, theft, assault) as the least serious disturbance to their teaching or the least frequently occurring (Elam, 1989; Huber, 1984; Levin, 1980a; Thomas, Goodall, and Brown, 1983; Weber and Sloan, 1986).

Thus, the schools of the late 1980s and early 1990s were perceived as experiencing less crime than the schools of the 1970s, and even though classroom misbehavior continued to be a major problem, it too was perceived as lessening. However, as we move into the late 1990s there are indications that these trends are reversing. As discussed earlier in this chapter, after an eight-year hiatus, discipline and violence shared first place in a public opinion poll of the most serious problem facing public education (Elam, Lowell, and Gallup, 1994) and continued to do so in 1997 (Rose, Gallup, and Elam, 1997). In 1997, a nationwide study (National Education Goals Panel, 1997) indicated that 36 percent of the tenth-graders and 15 percent of the teachers surveyed reported that they had been threatened or injured at school. Furthermore, vandalism, theft, and assault are no longer reported by teachers as the least frequently occurring disruptions (Rose, Gallup, and Elam, 1997). Indeed, there has also been an increase in teachers reporting that disruptions in their classrooms interfere with their teaching (National Education Goals Panel, 1997).

Just as crime is becoming more prevalent in schools so are weapons. In one survey, approximately 10 percent of eighth-, tenth-, and twelfth-graders questioned, reported that they had brought a weapon to school at least once during the previous month (National Education Goals Panel, 1994). A 1995 national survey of students between the ages of twelve and nineteen attending school reported that 13 percent of them knew a student who had brought a gun to school. In the same survey, 29 percent of the students reported the presence of street gangs in their schools (Chandler et al., 1998). The prevalence of weapons and gangs increases the likelihood that students will resort to violence to solve their conflicts.

Thus, as we move into the new millennium, every successful teacher will have to be able to recognize the genesis of potentially violent situations and manage disruptive classroom behaviors properly. Teachers must be able to defuse such situations and direct students toward more prosocial means of conflict resolution.

The Effect of Classroom Discipline Problems on Teaching and Learning

When classrooms are characterized by disruptive behavior, the teaching and learning environment is adversely affected. The amount of interference in the teaching and learning environment is related to the type, frequency, and duration of the disruptive behavior. Disruptive behavior also affects students' psychological safety, readiness to learn, and future behaviors.

In the course of the last decade, we have had the opportunity to interact with thousands of college students preparing to become teachers as well as thousands of in-service teachers and school administrators who want to improve their classroom management skills. One of the first questions we always ask is, "Why do students have to behave in a classroom?" At first we were somewhat embarrassed to ask such a basic question because we felt there was a universally obvious answer. However, to our surprise, the answer was not obvious to others. The answer, of course, involves the widely accepted learning principle that the more time spent on learning (time-on-task, or engaged time), the more learning will take place (Brophy, 1988). In other words, disruptive, off-task behavior takes time away from learning.

CASE 2.3 • *Discipline: A Costly Waste of Time*

Mr. Kay is a seventh-grade social studies teacher who teaches five classes a day. He is content to allow his students, on entering the room, to stand around and talk rather than prepare their materials for class. As a result, class usually does not begin until five minutes after the bell has rung.

Case 2.3 illustrates the tremendous amount of time that can be consumed over a school year by some very minor off-task behaviors. Over a period of a week, 25 minutes that could have been directed toward learning are not. Over the 40-week school year, 1,000 minutes are consumed by off-task behavior. This amounts to over 22 class periods, or approximately one-ninth of the school year, that could have been directed toward learning goals. If the calculations also consider the 120 students Mr. Kay teaches per day, 2,640 "student class periods" were not spent on learning social studies.

It has been reported that some teachers spend as much as 30 to 80 percent of their time addressing discipline problems (Walsh, 1983). This figure simply highlights a previously mentioned basic fact of teaching: To be a successful teacher, one must be competent in managing student behavior to maximize the time spent on learning.

Case 2.4 illustrates the fact that disruptive behavior can result in a "ripple effect." In other words, students learn misbehavior from observing misbehavior in other children (Baker, 1985). The off-task behaviors of Rebecca's friends draw her off task. This type of observational learning is often accelerated when the onlooking student notices the attention the disruptive student gains from both the teacher and his classmates.

Ripple effects are not limited to the initial misbehavior. The methods the teacher uses to curb the misbehavior and the targeted student's resultant behavior can cause a second ripple effect (Kounin, 1970). Studies have shown that rough and threatening teacher behavior causes student anxieties, which lead to additional dis-

CASE 2.4 • *The Ripple Effect*

Rebecca is a well-mannered, attentive fifth-grade student. For the first time since starting school, she and her two best friends are in the same class. Unlike Rebecca, her friends are not attentive and are interested more in each other than in class activities. The teacher often has to reprimand them for passing notes, talking to each other, and giggling excessively during class.

One day, Rebecca is tapped on the shoulder and is handed a note from her friend across the room. She accepts the note and sends one back. With this, her friends quickly include her in their antics. It takes the teacher a number of weeks to remove Rebecca from her friends' influence and reduce the off-task behaviors of the other two girls.

ruptive behaviors from onlooking students. Students who see disruptive students comply with the teacher's management technique and tend to rate their teacher as fair are themselves less distracted from their classwork than when they observe unruly students defying the teacher (Smith, 1969). Clearly the dynamics that come into play with even minor classroom disruptions are quite complex.

Common day-to-day off-task student behaviors such as talking and walking around exist in all classrooms to some degree. Although less common, some classrooms, indeed some entire schools, are plagued by threats, violence, and vandalism. A 1993 national survey found that nearly 50 percent of sixth- to twelfth-grade students at some point had witnessed bullying, robbery, or physical assault at school. The same survey found that one out of eight students reported being victimized at school (U.S. Department of Education, 1995). According to the survey, one half of the students polled used a variety of strategies to avoid being victimized, including avoiding certain locations in the school building, staying away from school-sponsored events, staying in groups while at school, and staying at home rather than attending school out of fear that someone might hurt or bother them. Obviously, when students are fearful for their own safety or the safety of their property, their ability to concentrate on their schoolwork is diverted. Fear creates a hostile learning environment, increases a feeling of mistrust in the school, and reduces students' confidence in their teachers' ability to manage students (Wayne and Rubel, 1982). Some studies indicate that a student's ability to learn in the classroom is reduced by at least 25 percent because of fear of other students (Dade County Public Schools, 1976; Lalli and Savitz, 1976).

In conclusion, minor and major misbehavior reduces learning time for both disruptive students and onlooking students. Less learning time equates to less learning. Although there is not a clear cause-and-effect relationship, there is a positive correlation between poor grades and all types of misbehavior (DiPrete, Muller, and Shaeffer, 1981).

Classroom discipline problems also have a negative impact on teacher effectiveness and career longevity. We believe that the overwhelming majority of teachers choose to enter the profession because they enjoy working with children and are intrinsically motivated when they know that their efforts have contributed to the children's academic growth. Therefore, teachers are emotionally vulnerable to discipline problems. They put long hours of preparation into what they hope will be interesting, motivating, and meaningful lessons. When such efforts are met by disinterested, off-task students, teachers begin to have negative attitudinal changes.

No matter how careful teachers are not to allow their personal feelings to play a role in their interactions with students, it is inevitable that some of their personal feelings will influence their behavior. Indeed, studies have shown that teachers interact differently with disruptive students than they do with nondisruptive students (Walker, 1979). Such differential treatment is fueled by the negative beliefs and feelings many teachers have toward disruptive students and the disparaging labels they assign to these students (Brendtro et al., 1990). Unfortunately, differential treatment only serves to escalate inappropriate student behavior. Even the most chronic disruptive student spends some time engaged in appropriate behavior. However, occasionally a teacher may become so angry at certain students that he tends to overlook the appropriate behavior and focuses only on the disruptive behavior. When this occurs, the teacher misses the few opportunities he has to begin to change disruptive behaviors to acceptable ones. At least two studies have concluded that teachers are much more likely to reprimand inappropriate behavior than to approve of appropriate behavior when interacting with disruptive students (Walker and Buckley, 1973, 1974). As a result, the student soon learns that when he behaves appropriately nothing happens, but when he misbehaves, he is the center of both the teacher's and students' attention.

Any teacher can attest to the fact that students easily realize when rules and expectations are not consistently enforced or obeyed by either the teacher or the students. Even so, because teachers are so emotionally tied to the disruptive students, they often set and enforce standards for these students that are different from those for the rest of the class. Often these standards are so inflexible and unrealistic that they actually reduce the chance that the disruptive student will behave appropriately.

Since disruptive students have a history of inappropriate behaviors, they must be given the opportunity to learn new behaviors. The learning process is usually best accomplished in small, manageable steps that enable the student to have a high probability of success. This process requires behavioral standards to be realistic and the same as those for the rest of the class. The teacher must recognize and encourage what at first may be infrequent and short-lived appropriate behaviors. When behavioral standards are stricter for some students than for others, the teacher risks losing the

Management problems are a major cause of job-related stress for teachers.

confidence and support of even the nondisruptive students while the disruptive student gains peer support.

As teachers begin to experience more discipline problems, their motivation to teach is often replaced by, at best, a "who cares?" attitude. If conditions do not improve, this attitude may develop into a "get even" attitude. When a "get even" attitude overrides a teacher's motivation to assist students in learning, supportive and effective teacher behaviors are replaced by revengeful behaviors. Once a teacher operates from a basis of revenge, teaching effectiveness ceases and teacher–student power struggles become commonplace. Such power struggles often further fuel and escalate disruptive behavior and place the teacher in a no-win situation (Dreikurs, 1964).

Children who display disruptive behaviors are constant reminders to teachers that the classroom environment is not what they would like it to be. The time and energy needed to cope with some disruptive students can be both physically draining and emotionally exhausting. Stress related to classroom management is one of the most influential factors in failure among novice teachers (Levin, 1980a; Vittetoe, 1977) and a major reason why they leave the profession (Canter, 1989).

Those teachers who do weather their first few years of teaching report that students who continually misbehave are the primary cause of job-related stress (Feitler and Tokar, 1992). According to the National Institute of Education (1980), teachers who report that they would not choose the teaching profession if they had to choose

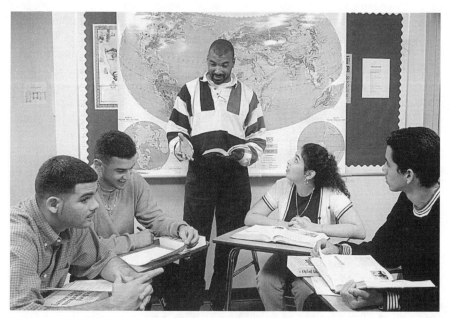

Teachers who are effective managers have greater job satisfaction.

a profession again were much more likely to have experienced discipline problems than teachers who would choose teaching again. Teachers who manage their classrooms effectively report that they enjoy teaching and feel a certain confidence in their ability to affect student achievement (Levin et al., 1985). Such feelings of efficacy lead to improvements in the teaching–learning process and job satisfaction, which ultimately result in gains in student achievement.

Summary

This chapter has answered three questions that are critical for an understanding of discipline and classroom management: What is a discipline problem? What is the extent of the problem in today's schools? What is the effect of discipline problems?

After a discussion of the contemporary definitions of discipline and their shortcomings, an operational definition was provided: A discipline problem is any behavior that (1) interferes with the teaching act; (2) interferes with the rights of others to learn; (3) is psychologically or physically unsafe; or (4) destroys property. According to this definition, teachers as well as students are responsible for appropriate behavior.

In response to the second question, we explored the belief that today's schools are plagued by violence, crime, and disruptive classroom behavior. Early studies were characterized by incomplete and in some cases unreliable data. Studies in the 1980s, which differentiated between crime and classroom misbehavior, characterized the schools as having less crime than in the 1970s. Common classroom misbehavior also seemed to have lessened during this period, even though such behaviors still posed serious and perplexing problems for teachers. However, recent studies indicate that the schools of the late 1990s may have experienced not only an increase in disruptive classroom behavior but also an increase in student violence.

Finally, it was shown that disruptive behavior reduces the time spent on learning, encourages misbehavior in onlooking students because of a ripple effect, and may cause fear in other students, with a resultant decrease in school attendance and academic achievement. Teachers are also adversely affected by disruptive behavior, suffering decreased effectiveness, increased job-related stress, and decreased career longevity.

References

Baker, K. (1985). Research evidence of a school discipline problem. *Phi Delta Kappan, 66,* 7, 482–488.

Bauer, G. L. (1985). Restoring order to the public schools. *Phi Delta Kappan, 66,* 7, 488–490.

Bayh, B. (1977). *Challenge for the Third Century: Education in a Safe Environment—Final Report on the Nature and Prevention of School Violence and Vandalism.* Washington DC: U.S. Government Printing Office.

Brendtro, L. K., Brokenleg, M., and Van Bockern, S. (1990). *Reclaiming Youth at Risk: Our Hope for the Future.* Bloomington, IN: National Educational Service.

Brophy, J. (1988). Research on teacher effects: Uses and abuses. *The Elementary School Journal, 89,* 1, 3–21.

Canter, L. (1989). Assertive discipline—More than names on the board and marbles in a jar. *Phi Delta Kappan, 71,* 1, 57–61.

Chandler, K. A., Chapman, C. D., Rand, M. R., and Taylor, B. M. *Students' Reports of School Crime: 1989 and 1995.* U.S. Departments of Education and Justice. NCES 98-241/NCJ-169607. Washington, DC: 1998.

Curwin, R. L., and Mendler, A. N. (1980). *The Discipline Book: A Complete Guide to School and Classroom Management.* Reston, VA: Reston Publishing.

Dade County Public Schools. (1976). *Experiences of Teachers and Students with Disruptive Behavior in the Dade Public Schools.* Miami, FL.

DiPrete, T., Muller, C., and Shaeffer, N. (1981). *Discipline and Order in American High Schools.* Washington, DC: National Center for Education Statistics.

Doyle, W. (1978). Are students behaving worse than they used to behave? *Journal of Research and Development in Education, 11,* 4, 3–16.

Dreikurs, R. (1964). *Children the Challenge.* New York: Hawthorn.

Elam, S. M. (1989). The second Gallup/Phi Delta Kappa poll of teachers' attitudes toward the public schools. *Phi Delta Kappan, 70,* 10, 785–798.

Elam, S. M., Lowell, C. R., and Gallup, A. M. (1994). The 26th Annual Phi Delta Kappa/Gallup poll of the public's attitudes toward the public schools. *Phi Delta Kappan, 76,* 1, 41–56.

Emmer, E. T., Evertson, C. M., Sanford, J. P., Clements, B. S., and Worsham, M. E. (1989). *Classroom Management for Secondary Teachers,* 2nd ed. Englewood Cliffs, NJ: Prentice Hall.

Feitler, F., and Tokar, E. (1992). Getting a handle on teacher stress: How bad is the problem? *Educational Leadership, 49,* 456–458.

Feldhusen, J. F. (1978). Behavior problems in secondary schools. *Journal of Research and Development in Education, 11,* 4, 17–28.

Gallup, A. M. (1986). The 18th annual Gallup poll of the public's attitudes toward the public schools. *Phi Delta Kappan, 68,* 1, 43–59.

Harris, L. (1984). *Metropolitan Life Survey of the American Teacher.* New York: Metropolitan Life Insurance Company.

Hawes, J. M. (1971). *Children in Urban Society: Juvenile Delinquency in Nineteenth Century America.* New York: Oxford University Press.

Huber, J. D. (1984). Discipline in the middle school—Parent, teacher, and principal concerns. *National Association of Secondary School Principals Bulletin, 68,* 471, 74–79.

Kindsvatter, R. (1978). A new view of the dynamics of discipline. *Phi Delta Kappan, 59,* 5, 322–365.

Kounin, J. (1970). *Discipline and Group Management in Classrooms.* New York: Holt, Rinehart & Winston.

Lalli, M., and Savitz, L. D. (1976). The fear of crime in the school enterprise and its consequences. *Education and Urban Society, 4,* 401–416.

Langdon, C. A. (1997). The fourth Phi Delta Kappa poll of teachers' attitudes toward public schools. *Phi Delta Kappan, 79,* 3, 212–221.

Levin, J. (1980a). Discipline and classroom management survey: Comparisons between a suburban and urban school. Unpublished report, Pennsylvania State University, University Park.

Levin, J. (1980b). Lay vs. teacher perceptions of school discipline. *Phi Delta Kappan, 61,* 5, 360.

Levin, J., Hoffman, N., Badiali, B., and Neuhard, R. (1985). Critical experiences in student teaching: Effects on career choice and implications for program modification. Paper presented to the Annual Conference of the American Educational Research Association, Chicago.

Mansfield, W., Alexander, D., and Farris, E. (1991). Teacher survey on safe, disciplined, and drug free schools. Washington, DC: U.S. Department of Education, National Center for Educational Statistics.

Mennell, R. M. (1973). *Thorns & Thistles: Juvenile Delinquents in the United States 1825–1940.* Hanover, NH: The University Press of New England.

Moles, O. (1983). Trends in interpersonal crimes in schools. Paper presented at the Annual Meeting of the American Educational Research Association, Montreal.

National Education Association. (1983). *Nationwide Teacher Opinion Poll 1983.* Washington, DC: NEA Research Memo.

National Education Goals Panel. (1997). *The 1997 National Education Goals Report: Building a Nation of Learners.* Washington, DC: Superintendent of Documents, U.S. Government Printing Office..

National Education Goals Panel (1994). *The National Education Goals Report: Building a Nation of Learners, 1994.* Washington, DC: Superintendent of Documents, U.S. Government Printing Office.

National Institute of Education. (1977). *Safe Schools—Violent Schools.* Washington, DC. U.S. Department of Health, Education, and Welfare.

National Institute of Education. (1980). *Teachers Opinion Poll.* Washington, DC: U.S. Department of Health, Education, and Welfare.

Rose, L. C., Gallup, A. M., Elam, S. M. (1997). The 29th annual Phi Delta Kappa/Gallup poll of the public's attitudes toward the public schools. *Phi Delta Kappan, 79,* 1, 41–58.

Schlossman, S. L. (1977). *Love and the American Delinquent: The Theory and Practice of "Progressive" Juvenile Justice, 1825–1920.* Chicago: University of Chicago Press.

Shrigley, R. L. (1979). Strategies in classroom management. *The National Association of Secondary School Principals Bulletin, 63,* 428, 1–9.

Smith, O. B. (1969). Discipline. In R. L. Ebel, *Encyclopedia of Educational Research,* 4th ed. New York: Macmillan.

Stipek, D. J. (1998). *Motivation to Learn: From Theory to Practice,* 3rd ed. Boston: Allyn and Bacon.

Thomas, G. T., Goodall, R., and Brown, L. (1983). Discipline in the classroom: Perceptions of middle grade teachers. *The Clearinghouse, 57,* 3, 139–142.

U.S. Department of Education. (1995). Student strategies to avoid harm at school. *Statistics in Brief.* Washington, DC: Office of Education Research and Improvement. NCES 95-203.

U.S. Department of Education. (1986). Discipline in public secondary schools. *Bulletin.* Washington, DC: Office of Educational Research and Improvement.

Vittetoe, J. O. (1977). Why first-year teachers fail. *Phi Delta Kappan, 58,* 5, 429.

Walker, H. M. (1979). *The Acting-Out Child: Coping with Classroom Disruption.* Boston: Allyn and Bacon.

Walker, H. M., and Buckley, N. K. (1973). Teacher attention to appropriate and inappropriate classroom behavior: An individual case study. *Focus on Exceptional Children, 5,* 5–11.

Walker, H. M., and Buckley, N. K. (1974). *Token Reinforcement Techniques: Classroom Applications for the Hard to Teach Child.* Eugene, OR: E-B Press.

Walsh, D. (1983). Our schools come to order. *American Teacher, 68,* 1.

Wayne, I., and Rubel, R. J. (1982). Student fear in secondary schools. *Urban Review, 14,* 1, 197–237.

Wayson, W. W. (1985). The politics of violence in school: Doublespeak and disruptions in public confidence. *Phi Delta Kappan, 67,* 2, 127–132.

Weber, T. R., and Sloan, C. A. (1986). How does high school discipline in 1984 compare to previous decades? *The Clearinghouse, 59,* 7, 326–329.

Weiner, B. (1980). A cognitive (attribution)–emotion–action, model of motivated behavior: An analysis of judgments of help-giving. *Journal of Personality and Social Psychology, 39,* 186–200.

Exercises

1. Is it important that all teachers have a consistent definition of what types of student behaviors constitute discipline problems? Why or why not?

2. Do you agree with the definition of a discipline problem stated in this chapter? If so, why? If not, how would you modify it?

3. Give several examples of teacher behavior that would constitute a discipline problem.

4. Using the definition of a discipline problem stated in this chapter, categorize each of the following behaviors as a discipline problem or a nondiscipline problem and explain your reasoning.

Discipline Behavior	Nondiscipline Problem	Problem	Rationale
a. A student consistently tries to engage the teacher in conversation just as class is about to begin.			
b. A student continually comes to class one minute late.			
c. A teacher stands in the hallway talking to fellow teachers during the first three minutes of class.			
d. A student does math homework during social studies class.			
e. A student interrupts a lecture to ask permission to go to the bathroom.			
f. A student often laughs at answers given by other students.			
g. A student doesn't wear safety goggles while welding in industrial arts class.			
h. A first-grader continually volunteers to answer questions but never has an answer when he is called on.			
i. A fourth-grader refuses to wear a jacket during recess.			

Discipline Behavior	Nondiscipline Problem	Problem	Rationale
j. A seventh-grader constantly pulls the hair of the girl who sits in front of him.			
k. An eighth-grade boy spends half of the time allotted for group work encouraging a girl to go out with his friend.			
l. A ninth-grade student consistently uses the last two minutes of class for hair combing.			
m. An unkempt student can't get involved in group work because all students refuse to sit near him.			
n. A student continually asks good questions, diverting the teacher from the planned lesson.			
o. A student eats a candy bar during class.			
p. A student flirts with the teacher by asking questions about her clothes and personal life during class.			
q. A student consistently makes wisecracks that entertain the rest of the class.			

5. At this point in your reading, how would you handle each of the 17 behaviors listed? Why?

6. For each of the 17 behaviors, give at least one type of teacher behavior that might escalate the student behavior.

7. Think back to your days as a student; to what extent would you say that discipline was a problem in your school? What type of discipline problems were most common?

8. Do you feel that the discipline problem in schools has increased or decreased since you attended high school? On what evidence or information do you base your opinion?

9. Considering what a teacher's job entails and his relationship with students, why would he be prone to take discipline problems personally?

10. What are the dangers of personalizing student behavior? How might doing so affect the instructional effectiveness of a teacher?

11. How can teachers protect themselves from personalizing misbehavior?

12. Think back on your days as a student. Can you recall instances in which classroom discipline problems prevented you and others in the class from learning? How did you feel about the situation at the time?

13. When a student disrupts class and takes away the right of others to learn, does that student forfeit his right to learn? If you believe he does, what implications does that have for teacher behavior? If you believe he doesn't, what implications does that have for teacher behavior?

14. Do you think that youth violence is on the increase or is this just a common misperception brought about by the increased coverage of this topic by the media?

15. What would you do as the teacher if a student told you that another student in your class had brought a gun to school?

3

Understanding Why Children Misbehave

> **The Basics**
>
> ⬇
>
> **Nature of the Discipline Problem**
>
> ⬇
>
> **Understanding Why Children Misbehave**
> Understanding Societal Change and Its Influence on Children's Behaviors •
> Recognizing Student Needs • Understanding Developmental Changes and
> Accompanying Behaviors • Recognizing the Importance of Instructional Competence

Principles of Classroom Management

1. An awareness of the causes of misbehavior enables teachers to use positive control techniques rather than negative techniques which stem from erroneously viewing misbehavior as a personal affront.
2. Basic human needs such as food, safety, belonging, and security are prerequisites for appropriate classroom behavior.
3. The need for a sense of significance, competence, virtue, and power influences student behavior.
4. Societal changes beyond the schools' control greatly influence student behavior.
5. Cognitive and moral developmental changes result in normal student behavior that often is disruptive in learning environments.
6. Instructional competence can lessen the effects of negative outside influences as well as prevent the misbehavior that occurs as a result of poor instruction.

Introduction

"Kids aren't the way they used to be. When I went to school, kids knew their place. Teachers wanted to teach and students wanted to learn. The students respected their teachers, and believe me, they sure didn't fool around in school like they do today." Adults frequently make these statements as they remember the "way it used to be," but are they true? Not entirely!

There have always been some behavior problems in our schools if only because of students' normal developmental changes. There also have always been some schools and homes that have been unable to provide adequately for children's needs. Even so, recent rapid societal changes have caused new behavior problems and have compounded existing ones. There have been significant shifts in the family structure, the U.S. distribution of wealth and knowledge, the cultural and racial makeup of the population, and world economies, as well as advances in technology that were only fantasized a few decades ago. These changes are evident in students' thoughts, attitudes, and behavior. Nonetheless, students still are intrinsically motivated toward skill acquisition and competency (Stipek, 1993), and teachers still want to teach.

If, however, teachers want to maximize their teaching time, they must minimize the effect of societal changes on student behavior. Teachers must (1) not expect students to think and act the way they did years ago; (2) not demand respect from students solely on the basis of a title or position; (3) understand the methods and behaviors young people employ to find their place in today's society; and (4) understand the ongoing societal changes and the influence these changes have on students' lives. To assist teachers in reaching this goal, this chapter describes some of the main factors that have influenced students to change and provides an explanation of why students now behave as they do.

Societal Changes

For over 70 years now, it has been recognized that schools are microcosms of the larger society (Kindsvatter, 1978; Dewey, 1916). Therefore, discipline problems in the schools reflect the problems that face society. The social climate of the nation, city, or town and the community that surrounds each school has profound effects on students' perceptions of the value of education and their behavior in school (Menacker, Weldon, and Hurwitz, 1989).

It is widely recognized that our society is plagued by the ills of drug and alcohol use, crime and violence, unemployment, child abuse, adolescent suicide, and teenage pregnancy. It is no coincidence that as these problems increase, so do a school's discipline problems. This clear relationship between social problems and school discipline problems simply highlights the fact that many factors that contribute to discipline problems are beyond the schools' control (Bayh, 1978).

Even if there were no societal problems, disruptive behavior could still be expected in a school because it is an institution that brings together many of the conditions that facilitate misbehavior. Large numbers of young people, many of whom are still learning socially acceptable behaviors and would rather be elsewhere, are concentrated in one place for long periods of time. These young people come from a wide range of backgrounds, with different ethnic, racial, and parental attitudes and expectations concerning education. A school exposes all students to norm-violating behaviors and makes failure visible (Elliott and Voss, 1974; Feldhusen, 1978).

Children no longer grow up in a society that provides them with constant, consistent sets of guidelines and expectations. The intense, rapid technological advancements in mass communication of the last two decades have exposed young people to a multitude of varying viewpoints, ideas, and philosophies. With this exposure, the direct influence of parents, community, and school has begun to wane. Role models have changed. Schools are now faced with children who are exposed to more varied types of information than ever before. As a result these children think and act differently.

The Knowledge Explosion and the Erosion of Respect for Authority

Since the 1950s, when the Soviet Union launched *Sputnik,* the first satellite, there has been an unabating explosion in scientific knowledge and technological advancements. This explosion has resulted in products only dreamed of previously. Cellular and digital phones, VCRs, satellite dishes, CD-ROMs, powerful personal computers, FAX machines, the Internet, e-mail, and other telecommunication devices that are used for instantaneous worldwide personal communications and access to an ever-expanding array of databases are common today.

To understand how great the explosion of knowledge has been, consider this. In the early 1970s, less than 20 years after Sputnik's launch, it was estimated that by

The unabated knowledge explosion has influenced the erosion of respect for traditional authority figures.

the time children born in 1980 reached the age of 50, the world's knowledge would have increased 32 times, and 97 percent of all knowledge would have been learned since they were born (Toffler, 1970). With the advances that have been made in the last 25 years, these estimates are probably much too low. Nothing illustrates this better than the emergence of the "information superhighway" or Internet. The Internet provides any user of a personal computer with instantaneous access to an almost limitless range and quantity of global information.

Such a rapid expansion of knowledge has caused generation gaps characterized by discontinuities rather than mere differences. By the end of elementary school many children possess knowledge that their parents only vaguely comprehend. This is poignantly clear in such areas as personal computing, information retrieval, ecology, biotechnology, and astronomy. In addition, because of the almost instantaneous telecommunication of national and world events, children are keenly aware of the state of the present world. They see famine, terrorist attacks, political corruption, drug busts, and chemical spills on a daily basis.

Such knowledge has caused many young people to view adults as ineffective in managing their own world. These young people perceive past solutions to life's problems as irrelevant to the world in which they live. Therefore, respect, which was once given to adults because of their worldliness and expertise, has eroded, and adults exercise less influence on the young than they once did. When talking to adolescents, it is common to hear such statements as, "My parents don't understand," "Why do we have to do it by hand when there are calculators that can do it for you?" and "Why do I have to be honest when government officials are always lying?"

As the world becomes a more complex and frightening place and as young people perceive their parents and teachers to be less relevant sources for solutions, the future becomes for these young people more remote, uncertain, and unpredictable, producing such feelings as "live for today." More than 30 years ago, Stinchcombe (1964) demonstrated a direct relationship between adolescents' images of the future and their attitudes and behaviors. Those adolescents who saw little or nothing to be gained in the future from school attendance were likely to exhibit rebellious, alienated behavior. Unfortunately, there are even more young people today with this image of the future than there were in 1964. Clearly, then, a teacher's ability to maximize student success and demonstrate the present and future usefulness of the material to be learned plays an important role in students' perceived value of education.

The Knowledge Explosion, Teacher and Student Feelings of Frustration, and the Relevancy of Schooling

Students are not alone in their feelings of frustration. Teachers too perceive many school curricula to be irrelevant to today's world. They are frustrated because of the almost impossible task of keeping up with the expansion of knowledge and the new technologies. Changes in school curricula occur at a snail's pace when compared to the daily expansion of information and technological advances.

Many teachers have said that they find it impossible to keep abreast of developments in their content areas and the rapidly expanding array of new pedagogical

CASE 3.1 • *"This Is the Greatest Thing That Has Happened to Me in Twenty Years of Teaching"*

About five years ago at a national education conference, one of the authors met Mr. Lee, a 20-year veteran high-school earth science teacher. Mr. Lee said that he felt he was no longer reaching his students who were disinterested and turned off. In his opinion, every day was an endless hassle. He was not sure he wanted to return to the classroom the next year.

A few years later, surprisingly, Mr. Lee was seen again at another national education conference. He said that not only had he remained in the classroom but that his enthusiasm for teaching was as high as it had ever been. Mr. Lee went on to say that shortly after meeting us, he had challenged himself to restructure his course to reflect contemporary earth science.

He had used his yearly allotment to purchase a modem to connect his students to a real-time meteorological–oceanographic database that allowed them to access the same up-to-the-minute data that scientists used. It was, he said, the best strategy he had ever used. For the first time in many years, visitation night was crowded with parents who had come to see what was going on in their sons' and daughters' science class. Many of the parents commented that their children were coming home talking about the neat things they were doing in science for the first time ever.

Mr. Lee ended the conversation by telling us that he was so impressed by the educational impact of technology that he had decided to study instructional technology at the graduate level and had enrolled in a doctoral program.

models, many of which support the use of new technologies. In addition, many have found it difficult to integrate the new material into an already overloaded curriculum. While they truly desire to restructure their curricula in meaningful ways and to integrate technologies into their instructional practices, they often find that their schools lack the necessary resources or commitment to invest in the latest technologies, training, or teacher release time for curriculum development. Their feelings of frustration lead to job dissatisfaction and poor morale, which can spill into the classroom disguised as less than ideal teacher–student interactions. However, when schools are able to invest in the new technologies and teachers are properly trained in their use, powerful changes can occur for both teachers and students, as illustrated in Case 3.1.

Just as students are positively affected by contemporary and innovative educational programs that meet their needs, they are negatively affected by those that do not. Frustration is a natural outcome when instructional methodology does not change, and students are expected to learn more in shorter periods of time. Traditional instructional practices used to deliver outdated content become meaningless and boring to youth who are growing up in a world significantly different from that of their parents. What often is labeled by teachers as only a lack of motivation may actually involve the students' inability to feel any affiliation with what is going on in the classroom (Gabay, 1991). Lack of affiliation leads to boredom and off-task, disruptive classroom behaviors.

CASE 3.2 • *Who Really Cares?*

The question that would win the game seemed simple: What is the capital of Kansas? Even so, none of the adults who were playing could remember. Don said, "How do they expect you to remember such ridiculous facts? This is exactly what bothers me about these games." He then called his two daughters over and said, "Hey, you learn the state capitals in fifth grade, don't you? So what's the capital of Kansas?" Amy, who was in seventh grade, replied, "I hated that stuff. We had to memorize all 50 state capitals, take a stupid test, and we never used it again. Who really cares what the capital is!" Mary, who was finishing fifth grade, replied, "I don't remember, but it's not hard to find out. I can look it up on the school's computer tomorrow. It has a CD-ROM. It's incredible. I don't know how it works but we have a disk that has everything about geography on it. If you want, I can even print a map of the capital."

Teaching facts only is not sufficient. To prepare them for their futures rather than our past, students must be instructed in ways that facilitate their "learning how to learn" (see Chapter 5). Case 3.2 illustrates how students respond to different types of educational experiences, depending on their relevancy. Obviously, Mary has a much better attitude about capitals than her sister. Although neither sister knew the requested capital, Mary knew one way to find it and was willing to follow through. Could it be that the different attitudes are related to the different instructional strategies that had been used in the girls' classrooms? Unlike Amy, Mary had an opportunity to use appropriate instructional technology and was taught a skill that facilitates her ability to be a self-learner. In other words, Mary was "learning how to learn."

Television and Violence

Unlike any stimulus available earlier in human history, including radio, television transmits to a viewer incredible amounts of information and gives the viewer a "window on the world." Ninety-eight percent of all U.S. homes have at least one television set. The average American child spends as much or more time watching television—23 to 28 hours per week (American Psychological Association, 1993)—than she does in a classroom. Clearly, then, television has become a major source of information for and major influence on children. The inhabitants of the TV world, however, often act and think in ways that contrast sharply with the attitudes and behaviors of parents and teachers.

Most studies on the impact of television on children have concentrated on the amount of violence portrayed and its effects. In 1993 the American Psychological Association stated, "Nearly 4 decades of research on television viewing and other media have documented the almost universal exposure of American children to high levels of media violence" (p. 33). Content analysis of television shows in the early

1950s indicated that on the average there were 11 threats or acts of violence per hour. However, TV programs in 1992 set an all-time record for violence, with 32 acts per hour, in children's shows alone. Given the format for most TV programs in the United States—brief sequences of fast-paced action with frequent interruptions for unrelated commercial messages—it was predicted in 1993 that the average child would witness 8,000 televised murders and 100,000 acts of violence before finishing elementary school (*Congressional Quarterly,* 1993).

Violence is not solely a characteristic of fictional TV programming. The "eye-witness" local news format frequently features violent stories. Content analysis has indicated that stories about murder, rape, and assault are disproportionately covered as local news, while stories of international violence and crime predominate in national newscasts (Atkin, 1983).

Although in the 1950s some psychologists suggested that TV violence had a cathartic effect and reduced a child's aggressive behaviors, by the 1980s, laboratory and field studies had cast serious doubt on the cathartic hypothesis (Pearl, Bouthilet, and Lazar, 1982). The 1982 National Institute of Mental Health's report, "Television and Behavior: Ten Years of Scientific Progress and Implications for the Eighties," concluded that (1) research findings supported a causal relationship between television violence and aggressive behavior; (2) there was a consensus among researchers that television violence leads to aggressive behavior; (3) despite slight variations over the past decade, the amount of violence on television remained at consistently high levels; and (4) television cultivated television-influenced attitudes among viewers, heavy viewers being more fearful and less trusting of others than light viewers (Bouthilet and Lazar, 1982). The most definitive statement to date was made by the American Psychological Association in 1993: "There is absolutely no doubt that higher levels of viewing violence on television are correlated with increased acceptance of aggressive attitudes and increased aggressive behavior" (p. 33). Psychologists now suggest that the effects of TV violence may extend beyond viewers' increased aggressive behaviors to the "bystander effect," or the increased desensitization or callousness toward violence directed at others (*Congressional Quarterly,* 1993).

Some researchers have proposed that violence on TV produces stress in children. Too much exposure to too much violence over too long a time, they say, creates emotional upset and insecurity, leading to resultant disturbed behavior (Rice, 1981). A 1984 study has indicated that heavy TV viewing is associated with elementary school children's belief in a "mean and scary world" and that poor school behavior (restlessness, disruptiveness, inattentiveness, aggressiveness) is significantly correlated with the home TV environment (number of sets, hours of viewing, and type of programs) (Singer, Singer, and Rapaczynski, 1984).

Of course, there have been many theories about the relationship between TV viewing and children's behavior (Pearl, 1984). The observational modeling theory, which is now over 20 years old, is the most widely accepted. This theory proposes that aggression is learned from the models and real-life simulations portrayed on TV and is practiced through imitation (Bandura, 1973). In trying to explain the effects of TV on school behavior, Rice, Huston, and Wright (1982) have hypothesized that the stimuli of sound effects, exciting music, and fast-action images generate an arousal reaction, with an accompanying inability to tolerate the sometimes long conversations, explanations, and delays characteristic of the real world of school.

In addition to viewing violence on TV, children can participate vicariously in violence by playing today's video games. A recent study concluded that 80 percent of today's video games contain violence, a noted increase from earlier years (*Congressional Quarterly,* 1993). It has been hypothesized that the hands-on involvement of video games, more than the passive viewing of television or movies, leads to an increase in children's aggression. However, at this time no definitive research has been conducted.

Television and Alternative Role Models

Television also influences children's behaviors by presenting a wide range of alternative models and life-styles. For instance, Music Television (MTV), a very popular network with young people, broadcasts 24 hours a day the audio and video imagery of the latest rock music. What once were mostly inaudible lyrics are now visual depictions of songs, many of which concern drug and alcohol use, sexual promiscuity, hopelessness, and distrust of school and teachers.

The recent proliferation of "talk-shows," especially during late afternoon hours, presents children with a glamorized view of oftentimes dysfunctional family life as they attempt to determine who they are, what they can do, and how far they can go in testing the limits of their parents' and teachers' authority. Television communicates to children pluralistic standards, changing customs, and shifting beliefs and values.

While behavioral experimentation is both a prerequisite and a necessary component of the cognitive and moral developmental growth of young people, today's world is not as simple as it once was, and parents and teachers need to be aware of alternative models with which they compete.

Television's messages possibly have the most detrimental effects on children who live in poverty. These children usually are aware that they do not possess the things most other Americans have. They also know they lack the opportunities to obtain them in the near future. Thus, television's depiction of the "good life" may compound their feelings of hopelessness, discontent, and anger. Such feelings, coupled with the fact that many of these children feel they hold no stake in the values and norms of the more affluent society, lay the foundation for rage, which is often released in violent or aggressive behaviors directed at others (American Psychological Association, 1993). It is imperative for teachers to be aware of these outside influences on student behaviors in order to work constructively with and be supportive of today's youth.

Failure to Meet Children's Basic Needs

The Home Environment

Educators have long recognized the significant influence of home life on a child's behavior and on academic progress. As Case 3.3 illustrates, the home's ability to meet students' basic needs is particularly crucial.

CASE 3.3 • *Hanging on the Corner*

Teresa, a fifth-grade student, is on the school playground at 7:45 every morning, even though school doesn't start until 9:00. Often she is eating a bag of potato chips and drinking a can of soda. On cold, snowy mornings, she huddles in the doorway wearing a spring jacket and sneakers, waiting for the door to be unlocked. She brags to the other students that she hangs out on the corner with the teenagers in her neighborhood until 12:00 or 1:00 A.M. The home and school coordinator who has investigated her home environment has confirmed this.

Teresa is the youngest of four children. Her father left the family before she started school. Her mother works for a janitorial service and leaves for work by 7:00 A.M. When she returns home in the evening she either goes out with her boyfriend or goes to sleep early, entrusting Teresa's care to her 16-year-old brother, who has recently quit school.

Teresa is two years below grade in both reading and mathematics. She is never prepared for class with the necessary books and materials, never completes homework assignments, and usually chooses not to participate in learning activities. Her classroom behavior is excessively off-task, characterized by noisy movements both in and out of her seat, calling out, and disruption of other students by talking to them or physically touching them. Occasionally she becomes abusive to her fellow students and her teacher, using a loud, challenging voice and vulgarities.

When considering Teresa's home environment, is it surprising that she has academic and behavior problems in school? Abraham Maslow's theory of basic human needs predicts Teresa's behavior. According to Maslow (1968), basic human needs align themselves into a hierarchy of the following levels:

1. Physiological needs: hunger, thirst, breathing
2. Safety and security needs: protection from injury, pain, extremes of heat and cold
3. Belonging and affection needs: giving and receiving love, warmth, and affection
4. Esteem and self-respect needs: feeling adequate, competent, worthy; being appreciated and respected by others
5. Self-actualization needs: self-fulfillment by using one's talents and potential

If lower-level needs are not met, an individual may experience difficulty, frustration, and a lack of motivation in attempting to meet the higher-order needs.

Maslow's hierarchy also represents a series of developmental levels. Although the meeting of these needs is important throughout an individual's life, a young child spends considerably more time and effort meeting the lower-level needs than an older child. From preadolescence on, assuming the lower-level needs are met, emphasis shifts to the higher-order needs of esteem and self-actualization. (Further discussion of self-esteem is found in a later section.)

Academic achievement and appropriate behavior are most likely to occur when a student's home environment has met her physiological, safety, and belonging needs. This enables her to begin to work on meeting the needs of esteem and self-actualization both at home and at school.

Let's now examine Teresa's home environment in light of Maslow's hierarchy of basic needs. Her breakfast of potato chips and soda, her clothing (a light jacket and sneakers) on cold days, the lack of a father at home, and a mother who is rarely present are indications that her physiological, safety, and belonging needs are not being met. Because of her inadequate home environment, she has attempted to meet her need for belonging and esteem by bragging about hanging out with teenagers and by using loud, vulgar statements in class and disturbing other students. Given her situation, it is surprising that Teresa still attends school on a regular basis. If her home environment remains the same, if she continues to achieve below grade academically, and if she continues to exhibit behavior problems, she probably will quit school at an early age, still unable to control her own behavior.

The results of a longitudinal study of third-, sixth-, and ninth-grade students (Feldhusen, Thurston, and Benning, 1973) provided clear evidence of the importance of the home environment on school behavior. Persistently disruptive students differed substantially from persistently prosocial students in a number of home and family variables:

1. Parental supervision and discipline were inadequate, being too lax, too strict, or erratic.
2. The parents were indifferent or hostile to the child. They disapproved of many things about the child and handed out angry, physical punishment.
3. The family operated only partially if at all, as a unit, and the marital relationship lacked closeness and equality of partnership.
4. The parents found it difficult to discuss concerns regarding the child and believed that they had little influence on the child. They believed that other children exerted bad influences on their child.

In its 1993 publication, *Violence and Youth*, the American Psychological Association offered examples of the family characteristics of children with anti-social behaviors that were quite similar to the Feldhusen et al. findings. The examples included parental rejection, inconsistent and physically abusive discipline, and parental support of their children's use of aversive and aggressive problem-solving approaches. The study found lack of parental supervision was one of the strongest predictors of children's later conduct disorders.

Case 3.3, Feldhusen's longitudinal study, and the American Psychological Association summary describe homes that could be considered abusive or at least neglectful. However, many nonabusive or nonneglectful home environments also create situations that are quite stressful to children. This stress may be symptomatically displayed as behavior problems. Consider, for example, Case 3.4.

While Seth's home environment is significantly different from Teresa's, it too has a detrimental effect on behavior in school. Seth's situation is one that an increasing

CASE 3.4 • *Marital Conflict*

Seth was a typical eleventh-grade student from a middle-class home who attended a suburban high school. For the most part he was motivated and attentive. Occasionally he had to be reminded to stop talking or to take his seat when class started. His grades were B's with a few C's. He planned to attend a state college and major in liberal arts. Teachers enjoyed having Seth in their classes.

Now, at the end of eleventh grade, Seth has changed. He doesn't turn in homework, is often off-task, and his moti- vation is reduced. His future plans are to get a job after high school rather than to attend college.

Conferences with his teachers and counselors reveal that Seth's parents have begun to discuss divorce. Since Seth is the oldest of three children, he often is involved in discussions with his parents concerning how the family will manage in the future. Both his mother and father now ask him for assistance in meeting family responsibilities rather than asking each other.

---

number of children face. As former U.S. Secretary of Education, Terrel H. Bell, said in an address given in 1984 to educational leaders: "The problems of American education today are at least partly attributed to changes that have taken place over the past decade in the lifestyle, stability, and commitment of parents."

What changes have occurred in the home environment of American children? Between 1960 and 1993, the divorce rate increased over 100 percent. In 1993 the divorce rate was approximately 52 percent of new marriages (U.S. Bureau of the Census, 1994). Remarriage often creates additional problems for children (Visher and Visher, 1978). Any form of marital conflict increases the likelihood that children will develop some type of behavioral problem (Rutter, 1978).

Unmarried-couple households are also increasing with 75 percent of teen births occurring to unmarried girls. It is estimated that if the proportion of births to unmarried women continues, more than 40 percent of all babies born in 2001 will go home to single-parent homes (Children's Defense Fund, 1994, 1997).

Divorce not only changes the family structure, but also frequently results in a decrease in the family's standard of living, with an increasing number of children and their single mothers moving into poverty status (Levine, 1984). In 1992, 14.8 million children lived in female-headed households, 54 percent of which were at or below the poverty level. It is estimated that by the year 2001, 24 percent (17 million) of all children under the age of 18 will be poor (Children's Defense Fund, 1994). In 1995, 14.7 million children (21 percent) lived below the poverty line, more than in any year since 1965 (Children's Defense Fund, 1997). These children are at greater risk than others of devel- oping academic and/or behavioral problems (American Psychological Association, 1993; Children's Defense Fund, 1997; Gelfand, Jenson, & Drew, 1982; Parke, 1978).

If, as Levine (1984) has suggested, out-of-school experiences are stronger pre- dictors of school behavior than their inschool experiences, today's children need competent teachers more than ever before. Still, as the president of the Elementary School Principals Association recently noted, there never will be any lasting educational reform until there is parental reform (Whitmire, 1991).

The School Environment

Physiological Needs.   Students are in school to learn. They are continually asked to demonstrate their new understanding and skills. In asking them to do so, schools are attempting to aid students in a process that Maslow calls self-actualization. When students successfully demonstrate new learnings, they usually are intrinsically and extrinsically positively reinforced, which leads to the development of self-esteem and self-respect. Positive self-esteem further motivates students to learn, which results in the further development of self-actualization. The self-esteem, learning, self-actualization cycle can be maximized only if the home and schools create environments in which the lower-level needs—physiological, safety and security, belonging and affection—are met.

Case 3.5 illustrates how a young child attempts to meet the physiological need of movement and activity. For some young children, no school activity takes more energy than sitting still. When the teacher demanded that Sarah sit and eventually removed recess, Sarah's physiological need was no longer being met. This resulted in Sarah's excessive movement around the room. When Sarah's needs were met, the disruptive behaviors stopped.

The importance of meeting students' physiological needs as a prerequisite to learning should be evident to everyone. Ask any teacher how much learning occurs

CASE 3.5 • *Forgetting to Sit Down*

Sarah, a second-grade student, is a bright, happy, active child. She is always the first one ready for recess and the last one to stop playing. When going to or from school, she is often seen skipping, jumping, or doing cartwheels.

Sarah's desk is second from the front. When given seat work, she either stands at her desk or half stands with one knee on the chair. Her teacher always reminds her to sit, but no sooner has she sat down then she is back up on her feet.

After a good number of reminders, Sarah is kept in from recess. When this occurs, she begins to walk around the room when class is in progress. This leads to further reprimands by her teacher. Finally her parents are notified.

Sarah's parents inform her teacher that at home Sarah is always jumping rope, playing catch, dancing, and even standing rather than sitting for piano lessons and practice. She even stands at the table at mealtimes. It is decided that Sarah's seat will be moved to the back of the room so that her standing doesn't interfere with the other students. After this is explained to Sarah, she agrees to the move. The reprimands stop. Sarah continues to do excellent work, and by the end of second grade, she is able to sit in her seat while working.

on the first cold day of fall before the heating system is functional or on the first hot day of early spring before the heating system has been turned off. Unfortunately, many of our nation's schools are not new, and it is only recently that public attention has turned to correcting the dilapidated conditions that exist in many urban and rural schools. At a minimum every classroom in every school should have adequate space and proper lighting and ventilation.

Somewhat less evident, but no less important than a school's environmental conditions, are concerns about hunger, overcrowding, noise, and frequent interruptions. Teachers have long known that students are less attentive in classes held just before lunch. When schools are overcrowded and/or lunch facilities are inadequate, lunch can span a three-hour period. Some students may eat lunch before 11:00 A.M.,

CASE 3.6 • *There Must Be a Better Way*

One university requires its secondary student teachers to follow a student's schedule of classes for an entire day. Student teachers are required to record their reactions to this experience. What follows are some common reactions:

No sooner were we in our seats in the first-period class than the V.P. was on the intercom system. She spent at least five minutes with announcements mostly directed for the teachers' attention. The speaker was loud and very annoying. After the announcements most of the students were talking among themselves. By the time we got down to work, 15 minutes had passed. Halfway through the period a student messenger interrupted the class when he brought the morning office notices to the teacher. And believe it or not, five minutes before the end of class the V.P. was back on the intercom with additional announcements. It was quite evident to me that these interruptions were a direct cause of inattentiveness and reduction in effective instruction. Much time was wasted during the announcements and in obtaining student on-task behavior after the interruptions. There must be a better way.

Probably the most eye-opening experience I had was remembering how crowded and noisy schools can be. This was most evident to me when we changed classes. We had three minutes between classes. The halls were very crowded, with frequent pushing, shoving, and just bumping into each other. The noise level was so loud that it really bothered me. On arriving at the next class all I really wanted to do was to sit quietly for a few minutes before starting to work. The changes from hallways to classrooms are dramatic. I can see why it is difficult for some students to settle down and get on task at the beginning of class. As bad as the hallways were, it didn't prepare me for lunch. The lunch room was even noisier. By the time I waited in line I only had 15 minutes to eat and then back to the hallways to class. By the end of the day I was drained.

CASE 3.7 • *Too Much Noise*

Karen is a third-grade student who is well behaved and does well academically. One day all of the third-grade classes are taken to the all-purpose room to observe a film. The classes are dismissed simultaneously, and the children in the hallway are very noisy because of excitement. Karen is seen walking in the hallway with her hands over her ears. When she enters the room, she goes directly to the back corner and sits against the wall. The teacher asks her what is the matter. She says the noise hurts her ears; she feels like crying and she doesn't want to be there if it is going to be so noisy.

After the teachers quiet the students, Karen rejoins her class. Referral to an ear specialist discloses that Karen has no problems with her hearing that would have caused such a reaction.

whereas others may not eat until after 1:00 P.M. This can produce a group of students whose long wait for lunch leaves them inattentive to learning tasks.

Interruptions, noise, and overcrowding produce in students, regardless of age, emotional uneasiness that may result in nervousness, anxiety, a need to withdraw, or overactivity. In both of these cases, emotional uneasiness interferes with on-task behavior and reduces the effectiveness of the teaching/learning environment. Consider, for example, Cases 3.6 and 3.7. Schools must pay particular attention to minimizing distractions if they want to reduce student off-task behavior.

Safety and Security Needs.   For the most part, schools create environments in which students feel safe from physical harm. There are, however, occasions when students, like Keith in Case 3.8, fear for their physical safety. Students in some schools sometimes are assaulted, coerced, bribed, or robbed. In 1997, 36 percent of tenth-grade stu-

CASE 3.8 • *Afraid of Going to School*

Keith, an eighth-grade student, achieves at an average level in his social studies class, which meets during the last period of the day. Approximately midway through the year Keith's behavior in this class begins to change. He goes from a student who is attentive and participates freely to one who rarely participates and has to be called back to attention by the teacher. He often is seen nervously looking out the window and is the first out of his seat and room at the end of class.

After a few days of such behavior, the teacher asks Keith to stay for a few minutes after class to discuss his behavior. At this point Keith tells his teacher that he has to be the first to leave school because Greg will beat him up if he sees him. Keith is fearful of Greg because Greg has threatened him for telling the gym teacher that he was throwing Keith's clothing around the locker room after gym class.

dents surveyed reported that they had been threatened or injured at school (National Education Goals Panel, 1997). This may not be surprising, as it has been estimated that a total of 270,000 guns are brought to school each day (American Psychological Association, 1993), and the presence of street gangs at school is increasing (Chandler et al., 1998). Also there are students in all schools who occasionally experience anxiety about walking to and from school, going to the restroom, changing in locker rooms, or changing classes. Nevertheless, the more students feel insecure about their physical safety, the less likely they will exhibit the on-task behaviors necessary for learning.

Belonging and Affection Needs. While these needs are most often met by family at home or by the students' peers in and out of school, there must be elements of caring, trust, and respect in the interpersonal relationships between teachers and students. In other words, there should be a caring, supportive classroom climate. Such a climate is more likely to be created by teachers who subscribe to a referent power base in the classroom. The development of various teacher power bases will be studied in Chapter 4.

Withall (1969) has stressed that the most important variable in determining the climate of a classroom is the teacher's verbal and nonverbal behaviors. Appropriate student behavior can be enhanced when teachers communicate the following to the learners:

Trust: "I believe you are able to learn and want to learn."

Respect: "Insofar as I try to help you learn, you are, by the same token, helping me to learn."

CASE 3.9 • *Turning Off Students*

Ms. Washington, a high-school science teacher, is quite concerned over what she perceives to be a significant decrease in student participation throughout the year. She views the problem as follows: "I ask a lot of questions. Early in the year many students volunteer but within a few weeks I find that volunteering has almost ceased and the only way I can get students to participate is to call on them."

Arrangements are made to observe the class to determine the causes of the problem. Teacher questions, student responses, and teacher feedback are recorded. An example of one such interaction:

Teacher Question: "We know that man is in the family of Hominidae. What is man's taxonomic order?"

Student Response: "Mammals."

Teacher Feedback: "No, it's not mammals. We had this material last week; you should know it. The answer is Primates."

Further observation reveals that about 70 percent of Ms. Washington's feedback is totally or partially negative. Students note that they don't feel like being put down because their answer isn't exactly what Ms. Washington wants. One student states, "I only answer when I know I'm correct. If I don't understand something I often just let it go rather than be drilled."

CASE 3.10 • *"I'm Going to Be Sorry When Fifth Grade Is Over"*

One afternoon last May I overheard a group of fifth-grade students say, "I'm going to be sorry when fifth grade is over." I stopped and asked them if they would be willing to tell me why they felt this way. The following were their comments:

"She lets us give our opinions."

"If we say something stupid, she doesn't say anything."

"She lets us decide how we are going to do things."

"She gives us suggestions and helps us when we get stuck."

"You can say how you feel."

"She gives us choices."

"She tells us what she thinks, but doesn't want us to think like her. Some teachers tell us their opinions, but you know that they really want you to think the same way."

"We learn a lot."

Caring: "I perceive you as a unique and worthwhile person whom I want to help to learn and grow." (Withall, 1979)

For students to learn effectively, they must participate fully in the learning process. This means they must be encouraged to ask and answer questions, attempt new approaches, make mistakes, and ask for assistance. However, learners only engage in these behaviors in settings in which they feel safe from being ridiculed or made to feel inadequate. Study Case 3.9. As the year progressed, Ms. Washington failed to demonstrate her trust, respect, and caring for her students. Thus, her students were discouraged from fully participating in the learning process.

Comments such as, "Why do you ask so many questions?" "You should know this; we studied it last week," or "Everyone should understand this; there should be no questions" serve no useful purpose. Indeed they hinder learner participation, confidence, and motivation and lead to off-task behavior. Glasser (1978) sees failure as the root of misbehavior, noting that when students don't learn at the expected rate, they get less "care" and recognition from the teacher. As the situation continues, students see themselves as trapped. Acceptance and recognition, it seems to them, can be gained only through misbehavior. In sharp contrast to the feelings of Ms. Washington's students are the feelings of the fifth-grade students in Case 3.10.

Children's Pursuit of Social Recognition and Self-Esteem

Social Recognition

Alfred Adler, the renowned psychiatrist, and Rudolph Dreikurs, Adler's student and colleague, believed that behavior can be best understood using three key premises.

1. People are social beings who have a need to belong, to be recognized, and to be accepted.
2. Behavior is goal directed and has the purpose of gaining the recognition and acceptance that people want.
3. People can choose how they behave; they can behave or misbehave. Their behavior is not outside their control.

Putting these key ideas together, Adler and Dreikurs theorized that people choose to try a wide variety of behaviors to see which behaviors gain them the recognition and acceptance they want. When socially accepted behaviors do not produce the needed recognition and acceptance, people choose to misbehave in the mistaken belief that socially unacceptable behaviors will produce the recognition they seek.

Applying these premises to children's conduct, Dreikurs, Grundwald, and Pepper (1982) have identified four goals of disruptive behaviors: attention getting, power seeking, revenge seeking, and the display of inadequacy. According to this theory, these goals, which are usually sequential, are strongest in elementary-aged children but are also present in adolescents.

Attention-seeking students make up a large part of the misbehaving population in the schools. These students may ask question after question, use excessive charm, continually need help or assistance, continually ask for the teacher's approval, call out, or show off. In time, the teacher usually becomes annoyed. When the teacher reprimands or gives these children attention, they temporarily stop their attention-seeking behavior. In Case 3.11, Bob was a child who felt that he was not getting the recognition he desired. He saw no chance of gaining this recognition through socially accepted or constructive contributions. He first channeled his energies into gaining attention. Like all attention-seeking students, he had the notion that he was important only when others took notice of him and acknowledged his presence. When attention-getting behavior no longer gives the students the recognition they want, many of them seek recognition through the next goal, power, which is exactly what Bob did when he began to confront the teacher openly.

Students who seek power through misbehavior feel that they can do what they want and that nobody can make them do anything they don't want to do. By challenging teachers, they often gain social acceptance from their peers. Power-seeking students argue, lie, ignore, become stubborn, have temper tantrums, and become disobedient in general to show that they are in command of the situation. Teachers feel threatened or challenged by these children and often feel compelled to force them into compliance. Once teachers enter into power struggles with power-seeking students, the students usually "win." Even if they do not succeed in getting what they want, they succeed in getting the teacher to fight, thereby giving them undue attention and time as well as control of the situation. If the teacher "wins" the power struggle, the winning reinforces the students' idea that power is what really counts.

With a power-seeking student, reprimands from the teacher result in intensified challenges or temporary withdrawal before new power-seeking behaviors reappear. As power struggles develop between a teacher and a student, both teacher controlling and student power-seeking behaviors usually become more severe and the student–teacher

CASE 3.11 • *Seeking Faulty Goals*

Bob is a sixth-grade student of average academic ability. On the first day of class when students are asked to choose seats, Bob chooses the one next to the window in the back of the room. Between classes he rarely interacts with classmates. Instead he either bolts out of the class first or slowly swaggers out last.

During instructional times he either nonchalantly leans back in his seat or jumps up and calls out answers. During seat work he often has to be reminded to begin, and once finished, he taps his pencil, wanders around the back of the room, or noisily moves his chair and desk.

Bob's behavior often improves for short periods of time after excessive teacher attention, ranging from positive reinforcement to reprimands. These periods of improvement are followed by a return to disruptive behaviors. Bob's attention-seeking behavior continues throughout the first half of the school year.

As time goes on, the teacher usually yells at Bob, sends him to the principal, or makes comments in front of the class that reflect her extreme frustration.

Eventually, the teacher's behavior is characterized by threats, such as, "You will stay after school longer every day until you begin to behave," or "Every day that you don't turn in your homework, you will have 20 more problems to do." Bob sees immediately the impossibility of some of the threats and boldly says, "If I have to stay after school longer each day, in two weeks I'll have to sleep here." There are tremendous amounts of laughter from his classmates at such comments. However, after a week or two, Bob says, "I'm not coming for your detention," and "You can't make me do homework if I don't want to." The teacher no longer feels annoyed but now feels threatened and challenged.

Whenever problems arise in the classroom, the teacher and students are quick to blame Bob. Occasionally he is accused of things that he has not done, and he is quick to shout, "I didn't do it; I'm always the one who gets blamed for everything around here." His classmates now show extreme annoyance with his behaviors, and Bob resorts to acts directed against individuals. He kicks students' chairs and intentionally knocks over others' books as he walks down the aisles.

One day one of the boys in the class accuses Bob of taking his book. Without warning, Bob flips the student's desk. The student falls backward, lands on his arm, and breaks it. As a result, Bob is suspended.

When Bob returns from his suspension, he is told that he will be sent to the office for any violation of a classroom rule. He is completely ignored by his classmates.

For the rest of the year Bob comes in, goes to the back of the room, does no work, and bothers no one. At first the teacher tries to get Bob involved, but all efforts are refused. The teacher thinks to herself that she has tried everything she knows. "If he wants to just sit there, let him. At least he isn't bothering anyone any more," she says.

---

relationship deteriorates further (Levin and Shanken-Kaye, 1996). If the student sees herself as losing the power struggle, she often moves to the next goal—seeking revenge.

When students perceive that they have no control over their environment, they experience an increased sense of inferiority and futility. They feel that they have been treated unfairly and are deeply hurt by what they consider to be others' disregard for their feelings. They seek revenge by hurting others, often not just those that they think have hurt them. For instance, Bob sought his revenge on random individuals who happened to be sitting along his aisle. Revenge-seeking children destroy property, threaten other students and sometimes the teacher, engage in extremely rough play, and use obscenities.

When working with these students, teachers feel defeated and hurt and have a difficult time being concerned with what is best for the student. Teacher reprimands usually result in an explosive display of anger and abusiveness from the student. Over time, the teacher feels a strong desire "to get even."

Unfortunately, revenge-seeking behaviors elicit dislike and more hurt from others. Revenge-seeking students continually feel a deep sense of despair and worthlessness. Their interactions with other people often result in negative feelings about themselves, which eventually move them to the last goal—the display of inadequacy. They cannot be motivated and refuse to participate in class activities. Their message is clear: "Don't expect anything from me because I have nothing worthwhile to give." They are often heard saying, "Why don't you just leave me alone, I'm not bothering anyone"; "Mind your own business"; "Why try, I'll just get it wrong"; or "I can't do it."

Teachers often feel that they have tried everything with these students. Further attempts usually result in very little, if any, change in the students' refusal to show interest, to participate, or to interact with others. Bob's teacher actually felt somewhat relieved that he no longer was a disturbing influence in class. However, if the teacher had been able to stop his progression toward the display of inadequacy, Bob would have had a much more meaningful and valuable sixth-grade learning experience, and the teacher would have felt much more professionally competent.

Most of the goals of misbehavior are pursued one at a time, but some students switch back and forth between goals. Goal-seeking misbehaviors can also be situational. The decision-making hierarchical approach to classroom management presented in this book offers many strategies for working with children seeking these four mistaken goals. In addition, specific management techniques for each goal are discussed in detail in Charles et al. (1995), Dreikurs, Grundwald, and Pepper (1982), Dubelle and Hoffman (1984), and Sweeney (1981).

Self-Esteem

Self-esteem, or a feeling of self-worth, is a basic need that individuals continually strive to meet. Without a positive sense of self-esteem, a child is vulnerable to a variety of social, psychological, and learning problems (Gilliland, 1986).

In his definitive work on self-esteem, Stanley Coopersmith (1967) wrote that self-esteem is made up of four components:

> *Significance:* a learner's belief that she is liked, accepted, and important to others who are important to her.
>
> *Competence:* a learner's sense of mastery of age-appropriate tasks that have value to her.

Power: a learner's ability to control important parts of her environment.

Virtue: closely akin to significance, a learner's sense of worthiness to another person's well-being because of the care and help she provides to the other person.

If families, teachers, or communities fail to provide prosocial opportunities that allow students to experience a sense of significance, competence, power, and virtue, students are likely to express their significance, competence, power, and virtue in negative, distorted ways (Levin and Shanken-Kaye, 1996).

It is possible to express the concept of self-esteem mathematically. When it is symbolized in this manner, it offers an explanation of why students choose to be disruptive.

$$\text{Self-Esteem} = \text{Significance} + \text{Competence} + \text{Power} + \text{Virtue}$$

Chronically disruptive students have low levels of significance because typically they are not liked or accepted by their teachers, peers, and sometimes even their parents. Their levels of competence are depressed because they rarely achieve academically, or are socially competent or involved in extracurricular activities. In addition, because these students rarely choose or are rarely selected by the teacher to interact responsibly with others, their sense of virtue is low. Therefore, as the self-esteem equation indicates, the only component left to build a chronically disruptive student's self-esteem is power. It is exactly this striving for power, or control of the environment, that is operating when students choose to behave disruptively. In fact the chronically disruptive student can be viewed as the most powerful individual in the classroom. How she behaves often determines the amount of time spent on learning in the classroom and whether the teacher leaves the classroom with a headache, or, in some cases, leaves the profession. It is, however, important to note that this is not prosocial power but distorted power. The display of distorted power provides the student with a distorted sense of significance and competence which is evident in a comment such as, "The other kids know that they can count on me to get Mr. Beal to go ballistic and liven this class up a bit."

As Case 3.12 illustrates, when a teacher interacts with a student without considering the student's self-esteem, she increases the likelihood that the student will use distorted power to preserve self-esteem. If the student's self-esteem is publicly threatened in front of her peers, the likelihood that she will use distorted power increases.

Stages of Cognitive and Moral Development

Not too long ago it was believed that children thought exactly the same way as adults think. Jean Piaget's work in the area of cognitive development, however, has shown that children move through distinct stages of cognitive and moral development. At each stage children think and interpret their environment differently than children at other stages. For this reason, a child's behavior varies as the child moves from one

CASE 3.12 • *"Get Out of My Face"*

Rob, Tom, Jason, Tanya, Margo, and Beth are talking in the hallway outside their seventh-period classroom door. Ms. Wertz comes out of her room and screams across the hall, "Jason, get to class immediately. A student like you should never be standing around wasting time. You need all the time in class you can get." Jason says, "Ms. Wertz, my class is right here and we have another two minutes. . . ." Before he can finish, Ms. Wertz interrupts, "Don't give me any excuses, you always have excuses." Again, Jason says, "Ms. Wertz, this isn't an excuse, this is my class." Ms. Wertz goes on, "Jason, you are nothing but trouble and someday you'll find out that you aren't such a big shot." Jason turns to Ms. Wertz and says "I don't even have you for a teacher this year so why don't you get out of my face and leave me alone?" Ms. Wertz refers Jason to the office, and later that day he is given three days of detention.

stage to another. An understanding of the stages of development enables a teacher to better understand student behavior patterns.

Cognitive Development

Throughout his life, Piaget studied how children interacted with their environment and how their intellect developed. To him, knowledge was the transformation of an individual's experience with the environment, not the accumulation of facts and pieces of information. His research resulted in the formulation of a four-stage age-related cognitive development theory (Piaget, 1970), which has significantly influenced the manner in which children are educated.

Piaget called the four stages of development the sensorimotor, the preoperational, the concrete operational, and the formal operational stages. The sensorimotor stage occurs from birth to approximately two years of age. It is characterized by the refinement of motor skills and the use of the five senses to explore the environment. This stage obviously has little importance for teachers working with school-age children.

The preoperational stage occurs from approximately two to seven years and is the stage most children have reached when they begin their school experience. Children at this stage are egocentric. They are unable to conceive that others may see things differently than they do. Although their ability to give some thought to decisions is developing, the great majority of the time they act only on perceptive impulses. Their short attention span interacts with their static thinking, resulting in an inability to think of a sequence of steps or operations. Their sense of time and space is limited to short duration and close proximity.

The concrete operational stage occurs from approximately seven to twelve years. Children are able to order and classify objects and to consider several variables simultaneously as long as they have experiences with "concrete" content. Step-by-step instructions are needed by these children if they are expected to work through lengthy procedures. What can be frustrating to teachers who do not understand the characteristics of this stage is that these children do not attempt to check their conclusions, have difficulty thinking about thinking (how they arrived at certain conclusions), and seem unaware of and unconcerned with inconsistencies in their own reasoning.

At about the age of twelve years, at the earliest, children begin to move into the formal operational stage. They begin to develop independent critical thinking skills, to plan lengthy procedures, and to consider a number of possible answers to problems. They no longer are tied to concrete examples but instead are able to use symbols and verbal examples. These children, who are adolescents, begin to think about their own and others' thinking, which leads them to consider motives; the past, present, and future; the abstract; the remote; and the ideal. The methodological implications for teaching students at each stage are somewhat obvious and have been researched and written about extensively (Adler, 1966; Gorman, 1972; Karplus, 1977).

Moral Development

Piaget related his theory of a child's cognitive development directly to the child's moral development. Through his work, Piaget demonstrated that a child is close to or at the formal operational stage of cognitive development before she possesses the intellectual ability to evaluate, consider, and act on abstract moral dilemmas. Thus, what an elementary school child thinks is bad or wrong is vastly different from what an adolescent thinks is wrong (Piaget, 1965).

Using Piaget's work as his basis, Laurence Kohlberg purposed that moral development progresses through six levels of moral reasoning: punishment–obedience, exchange of favors, good boy–nice girl, law and order, social contract, and universal ethical principles (Kohlberg, 1969, 1975).

Between the ages of four and six, children have a "punishment–obedience" orientation to moral reasoning. Their decisions are based on the physical consequences of an act; will they be punished or rewarded? Outcomes are paramount, and there is very little comprehension of a person's motive or intention. Children's egocentrism at this stage limits their ability to see other points of view or alternatives.

Between the ages of six and nine, children move into the "exchange of favors" orientation. At this level, judgments are made on the basis of reciprocal favors; you do this for me and I will do this for you. Fulfilling one's own needs comes first. Children are just beginning to understand the motives behind behaviors and outcomes.

Between the ages of ten and fifteen, children move into the "good boy–nice girl" orientation. Conformity dictates behavior and reasoning ability. Peer review is strong, and judgments about how to behave are made on the basis of avoiding criticism and pleasing others. The drive to conform with peers is so strong that it is quite common to follow peers unquestioningly but, at the same time, continually to ask "why" when requests are made by adults.

The "law and order" orientation dominates moral reasoning between the ages of fifteen and eighteen. Individuals at this stage of development are quite rigid.

Judgments are made on the basis of obeying the law. Motives are understood but not wholeheartedly considered if the behavior has broken a law. At this stage, teenagers are quick to recognize and point out inconsistencies in expected behavior. It is quite common to hear them say to adults, "Why do I have to do this? You don't." It is at this stage that adolescents begin to recognize the consequences of their actions.

According to Kohlberg, few people reach the last two levels of moral reasoning. The "social contract" orientation is reached by some between the ages of eighteen and twenty. At this level, moral judgments are made on the basis of upholding individual rights and democratic principles. Those who reach this level recognize that individuals differ in their values and do not accept "because I said so" or "that's the way it is" as rationales for rules.

The highest level of moral reasoning is the "universal ethical" orientation. Judgments are based on respect for the dignity of human beings and on what is good for humanity, not on selfish interests or standards upheld by authority.

As in cognitive development, the ages of any moral development stage are approximations. Individuals continually move back and forth between stages, depending on the moral situation at hand, especially at transitional points between stages.

Behavior: The Interaction of Cognitive and Moral Development

In order to understand how children perceive what is right and wrong, what cognitive skills they are able to use, and what motivates their social and academic behavior,

Some misbehavior can result when instruction is not matched with students' cognitive development stages.

teachers must know the stages of moral and cognitive growth. Teachers must also recognize common developmental behaviors that are a result of the interaction of the cognitive and moral stages through which the children pass. While this interaction does not and cannot explain all disruptive classroom behaviors, it does provide a basis on which we can begin to understand many disruptive behaviors. Table 3.1 summarizes the cognitive and moral stages of development, their characteristics, and associated behaviors.

At the beginning of elementary school, students are in the "preoperational" stage cognitively and the "punishment–obedience" stage morally. Their behavior is a result of the interplay of such factors as their egocentricity, limited sense of time and space, little comprehension of others' motives, and short attention span. At this stage, children become frustrated easily, have difficulty sharing, argue frequently, believe that they are right and their classmates wrong, and tattle a lot.

By middle to upper elementary school and beginning junior high or middle school, children are in the "concrete operational" stage cognitively and the "exchange of favors" to the "good boy–nice girl" stages morally. Early in this period, students form and reform cliques, act on opinions based on a single or very few concrete characteristics, and tell secrets. They employ many annoying attention-seeking behaviors to please the teacher. Later in the period the effects of peer conformity appear. Students are often off-task because they are constantly in conversation with their friends. Those who do not fit into the peer group are excluded and ridiculed.

Students still have little patience with long discussions and lengthy explanations. They are unaware of, or unconcerned about, their inconsistencies. They are

Age-specific behavior often is the result of the interaction of cognitive and moral development.

TABLE 3.1 *Cognitive and Moral Development with Common Associated Behaviors*

Cognitive Stage	Cognitive Abilities	Moral Stage	Moral Reasoning	Common Behaviors
Sensorimotor (0–2)	use of senses to "know" environment			
Preoperational (2–7)	difficulty with conceiving others' points of view (egocentric) sense of time & space limited to short duration/close proximity difficulty thinking through steps or decisions; acts impulsively	punishment–obedience (4–6)	actions based on physical outcome little comprehension of motives egocentric	inattentiveness easily frustrated difficulty sharing arguments during play
Concrete Operational (7–12)	limited ability to think about thinking often will not check conclusions unaware of and unconcerned with their own inconsistencies	exchange of favors (6–9)	actions based on reciprocal favors fulfilling one's own needs comes first beginning to understand motives	cliques attention-getting behavior exclusion of certain classmates inattentiveness during periods of discussion "know-it-all" attitude
		good boy–nice girl (10–15)	actions based on peer conformity	
Formal Operational (12–)	able to think about thinking can use independent critical thinking skills can consider motives; the past, present, and future; the abstract; and the ideal	law and order (15–18)	rigid judgments based on following the law motives and consequences recognized	point out inconsistencies between behaviors and rules challenge rules and policies demand rationale behind rules will not unquestioningly accept authority argumentative refuse to change even in face of punishment
		social contract (18–20)	actions based on upholding individual rights and democratic principles	
		universal ethical (few people reach this level)	actions based on respect for human dignity	

closed-minded, often employing such phrases as, "I know!" "Do we have to discuss this?" or "I don't care!" with a tone that communicates a nonchalant lack of interest.

By the time students are leaving junior high school and entering high school, most of them are in the "formal operational" stage cognitively and moving from the "good boy–nice girl" to the "law and order" stage morally. By the end of high school, a few of them have reached the "social contract" level.

At this stage, students can deal with abstractness and conceive of many possibilities and ideals as well as the reality of their environment. Although peer pressure is still strong, they begin to see the need and rationale for rules and policies. Eventually they see the need to protect rights and principles. They are now attempting to discover who they are, what they believe in, and what they are competent in.

Because students at this stage are searching for self-identity and are able to think abstractly, they often challenge the traditional values taught in school and home. They need to have a valid reason for why everything is the way it is. They will not accept "because I said so" as a legitimate reason to conform to a rule. Some hold to a particular behavior, explanation, or judgment, even in the face of punishment, if they feel that their individual rights have been challenged or violated. Unfortunately, many of these behaviors are carried out in an argumentative format.

There have been a number of studies that support the idea that normal developmental changes can lead to disruptive behavior. Jessor and Jessor (1977) found that the correlates of misbehavior in school are (1) growth in independence; (2) decline in traditional ideology; (3) increase in relativistic morality; (4) increase in peer orientation; and (5) increase in modeling problem behaviors. They concluded that the nor-

A teacher has total control over the use of effective teaching strategies.

mal course of developmental change is in the direction of greater possibility of problems. However, Clarizio and McCoy (1983) have found that normal problem behaviors that occur as a developmental phenomenon have a high probability of being resolved with increasing age. A study of 400 famous twentieth-century men and women, which concluded that four out of five had experienced difficulties and problems related to school and schooling (Goertzel and Goertzel, 1962), appears to support the Clarizio and McCoy findings.

Instructional Competence

At first glance it would seem that the teacher has little or no control over the five influences of misbehavior that have been discussed thus far. While it is true that a teacher cannot significantly alter the course of most of these societal, familial, and developmental

CASE 3.13 • *Not Being Able to Teach*

Ms. Cook loves mathematics and enjoys working with young people, which she often does in camp and youth organizations. After graduating with a B.S. degree in mathematics, she goes on to earn a master's degree in mathematics and becomes certified to teach at the secondary level. She obtains a teaching position at a progressive suburban junior high school.

Ms. Cook conscientiously plans for all of her algebra and geometry classes and knows the material thoroughly. Within a few months, however, her classes are characterized by significant discipline problems. Most of her students are out of their seats, talking, throwing paper, and calling out jokes. They come in unprepared and, in a few instances, openly confront Ms. Cook's procedures and competence. Even though she is given assistance, supervision, and support from the administration, Ms. Cook decides not to return for her second year of teaching.

In an attempt to understand the class' behavior, the students are interviewed at the end of the school year. The following are the most common responses concerning Ms. Cook's methods:

1. Gave unclear explanations
2. Discussed topics having nothing or little to do with the subject at hand
3. Kept repeating understood material
4. Wrote things on the board but never explained them and her board work was sloppy
5. Would say, "We already did this" when asked for help
6. Did not involve the class and only called on the same people
7. Had difficulty giving clear answers to questions
8. Didn't explain how to use the material
9. Always used her note cards
10. Could not determine why the class was having difficulty understanding the material
11. Either gave the answers to the homework or didn't go over it, so no one had to do it

events, she can control her instructional competence. Excellent instructional competence can minimize the effects of these ongoing events, maximize the learning potential in the classroom, and prevent misbehavior caused by poor instructional methodology.

Why does Ms. Cook in Case 3.13, who is knowledgeable and enthusiastic about her subject matter and enjoys working with young people, have such management problems? Why do otherwise well-behaved students misbehave to such an extent in one particular class? The students' responses indicate a reasonable answer: the teacher's lack of skill in basic instructional methodology.

Because of Ms. Cook's instructional skill deficiencies, her students did not accord to her *expert power,* the social authority and respect a teacher receives because she possesses special knowledge and expertise (French and Raven, 1960). (This and other authority bases are discussed in depth in Chapter 4.) Her inability to communicate content clearly, evaluate and remediate student misunderstandings, and explain the relevancy of the content to her students' lives caused her students to fail to recognize her expertise in the field of mathematics.

A teacher's ability to explain and clarify is foremost in developing authority. Kounin (1970) has found that teachers who are liked are described by students as those who can explain the content well, whereas those who are disliked leave students in some state of confusion. Kounin has also noted that when students like their teachers, they are more likely to behave appropriately and are more motivated to learn. As Tanner (1978) has stated, "Teacher effectiveness, as perceived by pupils, invests the teacher with classroom authority" (p. 67). To students, teacher effectiveness translates to "explaining the material so that we can understand it." When this occurs, students regard the teacher as competent, and the teacher is invested with authority.

Summary

Although there are innumerable influences of misbehavior in schools, this chapter has focused on some of the major ones.

Societal changes, most notably the effects of the knowledge explosion and the media revolution, have created an environment that is vastly different from that in which children of previous generations grew up. More children now than ever before live in single-parent homes. Also, more children today are living at or below the poverty level than in previous generations. Because of these and other factors, some children's basic needs, including the need for self-esteem, are not met by the home. Such out-of-school experiences are much more significant predictors of school behavior than children's in-school experiences. When a child's basic need for self-esteem is not met at home and/or is not met at school, discipline problems frequently result.

Throughout the school years, children's cognitive and moral development, as well as their continual need for social recognition, is reflected in their behavior. A teacher has little or no control over many of these developments. What she can control is her own instructional competence. Excellent instruction can ameliorate the effects of outside influences and prevent the misbehavior that occurs as a direct result of poor instruction. Effective teaching techniques are covered in detail in Chapter 5.

References

Adler, I. (1966, December). Mental growth and the art of teaching. *The Mathematics Teacher, 59,* 706–715.

American Psychological Association. (1993). *Violence and Youth: Psychology's Response,* Vol. 1. Washington, DC.

Atkin, C. (1983). Effects of realistic TV violence vs. fictional violence on aggression. *Journalism Quarterly, 60,* 4, 615–621.

Bandura, A. (1973). *Aggression: A Social Learning Analysis.* Englewood Cliffs, NJ: Prentice Hall.

Bayh, B. (1978). Seeking solutions to school violence and vandalism. *Phi Delta Kappan, 59,* 5, 299–302.

Bouthilet, P. D., and Lazar, J. (Eds.). (1982). *Television and Behavior: Ten Years of Scientific Progress and Implications for the Eighties.* Washington, DC: U.S. Department of Health and Human Services, National Institute of Mental Health.

Chandler, K. A., Chapman, C. D., Rand, M. R., and Taylor, B. M. (1998). *Students' Reports of School Crime: 1989 and 1995.* U.S. Departments of Education and Justice. NCES 98-241/NCJ-169607. Washington, DC.

Charles, C. M., Senter, G. W., and Barr, K. B. (1995). *Building Classroom Discipline,* 5th ed. New York: Longman.

Children's Defense Fund. (1997). *The State of America's Children Yearbook, 1997,* Washington, DC.

Children's Defense Fund. (1994). *The State of America's Children Yearbook, 1994,* Washington, DC.

Clarizio, H. F., and McCoy, G. F. (1983). *Behavior Disorders in Children,* 3rd ed. New York: Harper & Row.

Congressional Quarterly. (1993). TV violence. *CQ Researcher, 3,* 12, 165–187.

Coopersmith, S. (1967). *The Antecedents of Self-Esteem.* San Francisco: W. H. Freeman.

Dewey, J. (1916). *Democracy and Education.* New York: Macmillan.

Dreikurs, R., Grundwald, B., and Pepper, F. (1982). *Maintaining Sanity in the Classroom: Classroom Management Techniques,* 2nd ed. New York: Harper & Row.

Dubelle, S. T., and Hoffman, C. M. (1984). *Misbehaving—Solving the Disciplinary Puzzle for Educators.* Lancaster, PA: Technomic.

Elliot, D. S., and Voss, H. L. (1974). *Delinquency and Dropout.* Lexington, MA: Lexington.

Feldhusen, J. F. (1978). Behavior problems in secondary schools. *Journal of Research and Development in Education, 11,* 4, 17–28.

Feldhusen, J. F., Thurston, J. R., and Benning, J. J. (1973). A longitudinal study of delinquency and other aspects of children's behavior. *International Journal of Criminology and Penology, 1,* 341–351.

French, J. R. P., and Raven, B. (1960). In D. Cartwright and A. Zander (Eds.), *Group Dynamics: Research and Theory.* Evanston, IL: Row-Peterson.

Gabay, J. (1991, January). *ASCD Update.*

Gelfand, D. M., Jenson, W. R., and Drew, C. J. (1982). *Understanding Child Behavior Disorders.* New York: Holt, Rinehart & Winston.

Gilliland, H. (1986). Self concept and the Indian student. In J. Reyhner (Ed.), *Teaching the Indian Child.* Billings, MT: Eastern Montana College.

Glasser, W. (1978). Disorders in our schools: Causes and remedies. *Phi Delta Kappan, 59,* 5, 321–333.

Goertzel, V., and Goertzel, M. (1962). *Cradles of Eminence.* Boston: Little, Brown.

Gorman, R. M. (1972). *Discovering Piaget: A Guide for Teachers.* Columbus, OH: Merrill.

Jessor, J., and Jessor, S. L. (1977). *Problem Behavior and Psychosocial Development.* New York: Academic.

Jones, V. F. (1980). *Adolescents with Behavior Problems.* Boston: Allyn and Bacon.

Karplus, R. (1977). *Science Teaching and the Development of Reasoning.* Berkeley: University of California Press.

Kindsvatter, R. (1978). A new view of the dynamics of discipline. *Phi Delta Kappan, 59,* 5, 322–325.

Kohlberg, L. (1969). *Stages in the Development of Moral Thought and Action.* New York: Holt, Rinehart & Winston.

Kohlberg, L. (1975). The cognitive-developmental approach to moral education. *Phi Delta Kappan, 56,* 10, 610–677.

Kounin, J. S. (1970). *Discipline and Group Management in Classrooms.* New York: Holt, Rinehart & Winston.

Levin, J., and Shanken-Kaye, J. (1996). *The Self-Control Classroom: Understanding and Managing the Disruptive Behavior of All Students including Students with ADHD.* Dubuque, IA: Kendall-Hunt.

Levine, V. (1984, August). Time use and student achievement: A critical assessment of the National Commission Report. *Forum* (College of Education, The Pennsylvania State University), *11,* 12.

Maslow, A. (1968). *Toward a Psychology of Being.* New York: D. Van Nostrand.

Menacker, J., Weldon, W., and Hurwitz, E. (1989). School order and safety as community issues. *Phi Delta Kappan, 71,* 1, 39.

National Education Goals Panel. (1997). *The 1997 National Education Goals Report: Building a Nation of Learners.* Washington, DC: Superintendent of Documents, U.S. Government Printing Office.

Parke, R. D. (1978). Children's home environments: Social and cognitive effects. In I. Altman and J. F. Wohlwill (Eds.), *Children and the Environment.* New York: Plenum.

Pearl, D. (1984). Violence and aggression. *Society, 21,* 6, 15–16.

Pearl, D., Bouthilet, L., and Lazar, J. (Eds.). (1982). *Television and Behavior: Ten Years of Scientific Progress and Implications for the Eighties,* Vol. 2. Washington, DC: U.S. Government Printing Office.

Piaget, J. (1965). *The Moral Judgment of the Child.* Glencoe, IL: Free Press.

Piaget, J. (1970). Piaget's theory. In P. H. Mussen (Ed.), *Carmichael's Manual of Child Psychology,* Vol. 1. New York: Wiley.

Rice, M. L., Huston, A. C., and Wright, J. C. (1982). The forms and codes of television: Effects on children's attention, comprehension and social behavior. In D. Pearl, L. Bouthilet, and J. Lazar (Eds.), *Television and Behavior: Ten Years of Scientific Progress and Implications for the Eighties,* Vol. 2. Washington, DC: U.S. Government Printing Office.

Rice, P. F. (1981). *The Adolescent Development, Relationships, and Culture,* 3rd ed. Boston: Allyn and Bacon.

Rutter, M. (1978). Family, area, and school influences in the genesis of conduct disorders. In L. Herson, M. Berger, and D. Shaffer (Eds.), *Aggression and Anti-Social Behaviour in Childhood and Adolescence.* Oxford: Pergamon.

Singer, J. L., Singer, D. G., and Rapaczynski, W. S. (1984). Family patterns and television viewing as predictors of children's beliefs and aggression. *Journal of Communications, 34,* 2, 73–89.

Stinchcombe, A. L. (1964). *Rebellion in a High School.* Chicago: Quadrangle.

Stipek, D. J. (1993). *Motivation to Learn, from Theory to Practice,* 2nd ed. Boston: Allyn and Bacon.

Sweeney, J. J. (1981). *Adlerian Counseling Proven Concepts and Strategies,* 2nd ed. Muncie, IN: Accelerated Development.

Tanner, L. N. (1978). *Classroom Discipline for Effective Teaching and Learning.* New York: Holt, Rinehart & Winston.

Toffler, A. (1970). *Future Shock.* New York: Random House.

U.S. Bureau of the Census. (1994). *Statistical Abstract of the United States, 1994.* Washington, DC: U.S. Government Printing Office.

Visher, E. B., and Visher, J. S. (1978). Common problems of stepparents and their spouses. *American Journal of Orthopsychiatry, 48,* 252–262.

Whitmire, R. (1991, October). Educational declines linked with erosion of family. *The Olympian, 1.*

Withall, J. (1969, March). Evaluation of classroom climate. *Childhood Education, 45,* 7, 403–408.

Withall, J. (1979). Problem behavior: Function of social–emotional climate? *Journal of Education, 161,* 2, 89–101.

Exercises

1. Look back on your own school experiences. What are some instructional techniques your teachers used that had the potential to change disruptive student behaviors?

2. What if anything can schools and classroom teachers do to help students meet the following basic human needs: (a) physiological, (b) safety and security, and (c) belonging and affection?

3. Self-esteem can be conceptualized mathematically as follows:

   Self-Esteem = significance + competence + power + virtue

   How does the self-esteem formula help to explain why students behave disruptively inside and outside the classroom?

4. How does the self-esteem formula provide insight into the types of interventions that can lead to decreasing a student's disruptive behavior?

5. How does self-esteem relate to the success/failure ratio described in the preface to the second edition of this book?

6. Even though they are beyond the school's control, changes in society can influence student behavior in school. What changes in society during the last ten years do you feel have had negative influences on classroom behavior?

7. In your opinion, can television programs and films cause students to misbehave in the classroom? If so, list some specific examples to support your opinion. If not, explain why.

8. Explain why some educational researchers believe that cognitive development is a prerequisite for moral development.

9. Considering students' cognitive development, how might a teacher teach the following concepts in the third, seventh, and eleventh grades?
   a. Volume of a rectangular solid $= L \times W \times H$
   b. Civil rights and equality
   c. Subject–predicate agreement
   d. Gravity

10. How might inappropriate teaching of these concepts for the cognitive level of the students contribute to classroom discipline problems?

11. Considering students' moral development, what can we expect as typical reactions to the following events at each of the following grade levels?

Event	First	Fourth	Seventh	Twelfth
a. A student from a poor family steals the lunch ticket of a student from a fairly wealthy family.				
b. A teacher keeps the entire class on a detention because of the disruptive behavior of a few.				
c. A student destroys school property and allows another student to be falsely accused and punished for the vandalism.				
d. A student has points subtracted from her test score for talking after her test paper was already turned in.				

12. What are some normal behaviors (considering their developmental level) for elementary students, junior high or middle school students, and senior high students that can be disruptive in a classroom?

13. What might a teacher do to allow the normal behaviors (listed in the answer to question 10) to be expressed, while at the same time preventing them from disrupting learning?

14. Disruptive students often rationalize their inappropriate behavior by blaming it on the teacher, "I'll treat Mr. Lee with respect when he treats me with respect." Unfortunately, teachers often rationalize their negative behavior toward a student by blaming it on the student, "I'll respect Nicole when she respects me." Using the levels of moral development, explain why the student's rationalization is understandable but the teacher's is not.

4

Philosophical Approaches to Classroom Management

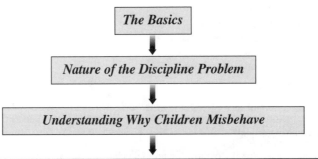

The Basics

⬇

Nature of the Discipline Problem

⬇

Understanding Why Children Misbehave

⬇

Philosophical Approaches to Classroom Management
Understanding and Employing Different Power Bases
Referent • Expert • Legitimate • Reward/Coercive
Understanding Theories of Classroom Management
Student-Directed • Collaborative • Teacher-Directed

Principles of Classroom Management

1. Theoretical approaches to classroom management are useful to teachers because they offer a basis for analyzing, understanding, and managing student and teacher behavior.
2. As social agents, teachers have access to a variety of power bases that can be used to influence student behavior.
3. The techniques a teacher employs to manage student behavior should be consistent with the teacher's beliefs about how students learn and develop.

Introduction

Teaching can be a threatening and frustrating experience, and all of us at some time entertain doubts about our ability to maintain effective classroom learning environments. For many teachers, however, these normal self-doubts, which are especially common early in a teaching career, lead to a frantic search for gimmicks, techniques, or tricks that they hope will allow them to survive in the real classroom world. This is indeed unfortunate as Case 4.1 illustrates. When classroom management problems are approached with a frenetically sought-after bag of tricks instead of a carefully developed systematic plan for decision making, teachers are likely to find themselves behaving in ways they later regret. The teachers who are most successful at creating a positive classroom atmosphere that enhances student learning are those who employ a carefully developed plan for classroom management. Clearly any such plan must be congruent with their basic beliefs about the nature of the teaching and learning process. When teachers use this type of plan, they avoid the dilemma that Ms. Knepp encountered.

There are multiple models or systems of classroom management and hundreds of techniques for promoting positive student behavior within these models. Most of these techniques are effective in some situations but not others, for some students but not others, and for some teachers but not others. "What most of the experts fail to mention is that the efficacy of a technique is contextually dependent. Who the teacher teaches and who the teacher is dictate what technique will have the greatest potential for addressing the complex management problems evidenced in classrooms (Lasley, 1989). Because every technique is based implicitly or explicitly on some belief system concerning how human beings behave and why, the classroom teacher must find prototypes of classroom management that are consistent with his beliefs and employ them under appropriate circumstances.

How can teachers ensure that their behavior in dealing with classroom management and classroom discipline problems will be effective and will match their beliefs about students, teachers, and learning? First, they can understand their own basic beliefs about classroom management. Second, they can develop, based on their beliefs, a systematic plan for promoting positive student behavior and dealing with inappropriate behavior. Chapters 6 through 9, which provide multiple options for dealing with any single classroom management problem, are designed to help teachers develop a systematic plan. Numerous options are provided to allow every teacher to develop a personal plan for encouraging appropriate student behavior and for dealing with unacceptable behavior in a manner congruent with his own basic beliefs about management. Because there are numerous options, the teacher can prioritize his options in a hierarchical format.

To help teachers and future teachers to lay the philosophical foundation for their own classroom management plan, this chapter offers an overview of a variety of philosophical approaches to classroom management. So that they may be considered in a more systematic and orderly fashion, the approaches are grouped under two major headings: teacher power bases and theories of classroom management. The first section discusses the various types of power or influence that are available to teachers to promote appropriate student behavior. The second section explains three theories of classroom management and their underlying beliefs and includes models and techniques for each of the theoretical approaches.

It is important to be aware of the inherent connection between the three theories and the four power bases. Each of the three theories relies on the dominant use of one or two power bases. Teachers can examine the foundations on which their own

CASE 4.1 • *The Tricks-of-the-Trade Approach*

Ms. Judy Knepp is a first-year teacher at Armstrong Middle School. Although most of her classes are going well, she is having a great deal of difficulty with her sixth-grade developmental reading class. Many of the students seem disinterested, lazy, immature, and rebellious. As a result of the class's continuous widespread chattering, Ms. Knepp spends the vast majority of her time yelling and reprimanding individual students. She has considered using detention to control students, but there are so many disruptive students that she doesn't know whom to give detention to first. The class has become such a battlefield that she finds herself hating to go to school in the morning.

After struggling on her own for a couple of long weeks, Ms. Knepp decides that she had better ask somebody for help. She is reluctant to go to any of the administrators because she thinks that revealing the problem will result in a low official evaluation for her first semester's work. Finally, she decides to go to Ms. Hoffman, a veteran teacher of 14 years with a reputation for striking fear into the hearts of her sixth-grade students.

After she tells Ms. Hoffman all about her horrendous class, Ms. Knepp waits anxiously for some words of wisdom that will help her to get the class under control. Ms. Hoffman's advice is short and to the point: "I'd just keep the whole class in for detention. Keep them until about 4:30 just one day, and I guarantee you won't have any more trouble with them. These kids think they're tough, but when they see that you're just as mean and tough as they are, they'll melt pretty quickly."

Ms. Knepp is dismayed. She immediately thinks, "That's just not fair. What about those four or five kids who don't misbehave? Why should they have to stay

in too?" She does not voice her objections to Ms. Hoffman, fearing Ms. Hoffman will see her as rude and ungrateful. She does ask, "What about parents who object to such punishment?" However, Ms. Hoffman assures her that she has never had any trouble from parents and that the principal, Dr. Kropa, will support the disciplinary action even if any parents do object.

Ms. Knepp feels trapped. She knows that Ms. Hoffman expects her to follow through, and she fears that Ms. Hoffman will tell the other veteran teachers if she doesn't take the advice. Like most newcomers, Ms. Knepp longs to be accepted.

Despite her misgivings, then, Ms. Knepp decides to follow the advice and to do so quickly before she loses her nerve. The next day, she announces that one more disruption—no matter who is the culprit—will bring detention for the entire class. For five minutes silence reigns, and the class actually accomplishes some work. Ms. Knepp has begun to breathe a long sigh of relief when suddenly she hears a loud "you pig" from the back right-hand corner of the room. She is positive that all the students have heard the epithet and knows that she cannot ignore it. She also fears that an unenforced threat will mean disaster.

"That does it. Everyone in this class has detention tomorrow after school." Immediately the air is filled with "That ain't fair," "I didn't do nothing," "You wish," and "Don't hold your breath." Naturally, most of these complaints come from the biggest troublemakers. However, several students who never cause trouble also complain bitterly that the punishment is unfair. Deep down, Ms. Knepp agrees with them, but she feels compelled to dismiss their complaints with a fainthearted, "Well, life just isn't always fair, and you might as well learn that now." She stonewalls it through the rest of

CASE 4.1 • continued

the class and is deeply relieved when the class is over.

When Ms. Knepp arrives at school the next morning, there is a note from Dr. Kropa in her box stating that Mr. and Mrs. Pennsi are coming in during her free period to talk about the detention of their son, Fred. Fred is one of the few students who rarely causes trouble. Ms. Knepp feels unable to defend her action. It contradicts her beliefs about fairness and how students should be treated. The conference is a dis-

aster. Ms. Knepp begins by trying to convince the Pennsies that she is right but ends by admitting that she too feels that she has been unfair to Fred. After the conference, she discusses the punishment with Dr. Kropa, who suggests that it is best to call it off. Ms. Knepp drags herself, half in tears, to her class. She is going to back down and rescind the punishment. She believes that the kids will see this as a sign of weakness, and she is afraid of the consequences.

classroom management plans rest by comparing their beliefs with those inherent in each of the various teacher power bases and theories of classroom management.

Teacher Power Bases

French and Raven (1960) have identified four different types of power that teachers as social agents may use to influence student behavior. The effective teacher is aware of the type of power he wants to use to influence student behavior and is also aware of the type of power that is implicit in each of the techniques available. It cannot be emphasized enough that when teachers' beliefs and behaviors are consistent, they are more likely to be successful than they are when they are not consistent. When beliefs and behavior are congruent, usually the teacher follows through and is consistent in dealing with student behavior because he (unlike Ms. Knepp) believes that it is the right thing to do, and students usually perceive the teacher as a genuine person who practices what he preaches. As you read the explanation of the four types of power, ask yourself which type or types fit your beliefs and which types you could use comfortably. Although every teacher probably uses each of the four types of power at some time, each teacher has a dominant power base that he uses most often.

The four teacher power bases are presented in a hierarchical format, beginning with those more likely to engender student control over their own behavior and proceeding to those that foster increasing teacher control. If a teacher believes, as we do, that one of the important long-range goals of schooling is to foster student self-direction, using those power bases at the top of the hierarchy as often as possible will be consistent with this belief. If a teacher does not share this belief, the hierarchical arrangement of power bases is not as important for him. Whatever one's beliefs about the long-range goals of education, it is still necessary to understand the four teacher power bases because no single one is effective for all students, all classrooms, or all teachers. Thus, effective classroom management requires the use of a variety of power bases.

Referent Power

Consider Case 4.2. The type of power Mr. Emig uses to influence student behavior has been termed *referent power* by French and Raven (1960). When a teacher has referent power, students behave as the teacher wishes because they like the teacher as a person. Students view the teacher as a good person who is concerned about them, cares about their learning, and demands a certain type of behavior because it is in their best interest.

There are two requirements for the effective use of referent power: (1) The teacher must perceive that the students like him, and (2) the teacher must communicate that he cares about and likes the students. He does this through positive nonverbal gestures; positive oral and written comments; extra time and attention; displays of sincere interest in students' ideas, activities, and especially, learning. Teachers with referent power are able to appeal directly to students to act a certain way. Examples of such direct appeals are, "I'm really not feeling well today. Please keep the noise level at a minimum," and "It really makes me angry when you hand assignments in late. Please have your assignments ready on time." These teachers might handle Ms. Knepp's problem with a statement such as, "You disappoint me and make me very angry when you misbehave and disrupt class time. I spend a great deal of time planning activities that you will enjoy and that will help you to learn, but I must spend so much time on discipline that we don't get to them. I would really appreciate it if you would stop the misbehavior."

Referent power must not be confused with the situation in which the teacher attempts to be the students' friend. A teacher who wants to be friends with students

CASE 4.2 • *The Involved Teacher*

Mr. Emig was envied by administrators and teachers alike at Spring Grove Junior High. Even though he taught eighth-grade English to all types of students, he never sent students to the office, rarely gave detentions, and never needed parent conferences to discuss student behavior. In fact, it seemed as if he never had any discipline problems with students.

Mr. Karr, the principal, decided that other teachers might be able to learn some techniques from Mr. Emig and so asked some of Mr. Emig's students why his classes were so well behaved. Students said that they liked Mr. Emig because he was always involved in activities with them. He sponsored the school newspaper, went on ski club trips, went to athletic events, coached track, chaperoned dances, and advised the student council. Because of his heavy involvement with them, students got a chance to see him as a person, not just as a teacher, and they felt that he was a really good person who cared a lot about kids. As a result, nobody hassled him in class.

usually is dependent on students to fulfill his personal needs. This dependency creates an environment in which students are able to manipulate the teacher. Over time, the teacher and students become equals, and the teacher loses the ability to influence students to behave appropriately. In contrast, the teacher who uses referent power is an authority figure and does make demands on students. Students carry out the teacher's wishes because they like the teacher as a teacher, not as a friend.

It is neither possible nor wise to use referent power all the time with all students. Indeed, using referent power with students who genuinely dislike the teacher may result in disaster. One need only consider the possible and probable response to direct appeals by students who see their primary goal as making the teacher's life miserable to understand this caution. However, when students make it clear that they like the teacher through their general reactions to him before, during, and after class, and when the teacher has communicated his caring and concern to students, the use of referent power can make classroom management easy.

Expert Power

Ms. Sanchez in Case 4.3 is a teacher who uses expert power to influence student behavior. When a teacher enjoys expert power, students behave as the teacher wishes because they view him as a good, knowledgeable teacher who can help them to learn. This is the power of professional competence. To use expert power effectively, two important conditions must be fulfilled: (1) The students must believe the teacher has both special knowledge and the teaching skills to help them acquire that knowledge, and (2) the students must value learning what the teacher is teaching. Students may value what they are learning for any number of reasons: The subject matter is inherently interesting, they can use it in the real world, they want good grades, or they want to reach some personal goal such as college or a job.

The teacher who uses expert power successfully communicates his competence through mastery of content material, the use of motivating teaching techniques, clear explanations, and thorough class preparation. In other words, the teacher uses his pro-

---

CASE 4.3 • *Her Reputation Precedes Her*

Ms. Sanchez is a chemistry teacher at Lakefront High School. Each year, Ms. Sanchez teaches an advanced placement (AP) chemistry course to college-bound seniors. For the last five years, none of her AP students has received less than a three on the AP exam. As a result, each student has received college credit for AP chemistry. Students in Ms. Sanchez's class recognize that she is very knowledgeable about chemistry and knows how to teach. If an observer walks into Ms. Sanchez's AP class, even during April and May, he will find the students heavily involved in class activities, with very little off-task behavior.

fessional knowledge to help students learn. When expert power is employed success-fully, students make comments similar to these: "I behave because he is a really good teacher," "She makes biology interesting," and "He makes you really want to learn." A teacher with an expert power base might say to Ms. Knepp's disruptive class: "I'm sure you realize how important reading is. If you can't read, you will have a rough time being successful in our society. You know that I can help you learn to read and to read well, but I can't do that if you won't behave as I've asked you to behave."

As is the case with referent power, a teacher may be able to use expert power with some classes and some students but not with others. A math teacher may be able to use expert power with an advanced calculus group but not with a remedial general math group; an auto mechanics teacher may be able to use expert power with the vocational-technical students but not with students who take auto mechanics to fill up their schedules.

One final caveat concerning this type of power: Whereas most primary school teachers are perceived as experts by their students, expert power does not seem to be effective in motivating these students to behave appropriately. Thus, unlike the other three power bases, which can be employed at all levels, the appropriate use of expert power seems to be confined to students above the primary grades.

Legitimate Power

The third type of power identified by French and Raven and utilized by Mr. Davis in Case 4.4 is legitimate power. The teacher who seeks to influence students through legitimate power expects students to behave appropriately because the teacher has the legal and formal authority for maintaining appropriate behavior in the classroom. In other words, students behave because the teacher is the teacher, and inherent in that role are a certain authority and power.

Teachers who wish to use a legitimate power base must demonstrate through their behavior that they accept the responsibilities, as well as the power, inherent in the role of teacher. They must be viewed by students as fitting the stereotypical image of teacher (e.g., in dress, speech, and mannerisms). Students must also believe that

---

CASE 4.4 • *"School Is Your Job"*

Mr. Davis looked at the fourth-graders in front of him, many of whom were talking or staring into space instead of doing the seat work assignment. He said, "You are really disappointing me. You're sitting there wasting precious time. School is not a place for wasting time. School is your job, just like your parents have jobs, and it is my job to see that you work hard and learn during school. Your parents pay taxes so that you'll have the chance to come to school and learn. You and I both have the responsibility to do what we're supposed to do. Now, cut out the talking and the day-dreaming, and do your math."

teachers and school administrators are working together. School administrators help teachers gain legitimate power by making clear through words and actions that students are expected to treat teachers as legitimate authority figures. Teachers help themselves gain legitimate power by following and enforcing school rules and by supporting school policies and administrators.

Students who behave because of legitimate power make statements such as, "I behave because the teacher asked us to. You're supposed to do what the teacher says." A teacher who employs legitimate power might use a statement in Ms. Knepp's class such as, "I do not like the way you people are treating me. I am your teacher. I will not put up with disrespectful behavior. I am responsible for making sure that you learn, and I'm going to do that. If that means using the principal and other school authorities to help me do my job, I'll do just that."

Because of the societal changes discussed in Chapter 3, most teachers rightly believe that today's students are less likely to be influenced by legitimate power than students of 30 or 40 years ago were. However, it is still possible to use legitimate power with some classes and some students. Groups of students who generally accept teacher-set rules and assignments without question or challenge are appropriate groups with whom to use legitimate power.

Reward/Coercive Power

Notice how the teacher in Case 4.5 is using reward and coercive power to influence student behavior. Although they may be considered two separate types of teacher authority, reward and coercive power are really two sides of the same coin. They are both based on behavioral notions of learning, foster teacher control over student behavior, and are governed by the same principles of application.

There are several requirements for the effective use of this power base: (1) the teacher must be consistent in assigning and withholding rewards and punishments; (2) the teacher must ensure that students see the connection between their behavior and the reward or punishment; (3) the rewards or punishments actually must be per-

---

CASE 4.5 • *Going to Recess*

"O.K., second-graders, it's time to put your spelling books away and get ready for recess. Now, we all remember that we get ready by putting all books and supplies neatly and quietly in our desks and then folding our hands on top of the desk and looking at me quietly. Let's see which row can get ready first. I see that Tammy's row is ready. O.K., Tammy's row, you can walk quietly out to the playground. Oh, no, wait a minute. Where are you going, Joe? You're not allowed to go out to recess this week because of your misbehavior on the bus. You can go to Mr. Li's room and do your math assignment. I'll check it when I get back."

ceived as rewards or punishments by the student (many students view a three-day out-of-school suspension as a vacation, not a punishment).

Teachers employing this base use a variety of rewards, such as oral or written praise, gold stars, free time, "good news" notes to parents, and release from required assignments, as well as a variety of punishments, including verbal reprimands, loss of recess or free time, detention, in-school suspension, out-of-school suspension, and corporal punishment.

Students who behave appropriately because of reward/coercive power are apt to say, "I behave because if I don't, I have to write out a stupid saying 50 times and get it signed by my parents." A teacher using reward/coercive power to solve Ms. Knepp's problem might say, "I've decided that for every five minutes without a disruption this class will earn one point. At the end of each week, for every ten points it has accumulated, the class may buy one night without homework during the following week. Remember, if there are any disturbances at all, you will not receive a point for the five-minute period." This point system is an example of a behavior modification technique. More information on the use of behavior modification in the classroom may be obtained from Axelrod (1983).

As is true for the other three power bases, reward/coercive power cannot be used all the time. As students become older, they often resent obvious attempts to manipulate their behavior through rewards and punishments. It is also difficult with older students to find rewards and punishments under the classroom teacher's control that are powerful enough to motivate them (see Chapter 6). (Still, some teachers have found their control of student time during school has allowed them to use reward/coercive power successfully with some students and some classes at all levels of schooling.) It should be noted that there are some inherent dangers in the use of reward/coercive power. Research has indicated that when students are rewarded for engaging in an activity, they are likely to perceive the activity as less inherently interesting in the future and are less likely to engage in that activity without external rewards (Lepper and Green, 1978). Also, overuse of punishment is likely to engender in students negative attitudes toward school and learning.

It is important for a teacher to recognize what power base he uses to influence students in a given situation and to recognize why that base is appropriate or inappropriate for the given students and situation. It is also important for the teacher to recognize the power base he uses most frequently as well as the power base he is comfortable with and would like to use. For some teachers, the two things may be quite different. Examining your beliefs about teacher power bases is one important step toward ensuring that your beliefs about classroom management and your actions are compatible. Table 4.1 offers a brief comparison of the four power bases on several significant dimensions.

Of course, most teachers use a combination of power bases. They use one for one type of class and students and another for another type of class and student. They may even use a variety of power bases with the same students. This may, indeed, be the most practical and effective approach, although combining certain power bases—for example, coercive and referent—may be difficult to do.

TABLE 4.1 *Teacher Power Bases*

	Referent	Expert	Legitimate	Reward/ Coercive
Motivation to behave	Student likes teacher as a person	Teacher has special knowledge	Teacher has legal authority	Teacher can reward and punish
Need for teacher management of student behavior	Very low	Very low	Moderate	High
Requirements for use	Students must like the teacher as a person	Teacher expertise must be perceived and valued	Students must respect legal authority	Rewards and punishments must be effective
Key teacher behaviors	Communicates caring for students	Demonstrates mastery of content and teaching skills	Acts as a teacher is expected to act	Has and uses knowledge of student likes and dislikes
Age limitations	Useful for all levels	Less useful at primary level	Useful at all levels	Useful at all levels but less useful at senior high level
Caveats	Teacher is not the student's friend	Heavily dependent on student values	Societal changes have lessened the usefulness of this power base	Emphasizes extrinsic over intrinsic motivation

Theories of Classroom Management

In this section, we will describe three theories of classroom management. In order to make the differences between the three theories clear, we will describe each theory as if it were completely independent of the others. In reality, however, the three theories are more like three points on a continuum moving from student-directed toward teacher-directed practices. On such a continuum, collaborative models represent a combination of the two end points. Of course, the classroom behavior of most teachers represents some blending of the three theories. As Bob Strachota (1966) has noted, "Theories about how to best help children learn and change have to be broad enough to encompass the vitality and ambiguity that come with life in a classroom. If relied on too exclusively, behaviorism or constructivism end up living awkwardly in school" (p. 133). Still, if a teacher's behavior is examined over time, it is usually possible to classify the teacher's

Punishment and rewards are often used by teachers; however, they may not be the most effective means to manage student behavior.

general approach to working with students and goals for classroom management into one of the theories on a fairly consistent basis.

Before reading the specific theories, determine your answers to the following nine basic questions about classroom management. Inherent in each theory are answers, either implicit or explicit, to these questions. If you are aware of your own beliefs about classroom management before you begin, you will be able to identify the theory that is aligned most closely with them.

1. Who has primary responsibility for managing student behavior?
2. What is the goal of classroom management?
3. How do you view time spent on management issues and problems?
4. How would you like students to relate to each other within your management system?
5. How much choice will you give students within your management system?
6. What is your primary goal in handling misbehavior ?
7. What interventions will you use to deal with misbehavior?
8. How important are individual differences among students to you?
9. What teacher power bases are most compatible with your beliefs?

Readers of earlier versions of this text will recognize that we have changed the labels of the three theories from *noninterventionist* to *student-directed*, from *interventionist* to *teacher-directed*, and from *interactionalist* to *collaborative*. We believe the new labels describe what the theories represent more clearly than the former labels, which were taken from Wolfgang and Glickman (1995). Because the student-directed approach is used less frequently in schools than the other two approaches and may be unfamiliar, more specific details are provided for it than for the other two.

Student-Directed Management

Advocates of the student-directed classroom management theory believe that the primary goal of schooling is to prepare students for life in a democracy, which requires citizens who are able to control their behavior, care for others, and make wise decisions. When the first two editions of this text were written, student-directed models of classroom management were drawn primarily from counseling models. Gordon's (1989) teacher effectiveness training, Berne's (1964) and Harris's (1969) transactional analysis, and Ginott's (1972) communication model relied almost exclusively on one-to-one conferencing between teacher and student to deal with behavior issues. Such models were difficult to implement in the reality of a classroom filled with 25 to 30 students, each with a variety of talents, needs, interests, and problems. As a result, most classrooms were dominated by teacher-directed management models. During the last five years, however, there has been considerable progress in developing student-directed management models that can be employed effectively within classrooms. Alfie Kohn (1996), Bob Strachota (1996), Ruth Charney (1992), Putnam and Burke (1994) and writers from the Developmental Studies Center and the Northeast Foundation for Children have provided a variety of practical strategies that classroom teachers can use effectively.

The student-directed theory of classroom management, which Ms. Koskowski in Case 4.6 uses to handle David's behavior, rests on two key beliefs: (1) students must have the primary responsibility for controlling their behavior; and (2) students are capable of controlling their behavior if given the opportunity to do so. Given these beliefs, student-directed models of management advocate the establishment of classroom learning communities, which are designed to help students become more self-directed, more responsible for their own behavior, more independent in making appropriate choices, and more caring toward fellow students and teachers. The well-managed classroom is one in which students care for and collaborate successfully with each other, make good choices, and continuously strive to do high quality work that is interesting and important to them.

When viewed from a student-directed perspective, time spent on management is seen as time well spent on equipping students with skills that will be important to them as adult citizens in a democracy. In attempting to develop a student-directed learning environment in which students develop self-regulation skills, collaborative social skills, and decision-making skills, the teacher relies heavily on several major concepts: student ownership, student choice, community, and conflict resolution and problem solving.

Student ownership is established in several ways. Although the teacher takes responsibility for the arrangement of the classroom and for the safety of the environment, students are often responsible for deciding how the room should be decorated, for creating the posters, pictures, and other works that decorate the walls, and for

CASE 4.6 • *Handling Disruptive David*

Ms. Koskowski, Ms. Sweely, and Mr. Green teach fourth grade at Longmeadow School. Although they work well together and like each other, they have very different approaches to classroom discipline. To illustrate their differing approaches, let's examine their behavior as each one deals with the same situation.

In the classroom there are three students at the reading center in the far right-hand corner and two students working quietly on insects at the science interest center near the chalkboard located in the front of the room. Five students are correcting math problems individually, and ten students are working with the teacher in a reading group. David, one of the students working alone, begins to mutter out loud, "I hate this math. It's too hard to do. I never get them right. Why do we have to learn about fractions anyway?" As his monologue continues, David's voice begins to get louder and clearly becomes a disruption for the other students.

Ms. Koskowski

Ms. Koskowski recognizes that David, who is not strong in math, is really frustrated by the problems on fractions. She walks over to him and quietly says, "You know, David, the other night I was trying to learn to play tennis, and I was getting really frustrated. It helped me to take a break and get away from it for a minute, just to clear my head. How about if you do that, now? Go, get a drink of water, and when you come back, you can get a fresh start." When David returns to his seat and

begins to work, Ms. Koskowski helps him to think through the first problem and then watches and listens as he does the second one on his own.

Ms. Sweely

As soon as she sees that David is beginning to interrupt the other students, Ms. Sweely gives the reading group a question to think about and walks toward David's desk. She puts her hand gently on his shoulder, but the muttering continues. She says, "David, you are disrupting others; please stop talking and get back to math." David stops for about five seconds but then begins complaining loudly again. "David, since you can't work with the group without disrupting other people, you will have to go back to the castle [a desk and rocking chair partitioned off from the rest of the class] and finish your math there. Tomorrow, if you believe that you can handle it, you may rejoin your math group."

Mr. Green

As soon as David's muttering becomes audible, Mr. Green says, "David, that behavior is against our class rules. Stop talking and concentrate on your math." David stops talking momentarily but begins again. Mr. Green walks calmly to David's desk and removes a small, round, blue chip. As he does, he says, "Well, David, you've lost them all now. That means no more recess for the rest of the week and no good-news note to your mom and dad."

Classroom meetings can help students realize that they have responsibilities to both themselves and the class.

maintaining the room. Throughout the year, students rotate through committees (the art supplies committee, the plants and animals committee, the clean-up committee, and so forth) that are responsible for various aspects of the class's work. Often these committees are structured so that students gain experience in planning, delegating, and evaluating their own work in a fair and equitable manner.

Students are also given a great deal of responsibility for determining classroom rules. Typically a class meeting is held during which the teacher and students discuss how they want their classroom to be. Students are asked to think about the ways they are treated by others that make them feel good or bad. These experiences are then used as a springboard for a discussion about how the students want to treat each other in the classroom. The students' words become the guidelines for classroom behavior.

Choice plays a key role in student-directed learning environments because it is believed that a student can learn to make good choices only if he has the opportunity to make choices. In addition to making choices about the physical environment of the room and the expectations for behavior, students are given choices about classroom routines and procedures, topics and questions to be studied in curriculum units, learning activities, and the assessment of their learning, including assessment options and criteria. Classroom meetings, which are viewed as important vehicles for establishing and maintaining a caring classroom community, provide more opportunities for choices. Agendas for the meetings, which may be planning and decision-making meetings, check-in meetings, or problem-solving and issues-oriented meetings, are often suggested by the students (Developmental Studies Center, 1996).

Through the physical arrangement of the room, class meetings, and planned learning activities, the teacher attempts to build a community of learners who know and care for each other and work together productively. A great deal of time is spent at the beginning of the year helping students to get to know each other through get-acquainted activities, meetings, and small group activities. Throughout the year, cooperative learning activities stressing individual accountability, positive interdependence, face-to-face interaction, social skill development, and group processing are utilized (see Chapter 6). These types of activities are emphasized because student-directed theorists believe that students learn more in collaborative activities and that when they know and care for those in their classroom community, they are more likely to choose to behave in ways that are in everyone's best interest.

Interpersonal conflict is seen as a teachable moment. Student-directed teachers realize that conflict is inevitable when individuals are asked to work closely together. In fact, the absence of conflict is probably a good indication that individuals are not working together very closely. Thus, these teachers believe that helping students to deal with interpersonal conflict productively is an important goal of classroom management. Conflict resolution, peer mediation, and interpersonal problem-solving skills are taught just as academic content is taught. Students are encouraged to use the skills when conflicts arise. Issues that concern the class as a whole—conflicts concerning the sharing of equipment, class cliques, and relationship problems—become occasions for using group problem-solving skills during class meetings. Some teachers even use class meetings to involve the entire class in helping to improve the behavior of a particular student. It is important to note that encouraging caring relationships and teaching ways to deal with conflict productively go hand-in-hand and demand ongoing efforts and consistency on the part of the teacher. If students do not know or care about each other, conflict is hard to resolve. Conversely, if students do not acquire the ability to resolve conflict productively, they are unlikely to build caring relationships with each other.

Student misbehavior is seen not as an affront to the teacher's authority but rather as the student's attempt to meet needs that are not being met. In response to misbehavior, the teacher tries to determine what motivates the child and to find ways to meet the unmet needs. A student-directed teacher would view the behavior problems in Ms. Knepp's class, Case 4.1, as a clear indication that student needs were not being met by the learning activities and curriculum. He probably would hold a class meeting to address the problem behaviors in the classroom. He would articulate his feelings and reactions to the class and would elicit student feelings about the class as well. Through a discussion of their mutual needs and interests, the teacher and the class would develop a solution to the problem that would probably include some redesign of the tasks that students were asked to perform.

Kohn (1996) suggests that the first questions the teacher should ask when a child is off task are: (1) What is the task? and (2) Is it really a task worth doing? Many teachers try to identify with the child. Strachota (1996) calls this " getting on their side." This strategy seems especially appropriate when coping with students who seem out of control and unable to behave appropriately. If a teacher can identify experiences in which he has felt out of control, he is usually more empathetic and helpful (see Chapter 9). In Case 4.6 Ms. Koskowski employs this strategy with David.

Student-directed teachers also believe in allowing students to experience the consequences of their behavior. Natural consequences (consequences that do not require teacher intervention) are the most helpful because they allow the student to experience the results of his behavior directly. However, sometimes the teacher must use logical consequences. The teacher's role in using consequences is neither to augment nor to alleviate the consequences but rather to support the child or the class as the consequences are experienced. This can be a difficult role for teachers and parents to play. Even when a teacher can predict that a given choice is going to lead to negative consequences, student-directed theorists argue, the student should experience the consequence unless it will bring great harm to the child. Students learn to make wise choices, according to student-directed theorists, by recognizing that their behavior inevitably has consequences for themselves and others.

Some student-directed theorists also believe that restitution is an important part of dealing with misbehavior when a behavior has hurt other students. In order to emphasize that the classroom is a caring community and that individual behavior has consequences for others, a student whose behavior has hurt others is required to make amends to those harmed. One strategy used by some teachers is called "an apology of action" (Forton, 1998) (see Chapter 8). In this strategy, the student who has been hurt is allowed to decide what the offending student must do to make restitution. The strategy not only helps students to recognize that inappropriate behavior hurts others but also can be a powerful way to mend broken relationships.

Referent and expert teacher power bases seem most compatible with student-directed management theory. Each power base emphasizes students' control over their own behavior. At the same time, the student-directed perspective adds a new dimension to the notion of expert power. Students must recognize the teacher's specialized knowledge and his ability to build a caring classroom community in which students are given the opportunity to make choices and take responsibility for directing their own behavior. Putting this philosophy into practice demands highly competent and committed teachers who truly believe that enabling students to become better decision makers who are able to control their own behavior is an important goal of schooling. These teachers must be committed to establishing more democratic classrooms that are true caring communities. A teacher who is not committed to these beliefs will be unwilling to invest the time and effort needed to establish a student-directed learning environment. Long-term commitment is one key to success.

It is important to note that student-directed classrooms are not laissez-faire situations or classrooms without standards. In fact, the standards for student behavior in most of these classrooms are exceptionally high. When student efforts fall short of meeting agreed-upon standards for behavior and work, the teacher plays the role of encourager, helping students to identify ways to improve. The teacher's role is not to punish the student with behavior or academic problems but rather to find ways to help the student overcome the problems.

Although potentially applicable at all grade levels, student-directed strategies seem most well suited for self-contained early childhood and elementary settings for several reasons. First, students and teachers in these settings typically spend a large portion of the day together, which gives them the opportunity to build close relationships with each other. Second, because the classes are self-contained, it is possible to build a community in which students really know and care about each other. Finally, teachers in these setting have greater control over the allocation of time during the day than most secondary teachers. Because they are not "bell bound," they are free to spend more time dealing with classroom management issues with individual students or the class as a whole. The current practice of teacher looping in which teachers stay with one group of students for two or three years (for example, from first through second or third grade) provides an outstanding opportunity to create a student-directed environment because teachers and students work together for an extended period of time. Secondary schools would seem to be well served by adopting similar structures to personalize the environment and make it more student-directed, e.g., block scheduling. At present, in many secondary schools, students and teachers spend only 45 minutes together per day, and an individual teacher may teach 150 students or more per day. In such environments, it is difficult, if not impossible, to get to know each other personally, to understand each other's needs, and to establish a caring community. Teachers who can do so are truly remarkable.

Collaborative Management

The collaborative theory of classroom management is based on the belief that the control of student behavior is the joint responsibility of the student and the teacher. Although those who adopt the collaborative approach to management often believe in many of the tenets of the student-directed theory, they also believe that the number of students in a class and the size of most schools make it impractical to put a student-directed philosophy into practice. Many secondary teachers, in particular, feel that the size of their classes and the limited time they have with students make it imperative for them to place the needs of the group above the needs of any individual student. Under the collaborative theory, then, students must be given some opportunity to control their own behavior because a long-range goal of schooling is to enable students to become mature adults who can control their own behavior, but the teacher, as a professional, retains primary responsibility for managing student behavior because the classroom is a group learning situation.

In Case 4.6 Ms. Sweely represents the collaborative management theory in action. Note that she tries to protect the reading group activity and, at the same time, deal with David. While the group is occupied, she uses touch interference (see Chapter 7) to signal David that he should control his behavior. When he cannot, she emphasizes the effect of his behavior on others and separates him from the rest of the group to help him recognize the logical consequences of being disruptive in a group situation. Thus, the teacher oriented toward the collaborative theory promotes individual control over behavior but sometimes subordinates this goal to the right of all students to learn.

When viewed from the collaborative perspective, the goal of classroom management is to develop a well-organized classroom in which students are (1) engaged in learning activities; (2) usually successful; (3) respectful of the teacher and fellow students; and (4) cooperative in following classroom guidelines because they understand the rationale for the guidelines and see them as appropriate for the learning situation. From the collaborative point of view, students become capable of controlling their own behavior not by simply following rules but rather by understanding why rules exist and then choosing to follow them because they make sense. Neither blind obedience to rules nor complete freedom in deciding what rules should exist is seen as the best route toward self-regulated behavior.

In collaborative classrooms rules and procedures are developed jointly by the teacher and students. Some teachers begin with a minimum list of rules, those that are most essential, and allow students to develop additional ones. Other teachers give students the opportunity to suggest rules but retain the right to add rules or veto suggested rules. Both of these techniques are intended to help the teacher maintain the ability to use his professional judgment to protect the rights of the group as a whole.

Teachers who adopt a collaborative approach to classroom management often give students choices in other matters as well. Typically the choices are not as open ended as those provided by student-directed advocates. For example, instead of allowing students to develop the criteria for judging the quality of their work, a collaborative teacher might present a list of ten potential criteria and allow students to choose the five criteria that will be used. Thus, the students are provided with choices, but the choices are confined to some degree by the teacher's professional judgment. This same system of providing choice within a given set of options may be followed in arranging and decorating the classroom or selecting topics to be pursued during academic units.

Advocates of a collaborative approach see time spent on classroom management issues as potentially productive for the individual but not for the class as a whole unless there is a major problem interfering with the learning of a large number of students. Thus, collaborative teachers, whenever possible, do not take time away from group learning to focus on the behavior of an individual or a few students. Interpersonal conflicts are treated in a similar way. They are not dismissed, but collaborative teachers usually do not use classroom time to deal with them unless they involve many students. When an interpersonal conflict arises, the teacher deals with the individuals involved when there is a window of time to do so. Class meetings are used to deal with management issues or conflicts involving large numbers of students. Collaborative teachers tend to view a class meeting as a means for solving problems rather than as an integral process for maintaining the classroom community.

While collaborative management advocates believe that outward behavior must be managed to protect the rights of the group, they also believe the individual's thoughts and feelings must be explored to get at the heart of the behavior. Therefore, collaborative teachers often use coping skills (see Chapter 7) to manage student behavior in a group situation and then follow up with a conference with the student. Because collaborative theorists believe that relating behavior to its natural or logical consequences helps students learn to anticipate the consequences of their behavior and thus become more self-regulating (see Chapters 6 and 8 for discussions of consequences), they advocate consequences linked as closely as possible to the misbehavior itself. A student who comes to school five minutes late, for example, might be required to remain five minutes after school to make up work.

The teacher power bases most compatible with collaborative management theories are the expert and legitimate bases. Each of these power bases rests on the belief that the primary purpose of schools is to help students learn important information and processes. Therefore, the teacher must protect the rights of the group while still nurturing the learning of individual students. A collaborative teacher in Ms. Knepp's class might decide to hold a class meeting to review the classroom expectations and the rationale for them, to answer any questions or concerns regarding those expectations, and to remind students that the expectations will be enforced through the use of logical consequences. The teacher might also allow the class to make some choices concerning upcoming activities and events from a list of options that he has presented. Three well-known collaborative management models come from the work of Dreikurs, Grundwald, and Pepper (1998), Glasser (1992), and Curwin and Mendler (1988).

Teacher-Directed Management

Advocates of the teacher-directed management theory believe that students become good decision makers by internalizing the rules and guidelines for behavior that are given to them by responsible and caring adults. The teacher's task, then, is to develop a set of guidelines and rules that will create a productive learning environment, to be sure that the students understand the rules, and to develop a consistent system of rewards and punishments that make it likely that students will follow the guidelines and rules. The goal of the teacher-directed theory is to create a learning environment in which management issues and concerns play a minimal role, to discourage misbehavior, and to deal with it as swiftly as possible when it does occur. In this theory, the teacher assumes primary responsibility for managing student behavior. Time spent on management issues is not seen as productive time because it reduces time for teaching and learning. The well-managed classroom is seen as one in which the management system operates efficiently and students are cooperative and consistently engaged in learning activities. The primary emphasis in teacher-directed classrooms is on academic content and processes.

In teacher-directed environments, the teacher makes almost all of the major decisions, including room arrangement, seating assignments, classroom decorations, academic content, assessment devices and criteria, and decisions concerning the day-to-day operation of the classroom. Students may be given a role to play in implementing teacher decisions—for example, they may be asked to create a poster—but they are usually restricted to implementing the teacher's decisions. Advocates of teacher-directed models view the teacher as a trained professional who understands students, teaching, and the learning process and therefore is in the best position to make such choices.

Usually the teacher presents his rules and a system of consequences or punishments for breaking them to students on the first or second day of school. Often students are asked to sign a commitment to obeying the rules, and frequently their parents are asked to sign a statement declaring that they are aware of the rules. Often punishments for misbehavior are not directly related to the misbehavior itself but rather are universal consequences that can be applied to a variety of transgressions. For example, the student's name may be written on the board, a check mark may be made in the grade book, or a call may be made to the student's parents. Often teachers also establish a set of rewards that are provided to the class as a whole if the rules are followed consistently by everyone. Punishments and rewards are applied consistently to ensure that the management system and rules are internalized by all.

Although teachers who follow teacher-directed approaches do use cooperative learning strategies, their management techniques usually are not focused on the creation of a caring classroom community in which caring is a primary motivator for choosing to behave appropriately. In a teacher-directed classroom, the primary relationship is usually the relationship between the teacher and individual students. Students tend to be seen as a collection of individuals who should not interfere with each other's right to learn or with the teacher's right to teach. Self-control is often viewed as a matter of will. If students want to control their own behavior, they can.

Given this, conflict is seen as threatening, nonproductive, and disruptive of the learning process. The teacher deals swiftly with any outward manifestations of a conflict but usually not with the thoughts and feelings that have resulted in conflict. Students have a right to feel upset, it is argued, but not to act in inappropriate ways. Using the predetermined list of punishments or consequences, the teacher redirects the misbehaving student to appropriate behavior by applying the appropriate consequence. For the most part, punishments are sequenced so that second or third offenses bring more stringent consequences than first offenses. While individual differences may play an important part in the academic aspects of classroom work, they do not play a major role in the management system. Consider the actions of Mr. Green in Case 4.6. As an advocate of teacher-directed management, he moves quickly to stop the misbehavior, emphasizes classroom rules, employs blue chips as rewards, and uses punishments in the form of loss of recess privileges and good-news notes.

Clearly reward and coercive power is the teacher power base that is most compatible with the teacher-directed theory. Advocates use clear, direct, explicit communication, behavior contracting, behavior modification, token economy systems, consistent reinforcement of appropriate behavior, and group rewards and punishments. A teacher following this theory might handle Ms. Knepp's dilemma by setting up a group management plan in which the group earned points for appropriate behavior. The points could then be exchanged for meaningful rewards. At the same time the teacher uses a predetermined set of punishments to punish any students who misbehaved.

The teacher who wants to use a teacher-directed approach should be aware of some important considerations. A thorough understanding of the principles of behavioral psychology is necessary in order to apply behavior modification appropriately. Individual student differences do play a role in the management system because they must be considered in developing rewards and punishments. After all, what is a reward to some individuals may be a punishment to others. Thus, most teacher-directed theorists are concerned with students' thoughts and emotions; however, the primary goal in dealing with misbehavior is management of the student's outward behavior not inner feelings. Therefore, individual differences do not play a role in determining what behaviors are acceptable. Finally, the effective use of behavior modification with secondary students tends to be much more difficult for several reasons: (1) the reactions of other students are more powerful than those of the teacher; (2) students have reached a higher stage of moral reasoning; and (3) in-school rewards are not as powerful as out-of-school rewards. Some well-known authors of classroom management systems derived from

TABLE 4.2 *Theories of Classroom Management*

Question	Student-Directed	Collaborative	Teacher-Directed
Primary responsibility for management	Student	Joint	Teacher
Goal of management	Caring community focus and self-direction	Respectful relationships, academic focus	Well-organized, efficient, academic focus
Time spent on management	Valuable and productive	Valuable for individual but not for group	Wasted time
Relationships within management system	Caring, personal relationships	Respect for each other	Noninterference with each other's rights
Provision of student choice	Wide latitude and freedom	Choices within teacher defined options	Very limited
Primary goal in handling misbehavior	Unmet need to be explored	Minimize in group; pursue individually	Minimize disruption; redirect
Interventions used	Individual conference, group problem solving, restitution, natural consequences	Coping skills, natural and logical consequences, anecdotal record keeping	Clear communication, rewards and punishments, behavior contracting
Individual differences	Extremely important	Somewhat important	Minor importance
Teacher power bases	Referent, expert	Expert, legitimate	Reward/coercive
Theorists	Charney, Faber and Mazlish, Gordon, Kohn, Strachota, Putnam and Burke	Curwin and Mendler, Dreikurs, Glasser	Axelrod, Cangelosi, Canter, Valentine

the teacher-directed perspective are Axelrod (1983), Canter (1992), Cangelosi (1997), and Valentine (1987).

Table 4.2 provides a summary of the three theories of management in terms of their answers to the nine basic questions about classroom management introduced at the beginning of this section.

Summary

The first section of the chapter provides an explanation of the four teacher power bases: referent, expert, legitimate, and reward/coercive. Each base is presented in terms of the underlying assumptions about student motivation to behave, the assumed need for teacher control over student behavior, the requirements for employing the base effectively, the key teacher behaviors in using the base, and limitations and caveats concerning its use.

The second section discusses nine basic questions that are useful for articulating beliefs about classroom management:

1. Who has primary responsibility for managing student behavior?
2. What is the goal of classroom management?
3. How do you view time spent on management issues and problems?
4. How would you like students to relate to each other within your management system?
5. How much choice will you give students within your management system?
6. What is your primary goal in handling misbehavior ?
7. What interventions will you use to deal with misbehavior?
8. How important are individual differences among students to you?
9. What teacher power bases are most compatible with your beliefs?

Articulating one's beliefs is the initial step toward developing a systematic plan for managing student behavior. These nine basic questions are used to analyze three theories of classroom management: student directed, collaborative, and teacher directed.

The information and questions provided in this chapter may be used by teachers to develop a plan for preventing classroom management problems and for dealing with disruptive student behavior that is congruent with their basic beliefs about teaching and learning.

References_____

Axelrod, S. (1983). *Behavior Modification for the Classroom Teacher.* New York: McGraw Hill.
Berne, E. (1964). *Games People Play: The Psychology of Human Relations.* New York: Avon.
Cangelosi, J. S. (1997). *Classroom Management Strategies: Gaining and Maintaining Students' Cooperation.* New York: Longman.

Canter, L., and Canter, M. (1992). *Assertive Discipline: Positive Behavior Management for Today's Classrooms.* Rev. ed. Santa Monica, CA: Canter Associates.

Charney, R. (1992). *Teaching Children to Care: Management in the Responsive Classroom.* Greenfield, MA: Northeast Foundation for Children.

Curwin, R. L., and Mendler, A. (1988). *Discipline with Dignity.* Alexandria, VA: Association for Supervision and Curriculum Development.

Developmental Studies Center. (1996). *Ways We Want Our Class to Be: Class Meetings That Build Commitment to Kindness and Learning.* Oakland, CA: Developmental Studies Center.

Dreikurs, R., Grundwald, B., and Pepper, F. (1998). *Maintaining Sanity in the Classroom: Classroom Management Techniques.* 2nd ed. Washington, DC: Taylor and Francis.

Faber, A., and Mazlish, E. (1995). *How to Talk So Kids Will Learn at Home and in School.* New York: Simon & Schuster.

Forton, M. B. (1998). Apology of action. *Responsive Classroom, 10,* 1, 6–7.

French, J. R. P., and Raven, B. (1960). The bases of social power. In D. Cartwright and A. Zander (Eds.), *Group Dynamics: Research and Theory.* Evaston, IL: Row-Peterson.

Ginott, H. (1972). *Between Teacher and Child.* New York: Wyden.

Glasser, W. (1992). *The Quality School: Managing Students without Coercion.* New York: Harper/ Collins.

Gordon, T. (1989). *Teaching Children Self-Discipline at Home and in School.* New York: Random House.

Harris, T. (1969). *I'm O.K., You're O.K.: A Practical Guide to Transactional Analysis.* New York: Harper & Row.

Kohn, A. (1996). *Beyond Discipline: From Compliance to Community.* Alexandria, VA: Association for Supervision and Curriculum Development.

Lasley. T. J. (1989). A teacher development model for classroom management. *Phi Delta Kappan, 71,* 1, 36–38.

Lepper, M., and Green, D. (1978). *The Hidden Costs of Reward: New Perspectives on Human Motivation.* Hillsdale, NJ: Erlbaum.

Putnam, J., and Burke, J. (1992). *Organizing and Managing Classroom Learning Communities.* New York: McGraw Hill.

Strachota, R. (1996). *On Their Side: Helping Children Take Charge of Their Learning.* Greenfield, MA: Northeast Foundation for Children.

Valentine, M. (1987). *How to Deal with Discipline Problems in the Schools: A Practical Guide for Educators.* Dubuque, IA: Kendall-Hunt.

Wolfgang, C, and Glickman, C. (1995). *Solving Discipline Problems: Methods and Models for Today's Teachers,* 2nd ed. Boston: Allyn and Bacon.

Exercises

1. If one of the long-term goals of classroom management and discipline is for students to gain control over their own behavior, what are some advantages and disadvantages of using each of the four teacher power bases to help students achieve that goal?

2. Given your knowledge of cognitive and moral development, what factors facilitate or limit the use of each of the four teacher power bases at (a) the primary elementary grades, (b) the intermediate elementary grades, (c) the junior high level, and (d) the senior high level?

3. Do you think there is any relationship between teacher job satisfaction and the power base the teacher uses most frequently to influence student behavior?

4. What specific teacher behaviors would indicate to you that a teacher was trying to use (a) referent power and (b) expert power?

5. Using referent authority successfully requires the teacher to communicate caring to students. (a) How can a teacher communicate caring without initiating personal friendships? (b) As you see it, is there a danger in initiating personal friendships with students?

6. How would teachers operating at each of the four authority bases respond to the following situations?

Behavior	Referent	Expert	Legitimate	Reward/Coercive
a. A student throws a paper airplane across the room.				
b. A student publicly shows disrespect for the teacher.				
c. A student makes funny noises while another student is giving an oral report.				

7. If one of the long-range goals of classroom management is to help students gain control over their own behavior, what are the advantages and disadvantages of each of the three theories of classroom management in helping students meet that goal?

8. Given your knowledge of cognitive and moral development, what factors facilitate or limit the use of each of the three theories of classroom management at (a) the primary elementary level, (b) the intermediate elementary level, (c) the junior high level, and (d) the senior high level?

9. How would each of the theories of classroom management respond to the following situations?

Behavior	Student-Directed	Collaborative	Teacher-Directed
a. A student uses power equipment in a dangerous way.			
b. A student chews gum loudly and blows bubbles.			
c. A student draws mustaches and beards on all the pictures in a textbook.			

10. Is there any danger in using techniques to manage student behavior that are not consistent with your basic beliefs about student learning and behavior?

11. Think of the best teacher that you have ever had. What authority base and classroom management theory was this teacher using the majority of the time?

12. Think of the worst teacher you have ever had. What authority base and classroom management theory was this teacher using the majority of the time?

5

The Professional Teacher

| The Basics |

↓

| *Nature of the Discipline Problem* |

↓

| *Understanding Why Children Misbehave* |

↓

| *Philosophical Approaches to Classroom Management* |

↓

The Professional Teacher
The Basics of Effective Teaching
• Lesson Design • Student Motivation: Teacher Variables • Teacher Expectations
• Classroom Questioning • Time-on-Task
Beyond the Basics
• Teaching for Understanding • Authentic Instruction • Thinking and Problem-
Solving Skills • Creating Learning Communities • Teaching for Multiple Intelligences
• Student Motivation: Student Cognition

Principles of Classroom Management

1. Student learning and on-task behavior are maximized when teaching strategies are based on what educators know about student development, how people learn, and what constitutes effective teaching.
2. Understanding and using the research on effective teaching enhances the teacher's instructional competence and helps to prevent classroom management problems.

Introduction

Frequently classroom management is conceptualized as a matter of control rather than as a dimension of curriculum, instruction, and overall school climate (Duke, 1982). In reality, classroom management is closely intertwined with effective instruction: "Research findings converge on the conclusion that teachers who approach classroom management as a process of establishing and maintaining effective learning environments tend to be more successful than teachers who place more emphasis on their roles as authority figures or disciplinarians" (Brophy, 1988a, p. 1). In the hierarchical decision-making model of classroom management presented in this text, the teacher must ensure that she has done all that she can to prevent problems from occurring before using coping techniques. This means that the teacher's classroom instructional behavior must match the behaviors defined as best professional practice—that is, those behaviors most likely to maximize student learning and enhance appropriate student behavior. If they do not, employing techniques to remediate misbehavior is likely to prove fruitless since the misbehavior will inevitably recur.

Unfortunately, one of the problems that has long plagued classroom teachers has been identifying the yardstick that should be used to measure their teaching behavior against best professional practice. Fortunately, there is now a reliable knowledge base, which when used appropriately, can help teachers to ensure that their behavior will enhance student learning and appropriate behavior.

This chapter presents a synopsis of that knowledge base. The chapter is divided into two parts. The first section, The Basics of Effective Teaching, explains research that emphasizes teacher behaviors that promote student achievement as measured by low-level, paper-and-pencil tests. The second section of the chapter, Beyond the Basics, examines more recent conceptualizations of teaching that focus primarily on student cognition and student performance on higher level cognitive tasks.

One of the major differences between section one and section two of this chapter concerns the emphasis placed on teacher versus student behavior. Early research on effective teaching was based primarily on the premise that the teacher is the most important actor in the classroom. Thus, this research focused on the overt behavior of the teacher during instruction. In the mid-1980s, however, researchers began to see the student as the most important actor and the student's thought processes as the key elements during instruction. As a result, the focus of the research switched from the overt behavior of the teacher to the covert behavior of the learner during instruction. This change in focus is most obvious in the research on student motivation. Indeed, it has led to the two sections on student motivation in this chapter. In the first section, the explanation focuses on student motivation as influenced by teacher behavior; in the second section, the explanation focuses on student motivation as influenced by student cognition.

The Basics of Effective Teaching

Most of the research findings discussed here were derived from studies of teacher behaviors that were effective in promoting student achievement as defined by lower-level cognitive objectives, which are efficiently measured by paper-and-pencil tests (Brophy, 1988b). It appears that general principles for teaching behavior derived from these studies apply to "instruction in any body of knowledge or set of skills that has been sufficiently well organized and analyzed so that: (1) it can be presented systematically, and then (2) practiced or applied during activities that call for student performance that (3) can be evaluated for quality and (4) can be given corrective feedback (where incorrect or imperfect)" (Rosenshine and Stevens, 1986, p. 49).

The research findings from which general principles have been drawn are the result of various long-term research projects that usually followed a three-step process. In step 1 of the process, teams of researchers observed classroom teachers who were considered to be either very effective or very ineffective. Effectiveness was most often defined as enhanced student achievement on paper-and-pencil tests. From the observations, it was possible to develop a list of teaching behaviors that were used frequently by the effective teachers but not by the ineffective teachers. Researchers hypothesized that at least some of these teaching behaviors were responsible for the success of the effective teachers.

In step 2, correlational studies were conducted to find positive relationships between the use of these "effective" teaching behaviors and student behavior or student learning as measured by paper-and-pencil achievement test scores. The correlational studies indicated that some of the effective teaching behaviors were positively related to student behavior and achievement, whereas others were not. Thus, the result of step 2 was to narrow the list of effective teaching behaviors to those that were used by effective teachers *and* had a positive relationship with student behavior or student achievement test scores.

In step 3, experimental studies were conducted. The researchers trained an experimental group of teachers to use the narrowed-down list of effective teaching behaviors consistently in their teaching. The achievement scores and classroom behavior of their students were then compared with the achievement scores and behavior of students taught by a control group of teachers, who had not been trained to use the effective teaching behaviors. The results of these experimental comparison studies showed that students of the experimental teachers had significantly higher achievement scores or significantly better classroom behavior.

Lesson Design

During the 1970s and 1980s, Madeline Hunter (1982), Barak Rosenshine (Rosenshine and Stevens, 1986), and other researchers spent a great deal of time trying to identify the type of lesson structure that was most effective for student learning. Although the various researchers tend to use their own specialized vocabulary, they agree that lessons that include the following components are the most effective in helping students to learn new material: a lesson introduction, clear explanations of the content, checks for student understanding, a period of coached practice, a lesson summary or closure, a period of solitary practice, and periodic reviews. As you read the discussion of these components that follow, remember that a lesson does not equal a class period. A lesson is defined as the amount of instructional time required for students to achieve a specific learning objective. Since a lesson may extend over several class periods, it is not essential to have all of these components in each class period. On the other hand, if one class period contains two lessons, one would expect the components to be repeated twice.

1. *Lesson introduction.* A good introduction makes students aware of what they are supposed to learn, activates their prior knowledge of the topic, focuses their attention on the main elements of the lesson to come, and motivates them to be interested in the lesson.

2. *Clarity.* Clear explanations of the content of the lesson proceed in step-by-step fashion, illustrate the content by using concrete examples familiar to the students, and are interspersed with questions that check student understanding. "Lessons in which learners perceive links among the main ideas are more likely to contribute to content learning than are lessons in which links among the main ideas are less easily perceived by learners" (Anderson, 1989, p. 102). Well-organized presentations help learners to process linking ideas by telling them what prior knowledge should be activated and by pointing out what pieces of information are important in using activated prior knowledge (Anderson, 1989). Techniques for ensuring that presentations are well organized include (a) using structured overviews, advance organizers, and statements of objectives near the beginning of the presentation; (b) outlining the content, signaling transitions between ideas, calling attention to main ideas, and summarizing subsections of the lesson during the presentation; and (c) summarizing main ideas near the end of the presentation.

3. *Coached practice.* Effective lessons include a period of coached or guided practice during which students practice using the skill or knowledge, either through written exercises, oral questions and answers, or some type of group work. This initial practice is closely monitored by the teacher so that students receive frequent feedback and correction. Feedback and correction can occur as frequently as after every two or three problems. Students should experience high amounts of success (over 75 percent) with the coached practice exercises before moving on to solitary practice. Otherwise, they may spend a large portion of the solitary practice period practicing and learning the wrong information or skill.

Wang and Palinscar (1989) cite "scaffolding" as an additional important aspect of the coached practice portion of lessons designed to help students acquire cognitive strategies (such as study skills, problem-solving skills, and critical thinking skills). They cite scaffolding as a process that underlies all of the elements of lesson design. "Scaffolding occurs when the teacher supports students' attempts to use a cognitive strategy; adjusts that support according to learner characteristics, the nature of the material, and the nature of the task; and treats the support as temporary, removing it as students show increased competence in using the cognitive strategy" (p. 79). In other words, the teacher plans instruction to move from modeling and instruction to feedback and coaching, and increasingly transfers control to students.

4. *Closure.* A good lesson summary or closure asks students to become actively involved in summarizing the key ideas that have been learned in the lesson and gives students some ideas about where future lessons will take them.

5. *Solitary practice.* Effective lessons also include a period of solitary or independent practice during which students practice the skill on their own and experience significant amounts of success (over 75 percent). This practice often takes the form of independent seat work or homework. The effectiveness of homework as a tool for promoting learning is directly related to whether it is checked and feedback is provided to students.

6. *Review.* Finally, periodic reviews conducted on a weekly and monthly basis help students to consolidate their learning and provide additional reinforcement.

These six research-based components, which are especially effective in lessons designed to impart basic information or specific skills and procedures, should not be viewed as constraints on the teacher's creativity and individuality. Each component may be embellished and tailored to fit the unique teaching situations that confront every teacher. Together, however, the components provide a basic framework that lessens student confusion about what is to be learned and ensures that learning proceeds in an orderly sequence of steps. When students try to learn more different content before they have mastered prerequisites and when they are not given sufficient practice to master skills, they become confused, disinterested, and much more likely to cause discipline problems in the classroom.

Student Motivation: Teacher Variables

Motivation refers to an inner drive that focuses behavior on a particular goal or task and causes the individual to be persistent in trying to achieve the goal or complete the task successfully. Fostering motivation in students is undoubtedly one of the most powerful tools the teacher has in preventing classroom discipline problems. When students are motivated to learn, they usually pay attention to the lesson, become actively involved in learning, and direct their energies to the task. When students are not motivated to learn, they lose interest in lessons quickly, look for sources of entertainment, and may direct their energies at amusing themselves and disrupting the learning process of others. There are many variables that a professional teacher can manipulate to increase student motivation to learn. According to a review of research on student motivation (Brophy, 1987), some of the most powerful variables are the following:

1. *Student interest.* Teachers can increase student motivation by relating subject content to life outside of school. For example, an English teacher can relate poetry to the lyrics of popular music, and a chemistry teacher can allow students to analyze the chemical composition of products they use. While there is no subject in which every topic can be related to the real world, games, simulations, videos, group work, and allowing students to plan or select activities can increase interest. Although these strategies can't be used effectively every day, they can be employed by all teachers at some time.

2. *Student needs.* Motivation to learn is increased when students perceive that learning activities provide an opportunity to meet some of their basic human needs as identified by Maslow (see Chapter 3). For example, simply providing elementary students with the opportunity to talk while the whole group listens can be an easy way to help meet students' needs for self-esteem. At the secondary level, allowing students to work together with peers on learning activities helps to meet students' needs for a sense of belonging and acceptance by others. At the most basic level, providing a pleasant, task-oriented climate in which expectations are clear helps to meet students' needs for psychological safety and security.

3. *Novelty and variety.* When the teacher has designed learning activities that include novel events, situations, and materials, students are likely to be motivated to learn. The popcorn lesson in Case 5.1 is an excellent example of the use of novelty to gain student attention. Once student attention has been captured, a variety of short learning activities will help to keep it focused on the lesson.

Human attention spans can be remarkably long when people are involved in an activity that they find fascinating. Most students, however, do not find typical school activities fascinating. Therefore, their attention spans tend to be rather short. For this reason, the professional teacher plans activities that last no longer than 15 to 20 minutes. A teacher who gives a lecture in two 15-minute halves with a 5-minute oral exercise interspersed is much more likely to maintain student interest than a teacher who gives a 30-minute lecture followed by the 5-minute oral exercise. TV soap operas are an excellent example of how changing the focus of activity every 5 to 10 minutes can hold an audience's attention.

4. *Success.* When students are successful at tasks they perceive to be somewhat challenging, their motivation for future learning is greatly enhanced. It is unreasonable to expect students who fail constantly to have any motivation to participate positively in future learning activities. Thus, it is especially important for teachers to create success for students who are not normally successful. Teachers help to ensure that all stu-

---

CASE 5.1 • *The Popcorn Popper*

As Mr. Smith's students walk into tenth-grade creative writing class, they hear an unusual noise. On the teacher's desk an electric popcorn popper filled with unpopped kernels is running. Soon the room is filled with the aroma of fresh popcorn. When the popping is finished, the teacher passes a bowl of popcorn around for everyone to eat. After the students finish eating, Mr. Smith asks them to describe out loud the sights, sounds, smells, taste, and feel of the popcorn. Mr. Smith then uses their accounts as an introduction to a writing exercise on the five senses.

dents experience some success by making goals and objectives clear, by teaching content clearly in small steps, and by checking to see that students understand each step. Teachers can also encourage success by helping students to acquire the study skills they need when they must work on their own—outlining, note taking, and using textbooks correctly. Still, the most powerful technique for helping students to succeed is to ensure that the material is at the appropriate level of difficulty. Material should be appropriate for the students, given the students' prior learning in that subject.

5. *Tension.* In teaching, tension refers to a feeling of concern or anxiety on the part of the student because she knows that she will be required to demonstrate her learning. A moderate amount of tension increases student learning. When there is no tension in the learning situation, students may be so relaxed that no learning occurs. On the other hand, if there is an overwhelming amount of tension, students may expend more energy in dealing with the tension than they do in learning. Creating a moderate amount of tension results in motivation without tension overload.

When a learning task is inherently interesting and challenging for students, there is little need for the teacher to add tension to the situation. When the learning task is routine and uninteresting for students, a moderate amount of tension created by the teacher enhances motivation and learning. Teacher behaviors that raise the level of tension include moving around the room, calling on volunteers and nonvolunteers to answer questions in a random pattern, giving quizzes on class material, checking homework and seat work, and reminding students that they will be tested on the material they are learning.

6. *Feeling tone.* Feeling tone refers to the emotional atmosphere or climate in the classroom. According to Madeline Hunter (1982), classroom feeling tone can be extremely positive, moderately positive, neutral, moderately negative, and extremely negative. An extremely positive feeling tone can be so sweet that it actually directs student attention away from learning, a neutral feeling tone is bland and nonstimulating, and an extremely negative feeling tone is threatening and may produce a tension overload. The most effective feeling tone is a moderately positive one in which the atmosphere is pleasant and friendly but clearly focused on the learning task at hand. The teacher can help to create such a feeling tone by making a room that is comfortable and pleasantly decorated, by treating students in a courteous and friendly manner, by expressing sincere interest in students as individuals, and by communicating positively with students both verbally and nonverbally. See how one teacher expresses his interest in students in Case 5.2.

Although a moderately positive feeling tone is the most motivating one, it is sometimes necessary to create, temporarily, a moderately negative feeling tone. If students are not doing their work and not living up to their responsibilities, it is necessary to shake them out of their complacency with some well-chosen, corrective comments. The wise teacher understands that undesirable consequences may result from a classroom feeling tone that is continuously negative and, therefore, works to create a moderately positive classroom climate most of the time.

7. *Feedback.* Because it provides both information that can be used to improve performance and a yardstick or criterion by which progress can be measured, feedback

CASE 5.2 • *Talking between Classes*

Mr. Dailey, the eighth-grade English teacher, does not spend the time in between classes standing out in the hallway or visiting with friends. Instead he uses the three minutes to chat with individual students. During these chats, he talks with students about their out-of-school activities, their hobbies, their feelings about school and his class in particular, their plans and aspirations, and everyday school events. He feels that these three-minute chats really promote a more positive feeling tone in his classroom and allow him to relate to his students as individuals.

---

also increases motivation. Feedback is most effective when it is specific and is delivered soon after or at the time of performance. Teachers usually provide feedback in the form of oral and written comments on tests and assignments. One additional way to use feedback as a motivator is to have students keep track of their own progress over time and to provide periodic opportunities for them to reflect on their progress.

8. *Encouragement.* Encouragement is a great motivator. It emphasizes the positive aspects of behavior; recognizes and validates real effort; communicates positive expectations for future behavior; and communicates that the teacher trusts, respects, and believes in the child. All too frequently, teachers and parents point out how children have failed to meet expectations. Pointing out shortcomings and focusing on past transgressions erode children's self-esteem, whereas encouraging communication, as defined by Sweeney (1981), enhances self-esteem. It emphasizes present and future behavior rather than past transgressions and what is being learned and done correctly rather than on what has not been learned.

Ms. Johnson in Case 5.3 would have had a far more positive impact on Heidi's motivation if she had pointed out the positive aspects of Heidi's work as well as the error in spelling. After all, a child who gets a 68 on an exam has learned twice as

CASE 5.3 • *Nonconstructive Feedback*

Ms. Johnson was handing back the seventh-graders' reports on their library books. Heidi waited anxiously to get her report back. She had read a book on archaeology and had really gotten into it. She spent quite a bit of time explaining in her report how neat it must be to be able to relive the past by examining the artifacts people left behind. When she received her book report, Heidi was dejected. The word *artifact*—Heidi had spelled it *artafact*—was circled twice on her paper with *sp* written above it. At the bottom of the paper, Ms. Johnson had written, "spelling errors are careless and are not acceptable." The only other mark Ms. Johnson had made on the paper was a grade of C.

much as she has failed to learn. For more on encouragement, see Dreikurs's *Children the Challenge* (1964).

How can you use these research findings to improve student motivation in your own classroom? Ask yourself the following questions as you plan classroom activities for your students:

1. How can I make use of natural student interests in this learning activity?
2. How can I help students to meet their basic human needs in this activity?
3. How can I use novel events and/or materials in this activity?
4. How can I provide for variety in these learning activities?
5. How can I ensure that my students will be successful?
6. How can I create an appropriate level of tension for this learning task?
7. How can I create a moderately pleasant feeling tone for this activity?
8. How can I provide feedback to students and help them to recognize their progress in learning?
9. How can I encourage my students?

This list of nine questions is also an important resource when discipline problems occur. By answering the questions, the teacher may find ways to increase the motivation to learn and decrease the motivation to misbehave.

Teacher Expectations

Teacher expectations influence both student learning and student motivation. In a famous study entitled *Pygmalion in the Classroom* (1968), Rosenthal and Jacobson began a line of inquiry that still continues and has yielded powerful insights concerning the effects of teacher behavior on student achievement. For their study, Rosenthal and Jacobson told teachers in an inner-city elementary school that they had developed an intelligence test designed to identify "intellectual bloomers," that is, students who were on the verge of taking a tremendous leap in their ability to learn. They also told these teachers that certain students in their classes had been so identified. This was a total fabrication. There was no such test. However, when Rosenthal and Jacobson checked student achievement test scores at the end of the year, the students identified as intellectual bloomers had actually bloomed. Compared to a matched group of their peers, the researcher-identified bloomers had made much greater gains in achievement. As a result, Rosenthal and Jacobson assumed that the teachers must have treated the bloomers differently in some way in the classroom, but they had no observational data to support this assumption. Although still considered controversial (Wineburg, 1987), the study provided the impetus for further research (Good, 1987).

Beginning in the 1970s, researchers such as Thomas Good and Jere Brophy conducted observational studies of teacher behavior toward students whom the teachers perceived as high achievers and students they perceived as low achievers. Multiple research studies found that teachers often unintentionally communicate low expectations toward students whom they perceive as low achievers. These lower expectations are communicated by behaviors such as:

1. Calling on low achievers less often to answer questions.
2. Giving low achievers less think time when they are called on.
3. Providing fewer clues and hints to low achievers when they have initial difficulty in answering questions.
4. Praising correct answers from low achievers less often.
5. Criticizing wrong answers from low achievers more often.
6. Praising marginal answers from low achievers but demanding more precise answers from high achievers.
7. Staying farther away physically and psychologically from low achievers.
8. Rarely expressing personal interest in low achievers.
9. Smiling less frequently at low achievers.
10. Making eye contact less frequently with low achievers.
11. Complimenting low achievers less often.

Some of these behaviors may be motivated by good intentions on the part of the teacher, who, for example, may give low achievers less think time to avoid embarrassing them if they don't know an answer. However, the cumulative effect is the communication of a powerful message: "I don't expect you to be able to do much." This message triggers a vicious cycle. Students begin to expect less of themselves, produce less, and confirm the teacher's original perception of them. While in many cases the teacher may have a legitimate reason to expect less from some students, communicating low expectations produces only negative effects.

Researchers have demonstrated that when teachers equalize response opportunities, feedback, and personal involvement, student learning can improve. The message is clear. Communicating high expectations to all learners appears to influence low achievers to learn more, whereas communicating low expectations, no matter how justified, has a debilitating effect (Good and Brophy, 1987).

Although empirical research in this area has been limited to the effects of teacher expectations on achievement, we believe that the generalizations hold true for student behavior as well. Communicating high expectations for student behavior is likely to bring about increased positive behaviors; communicating low expectations for student behavior is likely to bring about increased negative behavior. A teacher who says, "I am sure that all of you will complete all of your homework assignments carefully because you realize that doing homework is an important way of practicing what you are learning" is more likely to have students complete homework assignments than a teacher who says, "I know you probably don't like to do homework, but if you fail to complete homework assignments, it will definitely lower your grades." As Brophy (1988a) has noted: "Consistent projection of positive expectations, attributions and social labels to the students is important in fostering positive self-concepts and related motives that orient them toward prosocial behavior. In short, students who are consistently treated as if they are well-intentioned individuals who respect themselves and others and desire to act responsibly, morally, and prosocially are more likely to live up to those expectations and acquire those qualities than students who are treated as if they had the opposite qualities" (p. 11). Given the powerful research results in this area, all teachers should step back and reflect on the expectations they communicate to students through their verbal and nonverbal classroom behavior.

Classroom Questioning

Of all the instructional tools and techniques classroom teachers possess, questioning is perhaps the most versatile. According to Good and Brophy (1997) effective questions are clear, purposeful, brief, naturally sequenced, and thought provoking. When a teacher's questions have these characteristics, they may be used to assess readiness for new learning, to create interest and motivation in learning, to make concepts more precise, to check student understanding of the material, to redirect off-task students to more positive behavior, and to create the moderate amount of tension that enhances learning. The use of good questioning techniques is a potent means of keeping students actively involved in lessons and thereby minimizing disruptive behavior. Wilen (1986) has compiled a good summary of the research done on teacher questioning. Findings on classroom questioning indicate that the following behaviors help to promote student learning:

1. Ask questions at a variety of cognitive levels. Asking questions in a hierarchy that proceeds from knowledge and comprehension to application, analysis, synthesis, and evaluation promotes both critical thinking and better retention of basic information (Good and Brophy, 1997).
2. Call on volunteers and nonvolunteers to answer questions in a random rather than predictable order (*Note:* In working with first- and second-graders, research [Brophy and Good, 1986] indicates that the use of a predictable order in selecting students to answer questions is more effective than the use of a random order.)
3. After asking a question, allow students three to five seconds of Wait Time 1 before calling on someone to answer. This time is especially important when asking higher-level questions that require students to make inferences, connections, and judgments.
4. Have many students respond to a question before giving feedback. This may be done by asking for occasional responses from the entire group, by asking students to indicate their agreement or disagreement with answers by using signals, or by redirecting the question to obtain several individual answers.
5. After a student answers a question, wait three to five seconds before you respond. This planned silence, or Wait Time 2, tends to increase the number of students who respond, to increase the length of student answers, to increase the amount of student–student interaction, and to increase the diversity of student responses.
6. Vary the type of positive reinforcement you give and make it clear why student answers are worthy of positive reinforcement.
7. Ask follow-up or probing questions to extend student thinking after correct and incorrect responses. Some sample types of follow-up questions are (a) asking

Effective questioning techniques increase student participation.

for clarification, (b) asking students to re-create the thought process they used to arrive at an answer, (c) asking for specific examples to support a statement, (d) asking for elaboration or expansion of an answer, and (e) asking students to relate their answers to previous answers or questions.

Teachers who employ these techniques, which may be adapted to fit their own classroom context, are likely to improve student learning and to increase student involvement in the learning activities, thereby minimizing disruptive student behavior.

Maximizing Learning Time

One of the variables that affects how much students learn is the amount of time they spend learning. As Lieberman and Denham (1980) have found there is a statistically positive relationship between time devoted to learning and scores on achievement tests. This is not, however, a simple relationship. Other factors, such as the quality of instruction and the kinds of learning tasks, must be considered in assessing the potential impact of increased time spent on learning. In other words, spending more instructional time with a poor teacher or on poorly devised learning tasks will not increase student learning.

Assuming that the teacher is competent and the learning tasks are appropriate, students who spend more time learning will probably learn more and create fewer management problems because they are occupied by the learning activities. Two areas that teachers can control to increase the amount of time students spend learning are the time allocated to instruction and the rate of student engagement in the learning tasks.

Allocated Time.   Allocated time refers to the amount of time that the teacher makes available for students to learn a subject. Studies have found that the amount of time allocated to various subjects in elementary schools differs widely even among teachers in the same district at the same grade level (Karweit, 1984). For example, some teachers at the fourth-grade level allocate 12 hours per week to reading and language arts, whereas other fourth-grade teachers allocate 4 hours per week. Some fourth-grade teachers allocate 10 hours per week to math, and others allocate 3. Other factors being equal, the student who spends 12 hours per week in learning reading and language arts is going to learn a great deal more than the student who spends 3 hours per week.

In secondary schools, the amounts of time actually allocated to instruction also vary widely among teachers. The need to deal with routine attendance and housekeeping chores (for example, Who still owes lab reports? Who needs to make up Friday's test?) as well as the need to deal with disruptions that can range from discipline problems to public address announcements can steal large chunks of time from learning activities (see Chapter 2). Usually both elementary and secondary school teachers need to examine how much time they make available for students to learn the various subjects they teach. Elementary teachers should investigate how they allocate time to their various subjects. Secondary school teachers should investigate how to handle routine duties more efficiently and how to minimize disruptions.

Time-on-Task.   In addition to increasing allocated time, teachers need to maximize student time-on-task. "Research on teaching has established that the key to successful management (and to successful instruction as well) is the teacher's ability to maximize the time students spend actively engaged in worthwhile academic assignments and to minimize the time they spend waiting for activities to get started, making transitions between activities, sitting with nothing to do, or engaging in misconduct" (Brophy, 1988a, p. 3). Brophy's statement refers to the percentage of the total time allocated for learning that the student spends actually engaged in learning activities. Once again, research has provided some guidelines to increase student time-on-task.

1. The use of substantive interaction—a teaching mode in which the teacher presents information, asks questions to assess comprehension, provides feedback, and monitors student work—usually leads to higher student engagement than independent or small group work that is not led by the teacher.
2. Teacher monitoring of the entire class during the beginning and ending portions of a seat work activity as well as at regular intervals during the activity leads to higher engagement rates.
3. Making sure that students understand what the activity directs them to do, that they have the skills necessary to complete the task successfully, that each student has access to all needed materials, and that each student is protected from disruption by others leads to greater student time-on-task during seat work.

4. Giving students oral directions as well as written directions concerning how to do a seat work activity and what to do when they have finished the activity also leads to greater time-on-task during seat work.

5. Communicating teacher awareness of student behavior seems to lead to greater student involvement during seat work activities.

6. "Providing a variety of seat work activities with concern for students' attention spans helps keep students on task and allows the teacher more uninterrupted small group instruction" (Evertson, 1989, p. 64).

When students are on task, they are engaged in learning and less apt to disrupt the learning of others. The effective teacher uses these guidelines to increase student learning and to minimize disruptive student behavior.

Beyond the Basics

By the late 1980s, many educational researchers were beginning to express great dissatisfaction with the research that had been done on effective teaching. They were dissatisfied because it focused almost exclusively on low-level outcomes and generic teaching and learning strategies, paying little attention to contextual variables and to the subject matter being taught. Lee Shulman and his associates at Stanford (1987) began a line of research focused not on generic questions concerning good teaching but rather on good teaching of particular content in particular contexts. Their work was one of the major forces to give rise to the notions of teaching described in this section. As you will discover, these notions focus primarily on student cognition.

A second major impetus for a change in the focus of the research done on effective teaching came from conceptual change research in science (Pintrich, Marx, and Boyle, 1993). This line of research focused on the difficulty science teachers face in attempting to change the misconceptions that students bring to the classroom. For example, most students come to the classroom believing that the explanation for warmer weather in the summer is the fact that the sun is closer to the earth in the summer. Obviously, this is not true. The sun is actually closer to the earth in the winter. However, research indicates that even after they have the correct explanation, which they are able to reproduce for the test, most students leave the classroom believing that the sun is closer to the earth in the summer. Researchers have studied student learning of a number of scientific concepts including photosynthesis, electricity, gravity, and density with similar results—that is, students enter the classroom with misconceptions, learn the correct explanations for the test, and leave the classroom with their basic misconceptions completely unchanged. It is clear from these studies that we need to pay much closer attention than we have to date to the prior knowledge that students bring with them to the classroom as well as to the actual thought processes that take place during instruction.

The third major impetus for the current models of teaching and learning is the rise in popularity of constructivism as a philosophical set of beliefs about learning. Until recently educational thinking and research have been dominated by behaviorist and information processing views of learning which, although different in many respects, share a conception of the learner as a rather passive processor of information received from the external environment. In contrast, constructivism places its greatest emphasis on active construction of knowledge by the learner. Thus, constructivism places the learner squarely in the center of the learning paradigm and sees the role of the teacher as one of coaching, guiding, and supporting the learner when necessary. Indeed, among the tenets of constructivism are the following six: (1) knowledge is actively constructed, (2) knowledge should be structured around a few powerful ideas, (3) prior knowledge exerts a powerful influence on new learning, (4) restructuring of prior knowledge and conceptual change are key elements of new learning, and (6) knowledge is socially constructed (Good and Brophy, 1997). Given this view, it is not surprising that constructivism emphasizes conceptual-change teaching and the need to link new learning with prior knowledge. Using the constructivist paradigm, teachers must provide opportunities for students to make knowledge their own through question, discussion, debate, and other appropriate activities (Brophy, 1993).

The research on student cognition, constructivism, conceptual-change teaching, and subject-specific teaching have led to several changes in our thinking about instructional practice. Indeed, they have led to a new paradigm for learning that rests on the following: (1) teaching for understanding as the major goal for teaching; (2) using authentic instructional tasks as the basis for classroom learning; (3) emphasizing teaching frameworks that highlight the importance of thinking skills, problem solving, and student self-regulation; (4) moving from individual learning to the creation of learning communities; (5) teaching for multiple types of intelligence; and (6) emphasizing student cognitive variables rather than overt teacher behavior as the key aspect of student motivation in the classroom. In this section of the chapter, these concepts will be described individually even though they are interwoven and closely related to each other.

Teaching for Understanding

For much of the history of education in the United States, the goals for classroom learning have focused on the acquisition of factual information and routine skills and procedures. Although still important to some degree, these goals have become increasingly less sufficient for enabling students to function competently in today's technologically sophisticated, information-rich society. In order to function effectively in a global, interactive society, students need to go beyond memorization and routine skills to much deeper levels of understanding. Howard Gardner (Brandt, 1993) has asserted that our schools have never really taught for deep understanding. Instead, they have settled for what Gardner calls the "correct answer compromise," that is, students give agreed-upon answers that are counted as correct, but their real-world behavior indicates that they have failed to really understand the material. Gardner believes that we need to enable students to achieve a deep understanding of the material that they encounter in school. Deep understanding means being able to do a variety of thought-demanding tasks such as explaining a topic in one's own words, making predictions, finding exemplars in new contexts, and applying concepts to explain new situations (Brandt, 1993).

The first step in making deep understanding one of our goals for student learning involves the teacher coming to grips with the "content coverage" dilemma. Teaching for understanding involves time. Learners do not develop deep understandings of content overnight. They need opportunities to become engaged with the content in different contexts. They need the opportunity to see many examples, to ask many questions, to discuss ideas with peers and with the teacher, and to practice demonstrating their understanding in a variety of situations. As a result, it is simply not possible to cover the same amount of material that can be covered in a classroom in which student memorization is the goal. The teacher who wants to teach for understanding must be willing to take the time to allow students to become deeply involved with the material.

For those teachers who are willing to cover less material at deeper levels of student understanding, Perkins and Blythe offer a four-part framework that can be used to focus classroom learning on creating deep understanding (1994). The first part of the framework calls for the teacher to use "generative topics" as the focus for classroom learning. In order for a topic to qualify as generative, it must meet three criteria: (1) It must be an important topic in the discipline, (2) it must be able to be reasonably conveyed to learners at their particular developmental level, and (3) it must be able to be related to learners' lives and interests outside of school. The second part of the framework asks the teacher to set learning goals that require students to demonstrate their understanding. For example, students might identify examples of Newton's laws of motion in everyday sports events. The third part of the framework requires students to demonstrate their understanding through classroom activities such as discussions, debates, experiments, problem solving, and so forth. The final part of the framework calls for ongoing assessment of student progress using publicly shared criteria for success, frequent feedback by the teacher, and periodic opportunities for students to reflect on their own progress toward demonstrating a deep understanding of the particular topic.

Authentic Instruction

While the concept of teaching for understanding focuses on three separate but related elements (the content selected for instruction, the selected learning goals, and general strategies for assessing student learning), the concept of authentic instruction emphasizes actual classroom activities. When these two concepts are melded together in the classroom, the teacher has a powerful set of ideas for enhancing both student understanding and student interest in the teaching–learning process.

According to Newmann and Wehlage (1993), there are five key elements to authentic instruction. They have developed a continuum for each element that can be used by a teacher or an observer to determine the degree to which authentic instruction is happening in a classroom. The first continuum looks at the emphasis on higher-order thinking versus the emphasis on lower-order thinking. When authentic instruction is in progress, students are asked to manipulate, transform, and use information in new and unpracticed ways rather than to receive information and use it in repetitive and routine ways.

The second continuum, depth of coverage, is closely related to the concept of teaching for understanding. When authentic instruction is taking place, students encounter a small number of ideas but are expected to develop a deep level of understanding of the ideas as opposed to encountering many ideas that are dealt with only on the surface level.

The third continuum focuses on the connection of classroom activities to the world outside the classroom. Teachers using authentic instruction present real-world problems as topics of study, and students are expected to apply their knowledge to settings outside of the classroom. Information is not seen as useful *only* for continued success in school.

The fourth continuum, substantive conversation, focuses on the nature of the verbal interaction that occurs in the classroom. When authentic instruction takes place, both the learners and the teacher are engaged in dialogue and argumentation that is not scripted or controlled and that builds on participants' understandings as opposed to verbal interactions that are characterized primarily by lecture and short, preplanned, predictable conversations and interactions.

The final continuum focuses on the push for achievement in the classroom. When authentic instruction is in place, the classroom environment is marked by mutual respect, intellectual risk taking, and a widely accepted belief that all learners can learn, as opposed to a classroom environment that discourages effort and participation and in which only some students are viewed as capable learners.

Classrooms in which authentic instruction is employed differ from traditional classrooms not only in terms of the problems students are asked to solve but also in terms of the teacher's role in structuring student learning. Because authentic instruction forces students to solve real-world types of problems rather than simply apply previously learned formulas or concepts to solve textbook problems (Stepien and Gallagher, 1993), the problems are not well defined and are not usually confined to one specific discipline. In order to solve such problems, students must first define the problems, then gather additional information or acquire additional skills.

Consequently, teachers usually introduce these complex, ill-structured problems early in the learning sequence and then allow the instructional sequence to emerge from the way in which the problems are defined. In other words, lower-level knowledge and skills are not introduced as separate topics. The need to develop lower-level skills and acquire lower-level knowledge arises directly from the students' attempt to define and solve the problem that serves as the focus for learning. The old paradigm that held that students must first acquire a host of prerequisite knowledge before being introduced to problem-solving activities has been replaced by a paradigm that asserts that lower-level knowledge and skills should be acquired as a result of students needing specific information or specific skills in order to solve real-world problems.

In authentic instruction, the teacher is active early in the learning process, modeling appropriate problem-solving behavior, providing cues and information to the learner, and structuring the learning process. However, as time goes on and the student acquires a better understanding of the real-world problem and the information and skills needed to solve it, the student becomes more self-regulated and takes an active role in structuring her own learning (Brophy, 1993). As noted in the section on Lesson Design, this type of structuring is sometimes referred to as scaffolding.

Emphasis on Thinking and Problem-Solving Skills

Clearly, the concepts of teaching for understanding and authentic instruction place a great deal of emphasis on student thinking and problem-solving skills. However, because thinking and problem-solving skills are seen as tools for acquiring a deep understanding of content, they play a secondary rather than primary role in the conceptualization of the teaching and learning process. Thinking skills and problem-solving skills do play a primary role in the conceptualization of teaching developed by Marzano and his associates (1992). This conceptualization, entitled "dimensions of learning," provides a comprehensive framework for focusing teaching and learning on the development of higher-order thinking, problem solving, and understanding. Marzano assumes that the process of learning involves the interaction of five types of thinking, which he has called dimensions of learning.

Dimension one, entitled positive attitudes and perceptions about learning, states that all learning activities are filtered through the students' attitudes and perceptions. Therefore, effective teachers shape their lessons to foster positive attitudes and perceptions. They foster positive attitudes by helping students to feel accepted, by providing physical and psychological comfort (see Chapter 3), by creating a sense of order and routine in the classroom, by helping students to understand what they are required to do in performing classroom tasks, and by helping students to believe that they can be successful in completing those tasks.

Dimension two concerns the acquisition of new knowledge and skills. According to this dimension, early in the learning process, effective teachers help students to acquire new knowledge by encouraging them to relate the new knowledge to what they already know and by providing them with opportunities to organize the information in ways that will facilitate its storage in long-term memory. These teachers structure the acquisition of new skills by structuring the learning sequence, first helping students to build a cognitive model of the new skill, then gradually shaping skill performance to make it more refined, more automatic, and more internalized. This dimension corresponds nicely to the research on effective teaching described in the first section of this chapter.

Dimension three concerns the extension and refinement of knowledge by learners. Effective teachers help learners to refine and extend their knowledge by providing opportunities for them to use such thinking skills as comparing and contrasting information, classifying information and observations, analyzing arguments, constructing support for ideas and arguments, abstracting information, and analyzing diverse perspectives on issues and questions.

The final two dimensions concern using knowledge meaningfully and developing productive habits of mind. These two dimensions remind us that teachers should involve students in long-term, self-directed projects that require investigation, decision making, research, problem solving, and invention. Effective teachers should also be concerned with helping their students to develop sensitivity to feedback, a desire for accuracy, persistence in the face of difficulty, an unconventional view of situations, and an ability to avoid impulsive actions. It is the presence of these traits that helps learners to solve the complex problems and issues that they face both in the classroom and throughout their lives. When used as a framework for planning, implementing, and analyzing instruction, these five dimensions of learning serve as a valuable tool for enhancing student thinking, student problem solving, and student self-regulated learning.

Creating Communities of Learners

One of the most dramatic changes that has taken place in our thinking about teaching during the last ten years has been the emphasis we now place on the importance of building learning communities in the classroom. In the past, we emphasized individual student learning and interaction between individual students and the teacher. Note that the research on effective teaching described in the first section of this chapter focuses almost exclusively on individual student–teacher interaction. Early research on effective teaching viewed peers as superfluous to the learning process. However, because of the work on cooperative learning conducted by Roger and David Johnson (1993), Robert Slavin (1989–90), Spencer Kagan (1994), and others, we now believe that peers can play a tremendously important role in enhancing student learning and in developing positive classroom environments. For this reason, we now believe that the creation of a classroom learning community in which learners engage in dialogue with each other and the teacher is a critical step toward making classrooms productive learning environments (Prawat, 1993).

The creation of communities of learners often begins with lessons designed to involve students in cooperative learning activities. Cooperative learning should not be equated to simply putting students into groups. Cooperative learning activities share a set of common characteristics. Although the number of specific elements in cooperative learning differs among theorists (Johnson, Johnson, and Holubec [1993] favor five elements while Slavin [1989–90] favors three), there seem to be at least three elements that are critical to its success (Slavin, 1989–90). These three elements are face-to-face interaction, a feeling of positive interdependence, and a feeling of individual accountability. Face-to-face interaction requires placing students in close physical proximity to each other and ensuring that they are required to talk to each other in order to complete the assigned tasks. If students can complete the task without interacting with each other, they have been engaged in an individual learning activity rather than a cooperative learning activity.

Establishing a feeling of positive interdependence means that students believe each individual can achieve the particular learning goal only if all the learners in the group achieve the learning goal. Johnson, Johnson, and Holubec (1993), who refer to this as sinking or swimming together, have identified several types of interdependence that the teacher can work to create. Positive reward interdependence occurs when everyone is rewarded or no one is rewarded, and everyone gets the same reward. Positive resource interdependence occurs when each member of the group has only a portion of the information or materials needed to complete the task. A teacher is employing positive resource interdependence when each student has only one piece of the puzzle or one section of the required reading. Positive task interdependence occurs when a task is broken into a series of steps and is then completed in assembly-line fashion with each group member completing only one section of the total task. Positive role interdependence is the practice of assigning roles to individual group members, for example, consensus checker, writer, reader, time keeper, and so on. Obviously, each role must be important to the completion of the task. Finally, positive identity interdependence is established by allowing the group to form its own identity by creating a group name, decorating a group folder or flag, or developing a group motto or some other symbol that describes the group. The Johnsons and Holubec suggest that the teacher build as many of these types of positive interdependence into cooperative learning lessons as possible, in order to increase the likelihood of creating feelings of positive interdependence.

Individual accountability refers to each group member's feeling that she is responsible for completing the task and cannot rest on the laurels of the group or allow other members to do the work for her. Feelings of individual accountability can be established in a variety of ways, including assigning individual grades; giving individual tests, worksheets, and quizzes; or structuring tasks so that they must be completed by the group while making it clear that individual group members will be called on at random to answer questions about the task.

In addition to face-to-face interaction, positive interdependence, and individual accountability, the Johnsons believe two more elements—teaching social skills and processing group functioning—are crucial for the creation of cooperative learning activities. These two elements are described at length in Chapter 6 under the topic of using group norms to structure the classroom environment. As Case 5.4 illustrates, cooperative learning activities can have a positive impact on student motivation and behavior.

Teaching toward Multiple Intelligences

Due to the work of Howard Gardner (1983) and his colleagues in the last decade, many educators have come to realize that success in school has been unnecessarily restricted to those individuals who have talents in the areas of mathematical and verbal intelligence. Many of the tasks and learning activities performed in schools require learners to use verbal and mathematical reasoning while ignoring other avenues expressing talent. One need only look at standardized achievement tests, traditional IQ tests, and the Scholastic Aptitude Tests (SATs) to recognize our overdependence on verbal and mathematical ability. Fortunately, Gardner's theory of multiple intelligences and its application have helped us to recognize how other types of talent can be tapped.

Gardner's theory (1983) asserts that there are many types of human intelligence and that it is possible to group the various types into seven comprehensive categories: linguistic, logical-mathematical, spatial, bodily-kinesthetic, musical, inter-personal, and intra-personal. Every one of us, according to Gardner, possesses these types of intelligence to some degree. Those who exhibit high degrees of linguistic intelligence are able to use oral and written language effectively. They are often individuals who succeed in areas such as politics, sales, advertising, and writing. Individuals with strengths in the

CASE 5.4 • *Cooperative Learning in Biology*

As I walked into Mr. Higgins's seventh-period biology class, which was filled primarily with vocational technical students, I was surprised to see a variety of specimen samples lying on the lab tables. Mr. Higgins began class informing his students that they would be having a lab quiz—which he referred to as a "practical"—the next day that would constitute a major grade for the marking period. This news was met with shrugs of indifference by the students who were busily engaged in their own private conversations. Mr. Higgins continued speaking, "The practical will also be a cooperative learning team activity. Each of your individual scores on the quiz will be added together and averaged to form a team score. Your team score will be counted as part of the scores for our team competition. Just to review team standings so far, we have the Plumbers in first place with 93 points, followed by the Body Fixers with 88 points, the Hair Choppers with 87, and the Electricians in last place with 86 points. Don't forget that we have all agreed that

the winning team will be treated to a pizza party by the rest of the class. Now, you may go ahead and get started studying in teams for tomorrow's practical."

For a brief moment, the room fell completely silent. This was followed by the scrape of chairs and scuffling of feet as students moved into cooperative learning teams. Within minutes the students were busy looking at the specimens and relating them to the diagrams in their textbook. Students were clearly engaged in helping each other to memorize the various specimen parts that they would need to know for the quiz. Suddenly, one of the students from the Plumbers sat down and began to read a comic book. Within a few minutes, however, the other members of the team informed him that he was not going to sit there and do nothing. They assured him that they would help him to obtain a passing grade on the quiz whether he liked it or not. The student got to his feet with a look of resignation and resumed looking at the specimens.

---

area of logical-mathematical ability use numbers effectively and tend to use reason and logical arguments well. They are accountants, lawyers, scientists, and so on. Some individuals, for example, artists, architects, and interior designers, excel at tasks that require them to perceive and transform graphic and visual representations of reality. Athletes, dancers, and craftspeople such as mechanics fall into the category of bodily-kinesthetic intelligence. They are able to use their bodies to express feelings and ideas and are able to use their hands to produce things. Musicians, conductors, music critics, and composers have a special capacity to perceive and express musical form. Thus, they have a high degree of musical intelligence. Individuals who are very sensitive to the feelings, moods, and intentions of others display inter-personal intelligence. They are often quite successful in people-oriented occupations such as teaching, counseling, and psychology. Finally, there are certain individuals who seem to possess a high degree of self-knowledge and awareness. They understand themselves well and are able to act on that knowledge.

Although good teachers have always been aware of the variety of ways in which students demonstrate high ability, standard classroom practices and assessment devices have not allowed students to demonstrate their knowledge in ways compatible with their strengths. Recently, Thomas Armstrong (1994) and others have begun to help teachers figure out how to structure classroom activities and assessments to take full advantage of the range of intelligences that learners possess. According to Armstrong, learners who are linguistically talented benefit from activities such as storytelling, listening to and giving lectures, journal writing, and participating in classroom discussions. Students who have high aptitudes in mathematical-logical ability usually enjoy activities such as problem solving, observing and classifying, Socratic questioning, and experiments. Students who have strengths in spatial reasoning often profit from visual displays, color coding and color cues, and graphic representations such as semantic maps and webs. Students who are talented in the bodily-kinesthetic area profit from learning activities that include body movement, such as acting out stories and concepts, and using manipulatives. Learners who exhibit high degrees of musical ability usually learn more effectively when learning activities include songs, raps, chants, and the use of music as either a teaching tool or a background environment. Learners who are strong in inter-personal intelligence perform best when they are engaged in collegial interactions such as peer tutoring, cooperative learning, simulations, and board games. Finally, students who possess a high degree of intra-personal intelligence learn best when provided with opportunities for personal goal setting, for connecting school work to their personal lives, for making choices about learning activities, and for individual reflection on their own learning. These students often are exceptionally good at self-assessment.

Armstrong (1994) suggests that teachers ask themselves the following questions when planning a unit of instruction:

1. How will I use the spoken or written word in this unit?
2. How can I bring numbers, calculations, and logic into the unit?
3. How can I use visual aids, color, and symbolism in the unit?
4. How can I involve movement and create hands-on activities?
5. How can I use music or environmental sounds?
6. How can I involve students in peer tutoring, cooperative learning, and sharing?
7. How can I evoke personal feelings and connections and provide students with the opportunity to make individual choices about the unit?

Student Motivation: Student Cognition

In the first section of this chapter, we discussed theories and models of motivation that emphasized factors external to the student. Indeed, the focus of that section was on overt teacher behaviors that impact student motivation. In this section we will look at motivation from a different perspective, that of student cognition and its impact on motivation to learn. There are at present at least three theories of student motivation—

student cognition, attribution, and expectancy x value theory—that have interesting implications for teaching.

The primary developer of the social cognition theory of student motivation was A. Bandura (1986). Bandura took issue with the behavioral notions of motivation that emphasized external reinforcers. He asserted that the individual's thoughts play a central role not only in determining the individual's motivational levels but also in determining how the individual will perceive variables that are intended to be reinforcers. Bandura's research demonstrated that personal evaluation and self-satisfaction are potent reinforcers of behavior, in fact probably more potent than reinforcers provided by others. Bandura's research findings showed that involving students in personal goal setting and providing frequent opportunities for them to monitor and reflect on their progress toward these goals can increase student learning efforts. In fact, according to Bandura, external praise can diminish self-evaluation and create dependency on others, thereby reducing an individual's intrinsic motivation to succeed.

Bandura's work on personal evaluation and self-satisfaction led to a related concept that he called self-efficacy. Self-efficacy refers to an individual's expectation of success at a particular task. When feelings of self-efficacy are high, individuals are much more likely to exert effort toward task completion than they are when feelings are low because they believe they have the potential to be successful. When feelings of self-efficacy are low, efforts are diminished. Feelings of self-efficacy develop from judgments about past performance as well as from vicarious observations of others in similar situations. The greater the perceived similarity between the person we are observing (the model) and ourselves, the greater the impact their fate will have on our own feelings of self-efficacy.

When the social cognition theory is in action in the classroom, the task of the teacher is to focus encouragement on the improvement of individual effort and achievement over time. Teachers who wish to use this theory in the classroom should begin by engaging students in setting personal goals that are concrete, specific, and realistic. Teachers then involve students in monitoring their own performance toward the achievement of these goals. When students are successful, teachers encourage them to engage in self-reinforcement so that they will build positive feelings of self-efficacy toward the accomplishment of future tasks.

Attribution theory deals with student perceived causes of success and failure in school tasks. Clearly, student perceptions of why they succeed or fail at school tasks have a direct impact on their motivation to perform (Stipek, 1993). Research has identified five factors to which students are likely to attribute success or failure. These factors are ability, effort, task difficulty, luck, and other people such as the teacher (Ames and Ames, 1984). The only factor that can be controlled directly by the student is effort. When students attribute success to effort and failure to lack of effort or inappropriate types of effort, they are likely to exert additional effort in the future. "Students who believe that their personal efforts influence their learning are more likely to learn than those who believe that learning depends on teachers or other factors such as task difficulty or luck" (Wang and Palinscar, 1989).

When students attribute failure to lack of ability, the impact on future performance is devastating. Negative feelings of self-efficacy develop, and students see little value in making any effort since they believe that they are not likely to be successful. As negative judgments of ability become more internalized and self-worth more damaged, students stop making any effort as a defense mechanism. Not making the effort allows them to protect their self-concept from further damage. They can simply shrug their shoulders and claim, "I could have done it if I wanted to, but I really didn't think it was worth it." This face-saving device prevents the further ego damage that would result from additional negative ability attributions. To avoid setting up the vicious cycle of failure and lack of future effort, teachers need to recognize the danger of placing students in competitive situations in which they do not have the ability to compete, or of asking students to complete tasks that are too difficult for them.

The implications of attribution theory for classroom teaching are clear. Students need to be assigned tasks that are moderately challenging but within their capability. This may mean that the teacher has to break complex tasks into subtasks that the student can handle and provide a great deal of scaffolding for the student, especially early in the learning process. The teacher should encourage students to make the right kind of effort in completing classroom tasks. When students are successful, the teacher can attribute their success to this effort. When students are not successful, the teacher may want to focus attention on the lack of effort or on using inappropriate strategies. Research has demonstrated that teacher statements concerning attributions for success or failure are the key variable in influencing students to attribute success or failure to one variable rather than another. Case 5.5 illustrates the impact of changing attributions.

The expectancy X value theory proposes that the effort that an individual is willing to put forth in any task is directly related to the product of two factors: the belief that he will be successful and the value of the outcomes that will be gained through successful completion of the task (Feathers, 1982). A multiplication sign is used to indicate the interaction between the two factors. Note that if either of the two factors is 0, no effort will be put forth. Thus, if a students believes that he has the potential to be successful in academic work and values good grades and the other outcomes that accompany academic success, he will be highly motivated to put forth a strong effort. On the other hand, if the student doubts his ability to perform the academic tasks successfully or does not value good grades and the other outcomes attached to academic success, he is likely to put forth a limited effort. Teachers can increase a student's effort at success either by encouraging the learner to believe that he can be successful or by increasing the value of the outcomes.

Good and Brophy (1997) have suggested that teachers should take the following steps to take advantage of the expectancy X value theory in the classroom: (1) establish a supportive classroom climate, (2) structure activities so that they are at the appropriate level of difficulty, (3) develop learning objectives that have personal meaning and relevance for the students, and (4) engage students in personal goal setting and self-appraisal. Finally, for the expectancy X value theory to succeed, the teacher needs to help students recognize the link between effort and outcome suggested by attribution theory.

CASE 5.5 • *Three Years of History Rolled into One*

Mark was a senior who had failed tenth-grade history and eleventh-grade history and was now taking tenth-grade history, eleventh-grade history, and twelfth-grade history in order to graduate on time. The school counselor, who was working with him to improve his study skills, began by helping Mark to prepare for a test on the Egyptians. When the counselor asked what material seemed important for the test, Mark replied, "Well, I know that one thing he is going to ask is what the Egyptians used for cleaning instead of soap—sand." With this response it became clear to the counselor that Mark was not good at distinguishing important from unimportant material. Over the next couple of weeks, they spent a great deal of time looking at Mark's notes and his textbook, separating important from unimportant material.

Two days before the test, Mark had a list of important material to study and did a reasonably good job learning that material. Immediately after taking the test, Mark went to the counselor's office and announced, "You know what? I noticed something on the test." "What did you notice?" asked the counselor. "I noticed that the stuff I studied for, I knew, and the stuff I didn't study, I didn't know."

At first, the counselor thought that Mark was putting him on. However, as the conversation continued it became clear that Mark was serious. Until this point in his life, Mark had felt that success on tests was simply a matter of luck. If you happened to be paying attention to the right things in class, you did well on tests. If you were unfortunate enough to be daydreaming during key information, you did poorly. It was all a matter of luck in terms of when you were paying attention.

Armed with this information, the counselor now had a two-pronged approach to working with Mark. Not only did they work on identifying important information but also on attributing both success and failure to personal effort rather than to chance. As a result of this work, Mark managed to pass (albeit barely) all three histories and graduate on time.

Summary

Section one of this chapter presented an overview of the research on teaching that, as we see it, constitutes the basics of effective teaching. Section two of the chapter presented descriptions of several conceptualizations of teaching that have influenced our current understanding of best teaching practice. These conceptualizations focus on student cognition and higher-order thinking and understanding. Taken together, these two sections of the chapter provide the reader with a comprehensive understanding of current thinking concerning best teaching practice. All teachers have a professional obligation to examine their teaching behavior to ensure that it reflects best practice. This is a critical step toward making sure that the teacher has done all that can be done to prevent classroom management problems from occurring. Among the questions teachers should ask in assessing the congruence between their own teaching and best practice are the following:

Do the lessons I design include an introduction, clear presentation of content, checks for student understanding, guided practice, independent practice, closure or summary, and periodic reviews?

Have I used each of the following factors in trying to increase my students' motivation to learn: student interests, student needs, novelty and variety, success, student attributions, tension, feeling tone, feedback, and encouragement?

Have I communicated high expectations for learning and behavior to all students by equalizing response opportunities, providing prompt and constructive feedback on performance, and treating all students with personal regard?

Have I used classroom questioning to involve students actively in the learning process by asking questions at a variety of cognitive levels, using questions to increase student participation and to probe for and extend student thinking?

Have I maximized student learning by allocating as much time as possible for student learning and by increasing the percentage of student engagement in learning activities?

Am I teaching to enable students to develop a deep understanding of content rather than a surface-level knowledge?

Am I employing authentic instruction in terms of the learning activities I plan and carry out?

Am I using a comprehensive framework to help students develop thinking skills, problem-solving skills, and the capacity to regulate their own learning?

Am I building communities of learners?

Am I teaching so that students can demonstrate their learning by using a variety of intelligences?

Am I using student cognition to increase student motivation to learn?

The teacher who can answer yes honestly to each of these questions has made giant strides toward ensuring that the classroom will be a learning place for students in which discipline problems are kept to a minimum.

References

Ames, R., and Ames, C. (Eds.). (1984). *Research on Motivation in Education,* Vol. 1: *Student Motivation.* New York: Academic.

Anderson, L. M. (1989). Classroom instruction. In M. C. Reynolds (Ed.), *Knowledge Base for the Beginning Teacher.* New York: Pergamon.

Armstrong. T. (1994). *Multiple Intelligences in the Classroom.* Alexandria, VA: Association for Supervision and Curriculum Development.

Bandura, A. (1986). *Social Foundations of Thought and Action: Social Cognition Theory.* Englewood Cliffs, NJ: Prentice Hall.

Brandt, R. (1993). On teaching for understanding: A conversation with Howard Gardner. *Educational Leadership, 50,* 7, 4–7.

Brophy, J. E. (1987). Synthesis of research strategies on motivating students to learn. *Educational Leadership, 45,* 2, 40–48.

Brophy, J. E. (1988a). Educating teachers about managing classrooms and students. *Teaching and Teacher Education, 4,* 1, 1–18.

Brophy, J. E. (1988b). Research on teacher effects and abuses. *Elementary School Journal, 89,* 1, 3–21.

Brophy, J. E. (1993). Probing the subtleties of subject matter teaching. *Educational Leadership, 49,* 7, 4–8.

Brophy, J. E., and Good, T. L. (1986). Teacher behavior and student achievement. In M. C. Wittrock (Ed.), *Handbook of Research on Teaching,* 3rd ed. New York: Macmillan.

Dreikurs, R. (1964). *Children the Challenge.* New York: Hawthorne.

Duke, D. E. (1982). *Helping Teachers Manage Classrooms.* Alexandria, VA: Association for Supervision and Curriculum Development.

Evertson, C. M. (1989). Classroom organization and management. In M. C. Reynolds (Ed.), *Knowledge Base for the Beginning Teacher.* New York: Pergamon.

Feathers, N. (1982). *Expectations and Actions.* Hillsdale, NJ: Erlbaum.

Gardner, H. (1983). *Frames of Mind: The Theory of Multiple Intelligences.* New York: Basic Books.

Good, T. L. (1987, July–August). Two decades of research on teacher expectations: Findings and future directions. *Journal of Teacher Education,* 32–47.

Good, T., and Brophy, J. (1997). *Looking in Classrooms,* 4th ed. New York: Harper & Row.

Hunter, M. (1982). *Mastery Teaching.* El Segundo, CA: TIP Publications.

Johnson, D. W., Johnson, R. T., and Holubec, E. J. (1993). *Cooperation in the Classroom,* rev. ed. Edina, MN: Interaction Book Company.

Kagan, S. (1994). *Cooperative Learning: Resources for Teachers.* San Juan Capistrano, CA: Resources for Teachers.

Karweit, N. (1984). Time on task reconsidered: Synthesis of research on time and learning. *Educational Leadership, 41,* 8, 32–35.

Lieberman, A., and Denham, C. (1980). *Time to Learn.* Sacramento, CA: California Commission for Teacher Preparation and Licensing.

Marzano, R. J. (1992). *A Different Kind of Classroom: Teaching with Dimensions of Learning.* Alexandria, VA: Association for Supervision and Curriculum Development.

Newmann, F. and Wehlage, G. (1993). Five standards of authentic instruction. *Educational Leadership, 50,* 7, 8–12.

Perkins, D., and Blythe, T (1994). Putting understanding up front. *Educational Leadership, 51,* 5, 4–7.

Pintrich, P. R., Marx, R. W., and Boyle, P. (1993). Beyond conceptual change: The role of motivational beliefs and classroom contextual factors in conceptual change teaching. *Review of Educational Research, 63,* 2, 167–200.

Prawat, R. S. (1993). From individual differences to learning communities. *Educational Leadership, 49,* 7, 9–13.

Rosenshine, B., and Stevens, R. (1986). Teaching functions. In M. C. Wittrock (Ed.), *Handbook of Research on Teaching,* 3rd ed. New York: Macmillan.

Rosenthal, R., and Jacobson, L. (1968). *Pygmalion in the Classroom: Teacher Expectations and Pupil's Intellectual Development.* New York: Holt, Rinehart & Winston.

Shulman, L. S. (1987). Knowledge and teaching: Foundations of the new reform. *Harvard Educational Review, 57,* 1–22.

Slavin, R. E. (1989–90). Research on cooperative learning: Consensus and controversy. *Educational Leadership, 47,* 4, 52–54.

Stepien, W., and Gallagher, S. (1993). Problem based learning; as authentic as it gets. *Educational Leadership, 50,* 7, 17–20.

Stipek, D. (1993). *Motivation to Learn: From Theory to Practice,* 2nd ed. Boston: Allyn and Bacon.

Sweeney, T. J. (1981). *Adlerian Counseling: Proven Concepts and Strategies,* 2nd ed. Muncie, IN: Accelerated Development.

Wang, M. C., and Palinscar, A. S. (1989). Teaching students to assume an active role in their learning. In M. C. Reynolds (Ed.), *Knowledge Base for the Beginning Teacher.* New York: Pergamon.

Wilen, W. W. (1986). *Questioning Skills for Teachers,* 2nd ed. Washington DC: National Educational Association.

Wineburg, S. (1987). The self-fulfillment of the self-fulfilling prophecy. *Educational Researcher, 16,* 9, 28–36.

Exercises

1. Select a concept from any discipline with which you are familiar.
   a. Write a series of questions on the concept at each of the following levels: knowledge, comprehension, application, analysis, synthesis, and evaluation.
   b. Would there be any difference in the use of wait time in asking the six questions you wrote? Why?
   c. Why is a hierarchical ordering of questions important in classroom management?

2. Why is it better to ask the question first and then call on someone to answer it? Would there be any justification for doing it the other way around?

3. What specifically can teachers do to communicate high expectations for learning and behavior to students?

4. What would be the effect on student learning if the following were omitted from the teaching act:
   a. the introduction
   b. a check for understanding
   c. closure or summary

5. What are some things teachers can do to ensure that their explanation of content is clear?

6. Using your knowledge of students' cognitive and moral development, what are some important techniques for motivating students at each of the following grade levels: (a) primary elementary, (b) intermediate elementary, (c) junior high, and (d) senior high?

7. If you were observing a teacher, what specific behaviors would you look for to indicate that the teacher was attempting to maximize student time-on-task during (a) a lecture, (b) a discussion, and (c) a seat work activity?

8. How might secondary teachers handle routine chores such as taking attendance and receiving slips for excuses or early dismissals to maximize the time allocated for learning? What might elementary teachers do to ensure that all subjects receive the appropriate amount of allocated time?

9. Make a list of the topics taught in a given unit of instruction and identify those topics that can be considered generative topics to be taught at a deeper level of understanding.

10. Observe a class taught by a colleague or videotape a class that you teach and, using the five continua for authentic instruction identified by Newmann and Wehlage, assess the class.

11. List three or four habits of mind that you hope to cultivate in your students and briefly describe what you would do to help students develop these habits of mind.

12. Take a lesson you have taught using an individual lesson structure and redesign it as a cooperative learning lesson with all three critical elements of cooperative learning. Include as many types of positive interdependence as possible in the lesson.

13. Choose an assignment that you or a colleague have used in the past to assess student learning of a concept or topic. Identify how many types of intelligence were tapped by this assessment. Now, redesign the assignment to include all seven types of intelligence.

14. Carefully review the two bodies of knowledge on teaching presented in the two sections of this chapter (The Basics of Effective Teaching and Beyond the Basics) and answer the following questions:
   a. In what ways are the two similar?
   b. In what ways are the two different?
   c. Can the two be used compatibly in the same classroom?

6

Structuring the Environment

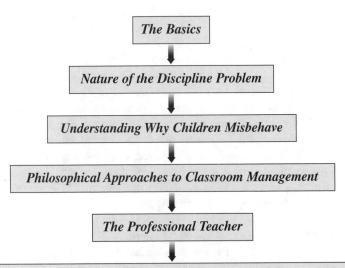

The Basics

⬇

Nature of the Discipline Problem

⬇

Understanding Why Children Misbehave

⬇

Philosophical Approaches to Classroom Management

⬇

The Professional Teacher

⬇

Structuring the Environment
Designing the Physical Environment • Establishing Classroom Guidelines
• Classroom Procedures • Classroom Rules
Determining Necessary Procedures and Rules
Developing Consequences
• natural • logical • contrived
Communicating Rules • Obtaining Commitments • Teaching Rules
The Cultural Embeddedness of Rules and Guidelines
• Creating Group Norms to Structure Appropriate Behavior

Principles of Classroom Management

1. When environmental conditions are appropriate for learning, the likelihood of disruptive behavior is minimized.
2. Students are more likely to follow classroom guidelines if the teacher models appropriate behavior and explains the relationship of the guidelines to learning, mutual student–teacher respect, and protection and safety of property and individuals.

3. Clearly communicating guidelines to students and obtaining their commitment to following them enhances appropriate classroom behavior.
4. Enforcing teacher expectations by using natural and logical consequences helps students to learn that they are responsible for the consequences of their behavior and thus are responsible for controlling their own behavior.
5. When classroom guidelines and rules match the culture of the students' home and community, the likelihood that students will behave appropriately is increased.
6. When the teacher creates group norms that are supportive of engagement in learning activities, the likelihood that students will behave appropriately is increased.

Introduction

Misbehavior does not occur in a vacuum. Psychologists have long believed that behavior is controlled or influenced by the events and conditions (antecedents) that precede it as well as by the events and conditions (consequences) that follow it.

Antecedents may increase the likelihood that appropriate behavior will take place, or they may set the stage for the occurrence of misbehavior. Therefore, when teachers act to prevent or modify inappropriate behavior, they must examine antecedents carefully before resorting to the delivery of consequences. The start of the school year and the introduction of novel learning activities are two critical times when antecedent variables must be carefully considered. Unfortunately, because their work load is heavy and planning time is limited, teachers often give only cursory attention to antecedent variables at these times. While it is understandable that many teachers decide to spend this time on designing learning activities, it must be stressed that learning activities are more successful when teachers have preplanned seating arrangements, supplies, and rules and procedures (Brophy, 1988a).

Because of the impact of antecedent variables on student behavior, teachers should take time to examine the two most crucial variables—the physical environment and classroom guidelines—if they do not take time to examine all of them. Teachers must also realize that classrooms are not culturally neutral and that it is important to consider how well the culture of the classroom and the culture of the students match. In this chapter, teachers will discover multiple ideas for creating group norms that are supportive of student engagement in learning activities and student achievement.

Designing the Physical Classroom Environment

Environmental Conditions

Clearly heating, lighting, ventilation, and noise affect behavior. Although teachers cannot install new lighting or remodel inefficient heating systems, they can ensure that the physical environment of the classroom is the most appropriate one for learning, given what is available. For instance, teachers can control lighting intensity. Dim lights, a flickering ceiling light, or inadequate darkening of the room for movies or filmstrips causes frustration, disinterest, and off-task behavior among students. Always checking on appropriate lighting before the start of a lesson can avoid these problems. Because many schools are on predetermined heating schedules, there are usually some days in every season when rooms may be uncomfortably hot or cold. While a teacher may not be able to adjust the thermostat, he can open windows to let in fresh air, turn off unnecessary lights to cool the room, and remind students to bring sweaters.

Depending on the school's location, outside noise may be uncontrollable, but inside noise is often manageable. As a group, teachers should insist that noisy repairs be completed either before or after school when possible. Teachers should also insist on predetermined times for public address announcements. Finally, school policy should dictate and enforce quiet hallway use by both teachers and students when classes are in session.

The importance of doing as much as possible to create environmental conditions conducive to learning cannot be stressed too much, as humans must be physically comfortable before their attention is voluntarily given to learning.

Use of Space

Although teachers have no control over the size of their classrooms, they usually can decide (except possibly in shops and labs) how best to utilize space within the classroom. Careful use of physical space makes a considerable difference in classroom behavior (Evans and Lovell, 1979).

Seating Arrangements. A teacher's first concern should be the arrangement of seating. No matter what basic seating arrangement is used, it should be flexible enough to accommodate and facilitate the various learning activities that occur in the classroom. If a teacher's primary instructional strategy involves a lot of group work, the teacher may put three or four desks together to facilitate these activities. On the other hand, if a teacher emphasizes teacher-directed lecture and discussion followed by individual seat work, the traditional rows of desks separated by aisles may be the appropriate seating arrangement. It is quite acceptable and often warranted for the teacher to change the primary seating arrangement to accommodate changing instructional activities.

An effective seating arrangement allows the teacher to be in close proximity to all students. This type of arrangement allows the teacher to reach any student in the class without disturbing other students and enables all students to see instructional presentations. An effort should be made to avoid having students face distractions, such as windows or hallways. Finally, seating should not interfere with high-usage areas, those areas where there are pencil sharpeners, sinks, closets, or wastepaper cans. Various seating arrangements for different learning activities are diagrammed and discussed, including their potential for discipline problems, in Howell and Howell (1979) and Rinne (1984).

Besides planning the location of seats and desks, which occupy most of the classroom space, the teacher must decide where learning centers, computers, storage cabinets, and large work tables are to be placed. Appropriate placement helps the classroom reflect the excitement and variety of the learning that is occurring. Because many people find a cluttered area an uncomfortable environment in which to work and learn, classrooms should be neat and uncluttered. A cluttered, sloppy, unorganized classroom suggests to students that disorganization and sloppiness are acceptable, which may lead to behavior problems.

Bulletin Boards and Display Areas.   The bulletin boards in Mr. Jaffee's room in Case 6.1 serve two purposes: They publicly recognize students' efforts, and they provide an opportunity for students to enrich their mathematics learning through their own efforts and ideas. This is in striking contrast to bulletin boards that are packed away unchanged at the end of each school year only to reappear again in September or bulletin boards that have only a few yellowed notices dated a few months earlier pinned to them.

The more bulletin boards are used to recognize students, as Ms. White does in Case 6.2, or to provide students with opportunities for active participation, the more likely they are to facilitate and enhance appropriate student behavior. Bulletin boards and display areas may also be used to post local or school newspaper articles mentioning students' names and to display students' work. A part of a bulletin board or other wall space may be set aside for a list of classroom guidelines. Remember that decisions about the use of classroom space and decorations may be shared with students to create a more student-directed learning environment.

Establishing Classroom Guidelines

There is at least one antecedent variable over which the teacher has major control and that is the development of classroom guidelines. Classroom guidelines are necessary

CASE 6.1 • *Fourteen to Ten, Music Wins*

Each of Mr. Jaffee's five classes has a bulletin board committee, which is responsible for the design of one bulletin board during the year. The only criterion is that the topic has to be mathematically related or its design has to use some mathematical skill.

The fifth-period bulletin board committee is ready to present three ideas to the class. Before the presentation, Mr. Jaffee reminds his students that they can vote for only one idea. Dana presents the first idea: "We would like to make a graph showing popular music sales of 1998." Tina presents the second idea: "I propose that we make bar graphs that compare the 1996

Olympic track and field outcomes to the world records." The third idea is presented by Jamie: "It would be interesting to have a display showing the many careers there are in mathematics."

After the class asks the presenting students questions about each idea, Mr. Jaffee calls for a vote. The popular music graph receives 14 votes, the Olympics 10, and not surprisingly, mathematics careers only 4. The committee immediately begins its research on popular music sales so that the bulletin board will be completed before parents' back-to-school night.

CASE 6.2 • *Having Your Name Placed on the Board Isn't Always Bad*

One by one the seventh-grade students enter Ms. White's room and cluster around the bulletin board. Today is the day after the test and the new "Commendable Improvements" list goes up. Cathy hollers, "Great; I made it!" Jimmy says, "Me too!" The list notes those students who have made improvements from one test to another regardless of test grade. Names appear on it in alphabetical order and do not reflect a grade ranking. The enthusiasm with which students greet this bulletin board surprises even Ms. White.

for the efficient and effective running of a classroom. After all, a classroom is a complex interaction of students, teachers, and materials. Guidelines help to increase the likelihood that these interactions are orderly and the environment is conducive to learning. Properly designed guidelines should support teaching and learning and provide students with clear expectations and well-defined norms, which in turn will give them the feeling of safety, security, and direction. A safe, secure atmosphere often provides students with the motivation and rationale to compete with those peer pressures that oppose behaviors conducive to learning (Jones and Jones, 1998).

Classroom Procedures

There are two types of classroom guidelines, procedures and rules. Procedures are routines that call for specified behaviors at particular times or during particular activities. Procedures are directed at accomplishing something, not at managing disruptive behavior. Examples of procedures include standard ways of passing out and turning in materials, entering and leaving the room, and taking attendance. Procedures reflect behaviors necessary for the smooth operation of the classroom and soon become an integral part of the running of the classroom.

Procedures are taught to students through examples and demonstrations. Properly designed and learned, procedures maximize on-task student behavior by minimizing the need for students to ask for directions and the need for teachers to give instructions for everyday classroom events. Certain important procedures, for example, steps to be followed during fire drills and appropriate heading information for tests and assignments, may be prominently displayed for students' reference.

Because students often do not learn and use a teacher's procedures immediately, feedback and practice must be provided. However the time spent on teaching the procedures is well invested and eventually leads to a successful management system (Brophy, 1988b). Often in art, science, and elementary classes, which are quite procedurally oriented, teachers have students practice the required procedures. In classrooms in which procedures are directly related to safety or skill development (such as equipment handling in industrial arts or science laboratory techniques), instructional objectives involving the procedures are used in addition to subject matter objectives. In these situations, the procedures become an integral part of the classroom instruction.

Classroom procedures have to be taught to students.

The use of natural and logical consequences is quite appropriate for students who fail to follow procedural guidelines. Natural consequences are outcomes of behavior that occur without teacher intervention. Examples of natural consequences are the inability of a teacher to record a student's grade if an assignment is handed in without a name and the incorrect results that occur because of inappropriate laboratory procedures (if not a safety hazard).

The use of logical consequences is much more common and has wider applicability in school settings than the use of natural ones. Logical consequences are outcomes that are directly related to the behavior but require teacher intervention to occur. Examples of logical consequences are students having less time for recess because they did not line up correctly to leave the room and students having to pay for the damage to their textbooks because of careless use.

Natural and logical consequences are powerful management concepts because the consequences that students experience are directly related to their behavior. In addition, because it is only the student who is responsible for the consequences, the teacher is removed from the role of punisher.

Classroom Rules

In contrast to procedures, rules focus on appropriate behavior. They provide the guidelines for those behaviors that are required if teaching and learning are to take place. Because they cover a wider spectrum of behavior than procedures, the development of rules is usually a more complex and time-consuming task.

The Need for Rules.   Schools in general and classrooms in particular are dynamic places. Within almost any given classroom, learning activities vary widely and may range from individual seat work to large group projects that necessitate cooperative working arrangements among students. While this dynamism helps to motivate student learning, human behavior is highly sensitive to differing conditions across situations as well as to changing conditions within situations (Walker, 1979). Evidence indicates that children in general and disruptive children in particular are highly sensitive to changing situations and conditions (Johnson, Boadstad, and Lobitz, 1976; Kazdin and Bootzin, 1972). Given this, the need for rules is apparent.

Rules should be directed at organizing the learning environment to ensure the continuity and quality of teaching and learning and not at exerting control over students (Brophy, 1988a). Appropriately designed rules increase on-task student behavior and result in improved learning.

Determining Necessary Rules.   A long list of do's and don'ts is one sure way to reduce the likelihood that rules will be effective. Teachers who attempt to cover every conceivable classroom behavior with a rule place themselves in the untenable position of having to observe and monitor the most minute and insignificant student behaviors. This leaves little time for teaching. Students, especially in upper elementary and secondary grades, view a long list of do's and don'ts as picky and impossible to follow. They regard teachers who monitor and correct every behavior as nagging, unreasonable, and controlling.

Teachers must develop individually or with students a list of rules that is fair, realistic, and can be rationalized as necessary for the development of an appropriate classroom environment (Emmer et al., 1997). To do this, the teacher, before meeting a class for the first time, must seriously consider the question "What are the necessary student behaviors that I need in my classroom so that discipline problems will not occur?" To assist in answering this question, keep in mind the definition of a discipline problem that appears in Chapter 2: *A discipline problem is any behavior that interferes with the teaching act, interferes with the rights of others to learn, is psychologically or physically unsafe, or destroys property.* Thus, any rule that is developed by the teacher or by the teacher and students jointly must be able to be rationalized as necessary to ensure that (1) the teacher's right to teach is protected, (2) the students' rights to learning are protected, (3) the students' psychological and physical safety are protected, and (4) property is protected. Rules that are so developed and rationalized make sense to students because they are not arbitrary. Such rules also lend themselves to the use of natural and logical consequences when students do not follow them.

Developing Consequences.   When students choose not to follow classroom rules, they should experience consequences (Canter, 1989). The type of consequences and how they are applied may determine whether or not students follow rules and whether or not they respect the teacher. Therefore, the development of appropriate consequences is as important as the development of the rules themselves.

Unfortunately teachers usually give considerably more thought to the design of rules than they do to the design of consequences. When a rule is not followed, teachers often simply determine the consequence on the spot. Such an approach may lead to inconsistent, irrational consequences that are interpreted by students as unfair, unreasonable, and unrelated to their behavior. This view of the teacher's behavior eventually undermines the teacher's effectiveness as a classroom manager and leads to more disruptive student behavior.

Although consequences should be planned in advance by the teacher, there is some debate about whether or not students should know in advance what the consequences will be. Some teachers feel that sharing potential consequences helps students to live up to teacher expectations and avoids later complaints about the fairness of the consequences. Other teachers believe that announcing consequences in advance gives students the impression that the teacher expects students not to live up to expectations. They prefer to act as if they have no need to think about consequences since they know that all the students will be successful in meeting both behavioral and academic expectations. There is no empirical answer to this debate. It is a matter of teacher beliefs and preference.

As we have already noted in the discussion of procedures, there are two types of consequences: natural and logical. Natural consequences, which occur without anyone's intervention and are the result of a behavior, are powerful modifiers of behavior. After all, have you ever

> Had an accident because you ran a red light or a stop sign?
>
> Injured your foot while walking barefoot?
>
> Locked yourself out of your house because you forgot your key?
>
> Lost or broken something because of carelessness?
>
> Missed a bus or train because of lateness?

All of these events usually lead to a change in behavior, and they all have certain characteristics. Each is an undesirable consequence, is experienced by all persons equally regardless of who they are, and comes about without the intervention of anyone else. Dreikurs (1964) has emphasized that children are provided with an honest and real learning situation when they are allowed to experience the natural consequences of their behavior.

Although students are more likely to experience natural consequences at home or in the general society than in school, allowing them to experience the natural consequences of their behavior, if at all possible, in classroom situations is a very effective management technique. It clearly communicates a cause-and-effect relationship between a student's chosen behavior and the experienced consequence and it removes the teacher from negative involvement with the students. Some examples of natural consequences in schools are

> Obtaining a low test grade because of failure to study.
>
> Losing assignments or books because of carelessness.
>
> Ruining a shop project as a result of the inappropriate use of tools.

Losing a ball on a roof or over a school fence because of playing with it inappropriately.

Of course, inherent ethical, moral, and legal restraints prohibit a teacher from allowing some natural consequences to happen. For instance, the natural consequences of failing to follow safety precautions in science laboratories or industrial arts classes may be serious bodily injury or even death. Obviously such a consequence must be avoided. Other natural consequences take a long time to occur. For example, the natural consequence of a student refusing to join a reading group may be a failure to gain necessary reading skills, which may eventually result in the student failing to get into college or to find meaningful employment. Consequences like these are not evident to the student at the time of the behavior.

When natural consequences are not appropriate or do not closely follow a given behavior, the teacher needs to intervene and apply a logical consequence. Have you ever

Been subjected to a finance charge because you were late paying a bill?

Received a ticket for a traffic violation?

Had a check returned for insufficient funds because you didn't balance your checkbook?

These are logical consequences. They are directly and rationally related to the behavior but they are usually the result of the purposeful intervention of another person. In school that person is usually the teacher, who optimally administers logical consequences in a calm, matter-of-fact manner. If logical consequences are imposed in anger, they cease to be consequences and tend to become punishments. Children are likely to respond favorably or positively to logical consequences because they do not consider such consequences mean or unfair, whereas they often argue, fight back, or retaliate when punished (Dreikurs, 1964). Logical consequences may be applied in two different ways. In the first way, the teacher prescribes the logical consequence without giving the student a choice:

"Joe, you spilled the paint; please clean it up."

"Sue, you continue to call out. When you raise your hand, you will be called on."

"Andy, you wrote on your desk. You will have to clean it up during recess."

In the second way, the teacher offers the student a choice of changing his behavior or experiencing the logical consequence. The use of this technique places the responsibility for appropriate behavior where it belongs, on the student. If the student chooses to continue the disruptive behavior, the logical consequence is forthcoming. If the student chooses to cease the disruptive behavior, there is no negative consequence:

"Sarah, you have a choice to walk down the hall without pushing or hold my hand."

"Heidi, you have the choice to stop disturbing Joey or change your seat."

"Mike, you have a choice to raise your hand or not be called on."

Notice that the phrasing for all the choices clearly identifies the student being addressed and the desired behavior as well as the logical consequence if the behavior does not change. Using the words "*you* have a choice" communicates to the student that the teacher is in a neutral position and thus serves to remove the teacher from arguments and power struggles with the student. This is crucial, especially in highly explosive situations. Natural or logical consequences often are not readily apparent to an extremely angry and upset student who has spewed vulgarities at his teacher during class. If, in response to this behavior, the teacher says, "Your behavior is unacceptable. If this occurs again, your parents will be contacted immediately," the student is made aware of exactly what will happen if he chooses to continue his behavior. Furthermore, the teacher remains neutral in the eyes of not only the student but also the rest of the class.

A third form of consequence is contrived consequence, more commonly known as punishment. The strict definition of punishment is any adverse consequence of a targeted behavior that suppresses the behavior. However in day-to-day school practice, punishment takes on two forms: removal of privileges and painful—physical or psychological—experiences. Either form may or may not suppress misbehavior.

If appropriately planned and logically related to the misbehavior, the removal of privileges becomes a logical consequence. For example, taking away a student's recess time because he has to complete classwork that was missed while daydreaming is a logical consequence. However, if the teacher cancels the student's participation in a trip to the zoo scheduled for the following week, it is a punishment and not a logical consequence because it is not directly related to helping the student complete his work.

Painful punishments may be physical (shaking, hitting, or pulling), psychological (yelling, sarcasm, or threats), or take the form of extra assignments (extra homework or writing something 100 times). Such punishments are often designed only to hurt and get even. The use of painful punishment has been and remains a highly controversial issue on the grounds of morality, ethics, law, and proven ineffectiveness (Jones and Jones, 1998; Kohn, 1993).

Research has indicated consistently that painful punishment suppresses undesirable behavior for short periods of time without affecting lasting behavioral change (Clarizio, 1980; Curwin and Mendler, 1988). Because avoidance or escape behavior is often a side effect of painful experiences, frequent punishment may only teach a child how to be "better at misbehaving." In other words, the child may continue to misbehave but find ways to avoid detection and thus punishment. Because it seldom is logically related to the behavior and does not point to alternative acceptable behavior, punishment deprives the student of the opportunity to learn prosocial, acceptable behavior. In addition, punishment reinforces a low level of moral development because it models undesirable behaviors. Students come to believe that it is appropriate to act in punishing ways toward others when one is in a position of authority (Clarizio, 1980: Curwin and Mendler, 1988; Jones and Jones, 1998).

Because it focuses the child's concern on the immediate effect, punishment does not help the child to examine the motivation behind the behavior and the consequences of the behavior for himself and others, which is important for him to do as he learns to control his disruptive behavior (Jones and Jones, 1998). It also limits the teacher's ability to help the child in this examination process because the child frequently does not associate the punishment with his or her actions but with the punisher. This often leads to rage, resentment, hostility, and an urge to get even (Dreikurs, Grundwald, and Pepper, 1982; Jones and Jones, 1998).

Although there has been an ever-increasing opposition to its use in schools, physical or corporal punishment is still used in many classrooms. Epstein (1979) has stated, "There is no pedagogical justification for inflicting pain. . . . It does not merit any serious discussion of pros and cons" (pp. 229–230). Similarly, Canter (1989) has stated, "[C]onsequences should never be psychologically or physically harmful to the students . . . corporal punishment should never be administered" (p. 58). Clarizio (1980) has stated, "[T]here is very little in the way of evidence to suggest the benefit of physical punishment in the schools but there is a substantial body of research to suggest that this method can have undesirable long-term side effects" (p. 141). Both Clarizio (1980) and Epstein (1979) have noted that some of the side effects of physical punishment are a dislike and distrust of the teacher and school; a feeling of powerlessness, with negative effects on a child's motivation to learn; and the development of escape and avoidance behaviors that may take the form of lying, skipping class, or daydreaming.

Those who advocate the use of physical punishment usually cite one of two myths (Clarizio, 1980). The first myth is that it is a tried-and-true method that aids students in developing a sense of personal responsibility, self-discipline, and moral character. The reality, however, is that studies have consistently indicated that physical punishment correlates with delinquency and low development of conscience. The second myth is that it is the only form of discipline some children understand. This has never been shown to be true. Perhaps it is a case of projection on the part of the teacher. In one study it was shown that teachers who relied heavily on physical punishment did not know other means of solving classroom management problems (Dayton Public Schools, 1973). Teachers must understand that if a technique has not worked in the past, more of the same technique will not produce desirable results.

Indeed, the unproven effectiveness of physical punishment and the risk of harmful side effects has caused some of the largest school districts in the country to prohibit corporal punishment (Philadelphia; Washington, DC; and Chicago), even though many of these school districts are plagued with discipline problems. The National Education Association and the American Federation of Teachers also have consistently supported the abolition of physical punishment.

For teachers who occasionally use mild forms of punishment, not physical, guidelines for minimizing possible harmful side effects are discussed by Clarizio (1980) and Heitzman (1983). Table 6.1 compares natural and logical consequences with punishment.

Communicating Rules. If the teacher decides to develop classroom rules by herself, she must communicate the rules clearly to the students (Canter, 1992; Evertson and Emmer, 1982; Jones and Jones, 1998). Clear communication entails a discussion of what the rules are and a rationale for each and every one (Good and Brophy, 1997).

TABLE 6.1 *Comparison of Consequences versus Punishment*

Natural/Logical Consequence	Punishment
Expresses the reality of a situation	Expresses the power of authority
Logically related to misbehavior	Contrived and arbitrary connection with misbehavior
Illustrates cause and effect	Does not illustrate cause and effect
Involves no moral judgment about person—You are O.K.; your behavior isn't	Often involves moral judgments
Concerned with the present	Concerned with the past
Administered without anger	Anger is often present
Helps develop self-discipline	Depends on extrinsic control
Choices often given	Alternatives are not given
Thoughtful, deliberate	Often impulsive
Does not develop escape and avoidance behaviors	Develops escape and avoidance behaviors
Does not produce resentment	Produces resentment
Teacher is removed from negative involvement with student	Teacher involvement is negative
Based on the concept of equality	Based on superior–inferior relationship
Communicates the expectation that the student is capable of controlling his own behavior	Communicates that the teacher must control the student's behavior

(Dreikurs, Grundwald, and Pepper, 1982; Sweeney, 1981)

When students understand the purpose of rules, they are likely to view them as reasonable and fair, which increases the likelihood of appropriate behavior.

The manner in which rules are phrased is important. Certain rules need to be stated so that it is clear that they apply to both the teacher and the students. This is accomplished by using the phrase, "We all need to" followed by the behavioral expectation and the rationale. For example, the teacher might say, "We all need to pay attention and not interrupt when someone is speaking because it is important to respect each other's right to participate and voice his views." Such phrasing incorporates the principle that teachers must model the behaviors they expect (Brophy, 1988a).

Although it is essential for the teacher to communicate behavioral expectations and the rationales behind them, in many cases this does not ensure student understanding and acceptance of the rules. A final critical strategy, then, is to obtain from each student a strong indication that he understands the rules as well as a commitment to attempting to abide by them (Jones and Jones, 1998).

Obtaining Commitments. When two or more people reach an agreement, they often finalize it with a handshake or a signed contract to indicate that the individuals intend to comply with the terms of the agreement. While agreements are often violated, a handshake, verbal promise, or written contract increases the probability that the agreement will be kept. With this idea in mind, it is a wise teacher who has his students express their understanding of the rules and their intent to abide by them.

Both Mr. Merit and Ms. Loy in Cases 6.3 and 6.4 are attempting to get their students to understand and agree to follow the classroom rules. However, notice that they use different methods because the maturity level of their students is different. Unlike Mr. Merit, Ms. Loy only asks her students to confirm that they understand the rules, not that they will abide by them. This is an important distinction that should be made when working with older students because it reduces the potential of a student confrontation during a time when the development of teacher–student rapport is critical.

CASE 6.3 • *"I Don't Know If I Can Remember"*

At the beginning of the school year, Mr. Merit has a discussion of class rules with his second-grade class. He explains each rule and gives examples. Members of the class are asked to give the reason for each rule. The class as a whole is encouraged to ask questions about the rules, and Mr. Merit in turn asks questions to assess their understanding of the rules.

After the discussion, Mr. Merit says, "All those who understand the rules please raise your hand." Next he says, "All those who will attempt to follow the rules please raise your hands." He notices that Helen and Gary do not raise their hands and asks them why. Helen says, "I'm not sure if I'll always remember the rules and if I can't

remember I can't promise to follow the rules." Mr. Merit replies, "Helen, I understand your concern, but I have written these rules on a poster, which I am going to place on the front bulletin board. Do you think that this will help you?" Helen answers, "Yes," and both Helen and Gary then raise their hands.

Mr. Merit shows the class the poster of rules, which is entitled "I Will Try to Follow Our Classroom Rules." One by one each student comes up and signs his or her name at the bottom of the poster. When all the students have signed it, Mr. Merit asks Helen to staple the poster to the front bulletin board.

CASE 6.4 • *"I'm Not Promising Anything"*

On the first day of class, Ms. Loy explains the classroom rules to her tenth-grade mathematics classes. She discusses with the class why these rules are necessary for the teaching and learning of mathematics.

Ms. Loy then says to the class, "I am going to pass out two copies of the rules that we just discussed. You'll notice that at the bottom is the statement 'I am aware of these rules and understand them,' followed by a place for your signature. Please sign one copy and pass it up front so I can collect them. Place the other copy in your notebook."

Alex raises his hand and says, "I can't make any promises about my future behavior in this class. I'm not sure what the class is even going to be like." Ms. Loy replies, "Please read what you are signing." Alex reads "I am aware of these rules and understand them" and says out loud "Oh, I see; I'm not promising anything." Alex then signs the sheet and passes it to the front.

CASE 6.5 • *Calling Out Correct Answers*

Mr. Martinez, a fourth-grade teacher, posts his classroom rules on the front bulletin board. One by one the student signs the poster, thus agreeing to follow the rules.

Mr. Martinez soon notices that Lowyn is having a difficult time remembering to raise her hand before answering questions. Instead, Lowyn just calls out the answers. At first Mr. Martinez ignores her answer. The next time she calls out, he makes eye contact with her and shakes his head in a disapproving fashion. Finally, he moves close to Lowyn and quietly says, "Lowyn, you have great answers, but you must raise your hand so that everyone has an equal chance to answer."

The next lesson begins, and Mr. Martinez asks the class, "Who can summarize what we learned about magnets yesterday?" Enthusiastically Lowyn calls out, "Every magnet has a north and south pole." Because Mr. Martinez has half

expected that Lowyn will continue to call out answers, he is prepared for the situation and says, "Class, please, put down your hands. Lowyn, please look at the rules on the bulletin board and find the one that you are not obeying." Lowyn answers, "Number four. It says we need to raise our hands to answer a question." Mr. Martinez responds, "Yes it does, and why do we need such a rule?" "So that everyone in the class has a chance to answer questions," she replies. Mr. Martinez then asks, "Lowyn, did you agree to follow these rules when you signed the poster?" "Yes," Lowyn says.

Mr. Martinez asks her to try harder in the future and tells her that he will help her by pointing to the rules if she calls out again. The first time Lowyn raises her hand Mr. Martinez calls on her, and says, "Lowyn, that was a great answer and thank you for raising your hand."

While many experts recommend having classroom rules on display or available for quick reference (Evertson and Emmer, 1982; Jones and Jones, 1981), it should be noted that merely displaying them has little effect on maintaining appropriate student behavior (Madsen, Becker, and Thomas, 1968). Teachers must refer to and use the displayed rules to assist individual students in learning the rules and developing self-control. Mr. Martinez in Case 6.5 understands this. He not only displays and teaches the rule to Lowyn but also reinforces the behavior when she finally does raise her hand. He understands that noting appropriate behavior and positively encouraging it enhances the likelihood of appropriate behavior in the future (Clarizio, 1980; Evertson and Emmer, 1982; Madsen, Becker, and Thomas, 1968).

Teachers also may employ student self-analyses to remind students of appropriate behavior and to help enhance their self-control. Indeed, self-analysis of one's behavior can be used by any student, although the actual manner of employment of the technique varies. Whereas Mr. Hite's smiley faces in Case 6.6 are appropriate for younger elementary students (see Figure 6.1), older students evaluate their behavior better by using rating continua. As with younger students, self-analysis is requested of all students or individual students as the need arises. Figure 6.2 is an example of a continuum rating scale that was successfully used to manage a seventh-grade art class.

Teaching and Evaluating.   Teachers do not expect students to learn a mathematical skill on its first presentation because they know students need practice and feedback.

CASE 6.6 • *The Smiley Face Self-Analysis*

Mr. Hite teaches first grade. After analyzing the types of behaviors he feels are necessary for the proper running of his class, he shares the rules with the children and explains what he calls the Smiley Face Procedure. "We all know what smiley faces are, and we are going to use smiley faces to help us learn and obey the classroom rules." Holding up a sheet of paper (see Figure 6.1), he continues, "As you can see, this sheet has faces next to each rule for every day of the week. At the end of class each day you will receive one of these sheets and you will circle the faces that are most like your behavior for the day."

Each day Mr. Hite collects the sheets and reviews them. When a pattern of frowns are observed or when he disagrees with a student's rating, he is quick to work with the student in a positive, supportive manner.

After a few weeks Mr. Hite discontinues the self-analysis sheets on a regular basis. They are, however, brought back into use whenever the class's behavior warrants it. Mr. Hite also uses the sheets for individual students who need assistance in self-control. When outdoor activities or new activities such as field trips occur throughout the year, Mr. Hite develops new sheets for the students.

CIRCLE THE APPLE THAT IS MOST LIKE YOUR BEHAVIOR TODAY

	MONDAY	TUESDAY	WEDNESDAY	THURSDAY	FRIDAY
Shared with Others					
Listened to the Teacher					
Listened While Others Talked					
Was Friendly to Others					
Worked Quietly					
Joined in Activities					
Stayed in My Seat					
Followed Directions					
Cleaned My Area					
Helped Put Away Materials					

FIGURE 6.1 *Smiley Face Self-Analysis*

FIGURE 6.2 *Behavior Self-Analysis for Art Class*

Name _____ Date _____

Class _____

Teacher–Student Evaluation

Class Behavior

1. Have you worked successfully with minimum supervision during the class period?

0% of the time		50% of the time		All the time
1	2	3	4	5

2. Have you been respectful and considerate to other students and their property?

0% of the time		50% of the time		All the time
1	2	3	4	5

3. Have you been cooperative with your teacher?

0% of the time		50% of the time		All the time
1	2	3	4	5

4. Have you used art materials properly?

0% of the time		50% of the time		All the time
1	2	3	4	5

5. Have you shown a high degree of maturity and responsibility through proper class behavior?

0% of the time		50% of the time		All the time
1	2	3	4	5

6. Have you been considerate of your classmates and teacher by talking softly, remaining in your seat, and helping classmates if help is needed?

0% of the time		50% of the time		All the time
1	2	3	4	5

7. Have you cleaned your area and put your materials away?

0% of the time		50% of the time		All the time
1	2	3	4	5

Frequently, however, teachers forget this when it comes to rules. They expect students to follow classroom rules immediately (Evertson and Emmer, 1982). But rules, like academic skills, must be taught (Brophy, 1988a; Canter, 1992; Evertson and Emmer, 1982; Jones and Jones, 1998). This entails practice and feedback. The amount of practice and feedback depends on the grade level and the novelty of the procedures and rules. Rules that students have not encountered before, such as rules for a science lab, take longer to learn than rules that are traditionally part of classroom settings.

New activities often require new procedures and rules. Since learning is not instantaneous, students will learn, understand, and abide by classroom rules only over time. It is not uncommon for teachers to spend entire lessons on how to conduct a debate, cooperatively work on a group project, safely operate machinery, set up and care for science apparatus, or behave on field trips or outdoor activities. In such cases specific objectives directed toward the procedures and rules are formulated and incorporated into the lesson plans. In these situations, they become an integral part of the course content, and therefore, their evaluation and consideration in grading decisions are warranted.

Some teachers, particularly those in the elementary grades, evaluate their students' understanding of rules through the use of written exams or student demonstrations (Curwin and Mendler, 1988). Secondary science and industrial arts teachers often insist that students pass safety exams and demonstrate the appropriate use of equipment before being given permission to progress with the learning activities.

To summarize, teachers must communicate to students the importance of the rules for learning and teaching. This is best accomplished through a no-nonsense approach that involves

1. Analyzing the classroom environment to determine the necessary rules and procedures needed to protect teaching, learning, safety, and property
2. Clearly communicating the rules and their rationales to students
3. Obtaining students' commitments to abide by the rules
4. Teaching and evaluating students' understanding of the rules
5. Enforcing each rule with natural or logical consequences

The Cultural Embeddedness of Rules and Guidelines

When teachers are establishing and teaching classroom rules and procedures, they need to remember that their students come from a variety of cultural backgrounds. Culture refers to the knowledge, customs, rituals, emotions, traditions, values, and norms shared by members of a population and embodied in a set of behaviors designed for survival in a particular environment. Because students come to the classroom from different cultural backgrounds, they bring with them different values, norms, and behavioral expectations. Traditionally, teachers have acted as if everyone shared the same cultural expectations and have ignored cultural differences. However, this does not appear to be a wise strategy. Schools and classrooms are not culturally neutral or culture free. Most schools follow the values, norms, and behavioral patterns of middle-class, white, European cultures. As Irvine (1990) has pointed out, however, these values and norms differ in significant ways from the values, norms, and behavioral expectations found in nondominant cultural groups such as African Americans, Hispanic Americans, and Native Americans.

Irvine has pointed out several specific differences in value orientation. Middle-class European American culture, which is the typical school culture, tends to value mastery over nature rather than living in harmony with nature. It tends to value impulse control rather than expressive movement and demonstrative behavior. It tends to value rugged individualism and standing on your own two feet rather than interconnectedness and helping others. It tends to value the use of reason rather than emotion during discussions and argumentation. It tends to value print-based communication over oral communication. It tends to value sedateness and passivity over verve and panache. Finally, it tends to value personal conformity rather than demonstrations of personal uniqueness. As a result of these differences in values and norms, the typical behavior patterns displayed by youngsters who come from a nondominant culture, while acceptable at home and in the community, are not acceptable in schools. Indeed, cultural differences in what is regarded as appropriate occur in many areas, including language patterns, nonverbal behavior, amount and freedom of movement, use of personal space, expression of emotions, and dress.

Because of these cultural differences, many children from underrepresented groups experience cultural dissonance or lack of cultural synchronization in school; that is, teachers and students are out of step with each other when it comes to their expectations for appropriate behavior. Cultural synchronization is an extremely important factor in the establishment of positive relationships between teachers and students. According to Jeanette Abi-Nader (1993), one of the most solidly substantiated principles in communication theory is the principle of homophily, which holds that the more two people are alike in background, attitudes, perceptions, and values the more effectively they will communicate with each other and the more similar they will become. A lack of cultural synchronization leads to misunderstandings between teachers and students that can and often do result in conflict, distrust, hostility, and possibly school failure (Irvine, 1990). "The typical experience in the school is a denigration of African and African American culture. Indeed there is a denial of its very existence. The language that students bring with them to school is seen to be deficient—a corruption of English. The familial organization is considered pathological. And the historical, cultural, and scientific contributions of African Americans are ignored or trivialized" (Ladson-Billings, 1994, p. 138).

To illustrate his discussion of the importance of cultural synchronization, Irvine has pointed out several differences in cultural style between whites and African Americans. We will use these differences in the following discussion simply as an illustration of the influence of culture on values, norms, and expectations. We recognize, as does Irvine, that these attributes are neither representative of all African Americans nor all white Americans. It would, of course, be possible to use any other nondominant cultural group to illustrate such differences. With these caveats in mind, we now turn to some of the differences in style identified by Irvine.

African Americans tend to be more high key, more animated, more intense, and more confrontational than whites. African Americans tend to appreciate social contexts in which overlapping speech and participatory dialogue are used rather than turn taking in which only one person is free to speak at any given time. African Americans tend to favor passionate, emotional argumentation in defense of beliefs as opposed to the nonemotional, uninvolved, logical argumentation preferred by whites. African Americans tend to have a relational, field-dependent learning style as opposed to the analytical, field-independent style of learning characteristic of most whites. While whites prefer confined or restricted movement, African Americans tend to learn better through freedom of movement. Finally, African Americans tend to have a much greater people focus than whites during learning activities and tend to favor modes of learning in which they are interactive with others. As a result of these differences in cultural style, African Americans often find their expressive behavior style criticized in contexts in which white standards of behavior prevail (Kochman, 1981).

In situations in which white teachers find themselves teaching students from a nondominant culture, the reactions of teachers and students to differences in cultural style tend to be quite different and not understood by the other party. Teachers sometimes revert to what Irvine calls cultural aversion; that is, they pretend not to notice that their students have a different racial and ethnic identity and act as if there were no cultural differences. This behavior tends to increase conflict because the teachers fail to attempt to understand reasons for the students' behavior. Students also engage in behavior that tends to exacerbate the problem. Engaging in cultural inversion, they decide that certain behaviors are characteristic of white culture and therefore are not appropriate for blacks (Ogbu, 1988). They view cultural differences as symbols of cultural identity that must be maintained rather than as obstacles to communication that can be overcome. Seen from this perspective, failure to conform with teacher expectations and lack of effort toward achieving teacher-valued goals can be regarded as a form of resistance against cultural assimilation. "Somehow they have come to equate exemplary performance in school with a loss of their African American identity; that is, doing well in school is seen as 'acting white.' The only option, many believe, is to refuse to do well in school" (Ladson-Billings, 1994, p. 11).

Differences in values, norms, and expectations resulting from cultural differences have several implications for teachers. First, teachers must understand that schools are culturally situated institutions. The values, norms, and behaviors promoted by schools are never culturally neutral. They are always influenced by some particular cultural mindset. Therefore, school and classroom rules and guidelines must be seen as culturally derived. Second, teachers should strive to learn more about the cultural backgrounds of the students they teach. This can be accomplished by observing how students believe in other contexts, by talking to students about their behavior and allowing them to teach about their behavior, by involving parents and community members in the classroom, and by participating in community events and learning more about the institutions in the students' home community. "Students are less likely to fail in school settings where they feel positive about both their own culture and the majority culture and are not alienated from their own cultural values" (Cummins [1986] in Ladson-

Billings, 1994, p. 11). Third, teachers should acknowledge and intentionally incorporate students' cultural backgrounds and expectations into their classrooms. When teacher rules and expectations are in conflict with student cultural expectations, it may be appropriate to reexamine and renegotiate rules and procedures. At the very least, students need to be provided with a clear rationale for why the rules and procedures are important. It goes without saying that the rationale for the rules should be in keeping with the four guidelines articulated earlier in the chapter. Finally, when students behave inappropriately, teachers should step back and examine the behavior in terms of the student's cultural background. Using a different set of cultural lenses to view behavior may shed a very different light on the teacher's perceptions of individual students. Obviously, misbehavior that results from differences in cultural background and expectations should be handled quite differently from misbehavior that signifies intentional disruption on the part of the student.

Creating Group Norms to Structure Appropriate Behavior

Although students and teachers bring their own cultural backgrounds with them, each classroom tends to develop its own culture, that is, certain norms develop over time that exert a great influence on student behavior. During the early years of schooling, it is the teacher's wishes and behavior that create the norms for student behavior. However, as students grow older, they become the dominant influence in establishing the cultural norms within the given classroom. According to Johnson, Johnson, and Holubec (1993), the relationships that develop among peers in the classroom exert a tremendous influence on social and cognitive development and student socialization. In their interactions with peers, children and adolescents learn attitudes, values, skills, and information that are unobtainable from adults. Interaction with peers provides support, opportunities, and models for personal behavior. Through peer relationships, a frame of reference for perceiving oneself is developed. In both educational and work settings, peers influence productivity. Finally, students' educational aspirations are influenced more by peers than by any other social influence (Johnson, Johnson, and Holubec, 1993).

Traditionally, teachers have ignored the notion of peer culture and group norms in the classroom. They have focused their attention on individual learners and have viewed influencing students to behave appropriately as an issue between the teacher and the individual student. As a result, the development of group norms among students has been left almost completely up to chance. However, there is growing evidence that teachers can intervene to create group norms that will promote prosocial behavior as well as lead to peer relationships that will enhance the four components of self-esteem identified earlier: significance, power, competence, and virtue. Cooperative learning lessons that include face-to-face interaction, positive interdependence, and individual accountability can help to establish positive group norms. When teachers make a concentrated effort to help students develop the social skills necessary to function effectively as group members during cooperative learning activities, they enhance the power of cooperative learning activities to create positive group norms.

Johnson, Johnson, and Holubec (1993) have identified four sets of skills—forming skills, functioning skills, formulating skills, and fermenting skills—that students need to develop over time in order to function most effectively as a group. When these skills are in place and groups function successfully, group norms develop that lead students to (1) be engaged in learning activities, (2) strive toward learning and achievement, and (3) interact with each other in ways that will facilitate the development of positive self-esteem.

Forming skills are an initial set of management skills that are helpful in getting groups up and running smoothly and effectively. These skills include moving into groups quietly without bothering others, staying with the group rather than moving around the room, using quiet voices that can be heard by members of the group but not by others, and encouraging all group members to participate.

Functioning skills are group-management skills aimed at controlling the types of interactions that occur among group members. These skills include staying focused on the task, expressing support and acceptance of others, asking for help or clarification, offering to explain or clarify, and paraphrasing or summarizing what others have said.

Formulating skills refer to a set of behaviors that help students to process material mentally. These skills include summarizing key points, connecting ideas to each other, seeking elaboration of ideas, finding ways to remember information more effectively, and checking explanations and ideas through articulation.

Finally, fermenting skills are a set of skills needed to resolve cognitive conflicts that arise within the group. These skills include criticizing ideas without criticizing people, synthesizing diverse ideas, asking for justification, extending other people's ideas, and probing for more information.

Johnson, Johnson, and Holubec (1993) suggest that teachers teach these social skills just as they teach academic content. Therefore, when teachers plan a cooperative learning activity, they must plan social skill objectives as well as the academic objectives. Making the social skills explicit as lesson objectives helps to focus both student and teacher attention on them. To do this the teacher should explain the skill before the activity begins and make sure students know what the skill looks like and sounds like as it is expressed in behavior. Once the teacher is convinced that students understand the meaning of the skill, students may practice the skill during the cooperative learning activity. While the students are practicing, the teacher moves from group to group monitoring the use of the skill. When the activity has been completed, the teacher engages each group in reflecting on how successfully the skill was used and in setting goals for improving their use of the skill in the future. Although teaching social skills in addition to academic content takes time, the time is well spent for two reasons. First, many of these skills are exactly the kinds of skills students will need to help them succeed as adults. Second, when students are skilled at interacting with each other in positive ways, group norms develop in the classroom that are supportive of prosocial behavior and of engagement in appropriate learning activities.

Summary

This chapter first examined two of the critical variables that influence behavior in the classroom: the physical environment and classroom guidelines. This discussion was followed by a consideration of the role of culture in the establishment of classroom guidelines and rules. The final section of the chapter discussed the creation of group norms that are supportive of appropriate behavior.

Although teachers have no control of the size of their classrooms, they can control the seating arrangement within the classroom and the use of bulletin boards. The seating arrangement should accommodate the learning activity. It must also permit all students to see instructional presentations and allow the teacher to be close to all students. Bulletin boards should reflect and add to the learning excitement occurring in the classroom. Properly used, they can provide students with the opportunity to enrich and actively participate in their learning and allow the teacher to recognize and display students' work and achievements.

Classroom guidelines are needed for routine activities (procedures) and for general classroom behavior (rules). When they are well designed, guidelines provide students with clear expectations. The teacher can increase the effectiveness of guidelines by (1) analyzing the classroom environment to determine what guidelines are needed to protect teaching, learning, safety, and property; (2) communicating the guidelines and their rationales to students; (3) obtaining student commitments to abide by the rules; (4) teaching and evaluating student understanding of the rules; and (5) enforcing each guideline with natural or logical consequences.

Classrooms and schools are never culturally neutral or value free; they are always situated within a particular cultural context. When the culture of the school and the culture of the students are synchronized, positive behavior increases and positive relationships are established between teachers and students. However, when teachers and students hold differing values, norms, and behavioral expectations, the potential for misunderstanding, conflict, and mistrust are greatly enhanced.

Each classroom also develops its own culture with its own set of group norms and values. Traditionally, teachers have ignored the communal aspects of classroom life, focusing instead on individual relationships. Evidence now indicates that the use of cooperative learning activities that contain all essential elements combined with the teaching of prosocial skills will lead to the establishment of group norms that are supportive of appropriate student behavior.

References

Abi-Nader, J. (1993). Meeting the needs of multicultural classrooms: Family values and the motivation of minority students. In M. J. O'Hair and S. J. Odell (Eds.), *Diversity and Teaching: Teacher Education Yearbook 1*. Fort Worth, TX: Harcourt, Brace, Jovanovich College Publications.

Brophy, J. (1988a). Educating teachers about managing classrooms and students. *Teaching and Teacher Education, 4,* 1, 1–18.

Brophy, J. (1988b). Research on teaching effects: Uses and abuses. *The Elementary School Journal,* *89,* 1, 3–21.

Canter, L. (1989). Assertive discipline—More than names on the board and marbles in a jar. *Phi Delta Kappan, 71,* 1, 57–61.

Clarizio, H. F. (1980). *Toward Positive Classroom Discipline,* 3rd ed. New York: Wiley.

Cummins, J. (1986). Empowering minority students. *Harvard Educational Review, 17,* 4, 18–36.

Curwin, R., and Mendler, A. (1988). *Discipline with Dignity.* Alexandria, VA: Association for Supervision and Curriculum Development.

Dayton Public Schools. (1973). Corporal punishment: Is it needed? *Schoolday, 5,* 1, 4.

Dreikurs, R. (1964). *Children the Challenge.* New York: Hawthorne.

Dreikurs, R., Grundwald, B. B., and Pepper, F. C. (1998). *Maintaining Sanity in the Classroom, Classroom Management Techniques,* 2nd ed. New York: Taylor and Francis.

Emmer, E. T., Evertson, C. M., Sanford, J. P., Clements, B. S., and Worsham, M. E. (1997). *Classroom Management for Secondary Teachers,* 4th ed. Boston: Allyn and Bacon.

Epstein, C. (1979). *Classroom Management and Teaching: Persistent Problems and Rational Solutions.* Reston, VA: Reston.

Evans, G., and Lovell, B. (1979). Design modification in an open-plan school. *Journal of Educational Psychology, 71,* 41–49.

Evertson, C. M., and Emmer, E. T. (1982). Preventive classroom management. In D. L. Duke (Ed.), *Helping Teachers Manage Classrooms,* pp. 2–31. Alexandria, VA: Association for Supervision and Curriculum Development.

Good, T., and Brophy, J. (1997). *Looking in Classrooms,* 4th ed. New York: Longman.

Heitzman, A. J. (1983). Discipline and the use of punishment. *Education, 104,* 1, 17–22.

Howell, R. G., Jr., and Howell, P. L. (1979). *Discipline in the Classroom: Solving the Teaching Puzzle.* Reston, VA: Reston.

Irvine, J. J. (1990). *Black Students and School Failure: Policy, Practices, Prescriptions.* Westport, CT: Greenwood.

Johnson, D. W., Johnson, R. T., and Holubec, E. J. (1993). *Cooperation in the Classroom,* 6th ed. Edina, MN: Interaction Book Company.

Johnson, S. M., Boadstad, D. D., and Lobitz, G. K. (1976). Generalization and contrast phenomena in behavior modification with children. In E. J. Mash, L. A. Hamerlynck, and L. C. Handy (Eds.), *Behavior Modification and Families.* New York: Brunner/Mazell.

Jones, V. F., and Jones, L. S. (1998). *Comprehensive Classroom Management: Creating Positive Learning Environments and Solving Problems,* 5th ed. Boston: Allyn and Bacon.

Kazdin, A. E., and Bootzin, R. R. (1972). The token economy: An evaluative review. *Journal of Applied Behavior Analysis, 5,* 343–372.

Kochman, T. (1981). *Black and White: Styles in Conflict.* Chicago: University of Chicago Press.

Kohn, A. (1993). *Punished by Rewards.* Boston: Houghton Mifflin.

Ladson-Billings, G. (1994). *The Dreamkeepers: Successful Teachers of African American Children.* San Francisco: Jossey Bass.

Madsen, C. H., Becker, W., and Thomas, D. R. (1968). Rules, praise and ignoring: Elements of elementary classroom control. *Journal of Applied Behavior Analysis, 1,* 139–150.

Ogbu, J. (1988). Class stratification, racial stratification, and schooling. In L. Weis (Ed.), *Class, Race and Gender in American Education.* Albany, NY: SUNY Press.

Rinne, C. H. (1984). *Attention: The Fundamentals of Classroom Control.* Columbus, OH: Merrill.

Sweeney, T. J. (1981). *Adlerian Counseling, Proven Concepts and Strategies,* 2nd ed. Muncie, IN: Accelerated Development.

Walker, H. M. (1979). *The Acting-Out Child: Coping with Classroom Disruption.* Boston: Allyn and Bacon.

Exercises

1. For each of the following activities, design a seating arrangement for 24 students that maximizes on-task behavior and minimizes disruptions.
   a. Teacher lecture
   b. Small group work (4 students per group)
   c. Open discussion
   d. Individual seat work
   e. Class project to design a bulletin board
   f. Teacher-led group work and simultaneous individual seat work
   g. Student group debate
   h. Teacher demonstration

2. Give examples of how a teacher can use the classroom environment (bulletin boards, shelves, walls, chalkboard, etc.) to create a pleasant atmosphere that increases the likelihood of appropriate student behavior.

3. With your present or future classroom in mind, determine the common activities that do or will regularly occur. Design appropriate procedures to accomplish those activities. How would you teach these procedures to the class?

4. a. With your present or future classroom in mind, determine what general student behaviors are necessary to ensure that learning and teaching take place and that students and property are safe.
   b. State a positive rule for each of the behaviors you previously listed.
   c. For each behavior, give a rationale you can explain to students that is consistent with the definition of a discipline problem and appropriate for the age of the students you do or will teach.
   d. For each behavior, determine a natural or logical consequence that will occur when the rule is broken.
   e. How will you communicate these rules to students?
   f. How will you obtain student commitment to these rules?

5. Determine a natural, logical, and contrived consequence for each of the following misbehaviors:
   a. Fourth-grade student who interrupts small group work
   b. Eleventh-grade student who continually gets out of his seat
   c. Seventh-grade student who makes noises during class
   d. Tenth-grade student who makes noises during class
   e. Twelfth-grade student who refuses to change his seat when requested to do so by the teacher
   f. First-grade student who interrupts reading group to tattle on a student who is not doing his seat work
   g. A group of sixth-grade students who drop their pencils in unison at a given time
   h. Ninth-grade student who threatens to beat up another student after class
   i. Eighth-grade student who continually pushes the chair of the student in front of him
   j. Tenth-grade student who does not wear goggles while operating power equipment

6. The following are examples of some rules developed for an eighth-grade science class. Identify and correct any problems in the rule, rationale, or consequences.

Rule	Rationale	Consequences
a. Don't be late to class	Because we have a lot of material to cover and we need the whole class period	a. Reminder by teacher b. Student required to get a note c. Student writes 100 times "I will not be late"
b. We all need to work without disrupting others	Because everyone has a right to learn and no one has a right to interfere with the learning of others	a. Reminder by teacher b. Student moved where he cannot disrupt others c. Student removed from class d. Student fails
c. We all have to raise our hands to answer questions or contribute to a discussion	Because I do not like to be interrupted	a. Student ignored b. Reminder by teacher c. Parents notified
d. We must use lab equipment properly and safely	Because it is expensive to replace	a. Pay for broken equipment b. Pay for equipment and additional fine

7. For each of the following scenarios, explain why the student behaved as he/she did:

a. Juanita, a Mexican American child, is being reprimanded by her teacher for not doing her homework. Despite repeated attempts by her teacher to get Juanita to look her in the eye, Juanita refuses to do so.

b. Eunsook, a student from Korea, is obviously upset about something. When Mr. Barber bends close to her and tries to find out what is happening, Eunsook simply clams up and does not say a word.

c. Justin, an African American first-grader, continually sings along and talks along with his teacher, Mrs. Gray, when she is telling stories to the class. Mrs. Gray finds Justin's behavior rude.

8. How do differences in cultural values, norms, and behavioral expectations influence the development of teacher expectations for student achievement?

9. For each of the following social skills, develop an explanation of what the social skill means for students at the third-grade level, at the seventh-grade level, and at the eleventh-grade level.

a. Encouraging everyone to participate

b. Paraphrasing what others have said

c. Seeking elaboration

d. Asking for justification for ideas

7

Managing Common Misbehavior Problems

Nonverbal Interventions

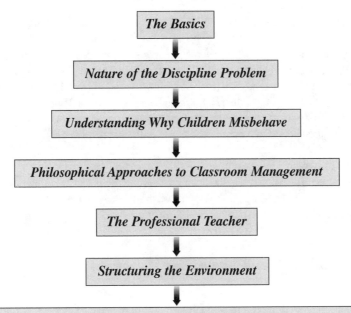

The Basics

↓

Nature of the Discipline Problem

↓

Understanding Why Children Misbehave

↓

Philosophical Approaches to Classroom Management

↓

The Professional Teacher

↓

Structuring the Environment

↓

Managing Common Misbehavior Problems: Nonverbal Interventions
Using Proactive Intervention Skills •
Using Preplanned Remedial Nonverbal Intervention
• planned ignoring • signal interference • proximity interference • touch interference

Principles of Classroom Management

1. Classroom management techniques need to be consistent with the goal of helping students to become self-directing individuals.
2. Use of a preplanned hierarchy of remedial interventions improves the teacher's ability to manage misbehavior.

151

3. The use of a hierarchy that starts with nonintrusive, nonverbal teacher behaviors gives students the opportunity to exercise self-control, minimizes disruption to the teaching/learning process, reduces the likelihood of student confrontation, protects students' safety, and maximizes the teacher's management alternatives.

Introduction

In most classrooms the majority of student misbehaviors are verbal interruptions, off-task behavior, and disruptive physical movements. These behaviors, which are sometimes called surface behaviors, are present in every classroom in every school almost every day. With proper planning, instructional strategies, and environmental structuring, the frequency of surface behaviors is reduced greatly. However, no matter how much time and energy the teacher directs toward prevention, surface behaviors do not disappear and to some extent are an ever-present, continuing fact of life for all teachers.

There are many intervention skills that the successful teacher may use to deal with surface behaviors in a manner that is effective, expedient, and least disruptive to the teaching/learning process. These skills are organized in a decision-making hierarchy of three tiers: (1) nonverbal behaviors, (2) verbal behaviors, and (3) consequences. Each tier consists of the individual skills, which are themselves hierarchically ordered. The dimensions on which these subhierarchies are developed are the degree of intrusiveness and the potential for disruption to the teaching/learning environment. When these intervention skills are applied in a preplanned, systematic manner, they have been shown to be quite effective.

This chapter discusses nonverbal skills, the first tier in the decision-making hierarchy. This group of skills is the least intrusive and has the least potential for disrupting the teaching/learning process while leaving the teacher with the maximum number of management alternatives for future use.

Prerequisites to Management

All too often teachers are quick to place total responsibility for inappropriate behavior on their students without carefully analyzing their own behavior. It is quite common to hear teachers say, "There's nothing I can do; all they want to do is fool around," or, "These kids are impossible; why even try!" Such comments clearly indicate that teachers have assigned all blame for student misbehavior to the students themselves. However, effective teaching and maximum learning occur in classrooms when teachers and students understand that teaching/learning is the responsibility of both the student and the teacher.

The responsibilities of the students are obvious. Students must prepare for class, study, ask questions to enhance their understanding, and remain on-task. Many of the preventive techniques discussed in previous chapters, as well as the management techniques to be discussed in this chapter, assist students in accepting responsibility for their learning. However, students more readily accept their responsibilities when it is clear to them that the teacher is fulfilling her responsibilities. These professional responsibilities, which have been discussed in previous chapters, are the basic minimum competencies that all teachers must possess. They are the prerequisites to appropriate classroom management.

1. The teacher is well prepared to teach. Prior to class she has designed specific learning objectives and effective teaching strategies based on accepted principles of learning.
2. The teacher provides clear directions and explanations of the learning material.
3. The teacher ensures that students understand evaluation criteria.
4. The teacher clearly communicates, rationalizes, and consistently enforces behavioral expectations.
5. The teacher demonstrates enthusiasm and encouragement and models the behaviors expected from students.
6. The teacher builds positive, caring relationships with students.

When teachers reinforce the concept of shared responsibility for teaching and learning through their behavior, management techniques, if needed, are more likely to be effective in encouraging appropriate student behavior.

Surface Behaviors

The most common day-to-day disruptive behaviors are verbal interruptions (talking, humming, laughing, calling out, whispering), off-task behaviors (daydreaming, sleep-

Surface behaviors are the most common type of disruptive behaviors that teachers must manage on a day-to-day basis.

CASE 7.1 • "... 3, 2, 1, Blast Off"

The students in Mr. Berk's seventh-grade English class have science before English. Today, their science teacher illustrated the concept of propulsion by folding a piece of tin foil around the tip of a match. When he heated the tin foil, the match was ignited and accelerated forward.

During English class, Mickey, seated in the back row, decides to try the propulsion experiment. It is not long before many students are aware of Mickey's activity and are sneaking glances at him. Mickey is enjoying the attention and continues to propel matches across his desk.

It does not take Mr. Berk long to become aware that many of his students are not paying attention. Instead of attempting to determine what the distraction is, he reacts impulsively. He sees Terri turn around to look at Mickey and says, "Terri, turn around and pay attention!" Terri immediately fires back. "I'm not doing anything." The class begins to laugh, because only Mr. Berk is unaware of the aerospace activity in the back of the room.

ing, combing hair, playing with something, doodling), physical movement intended to disrupt (visiting, passing notes, sitting on the desk or on two legs of the chair, throwing paper), and disrespect (arguing, teasing, vulgarity, talking back) (Huber, 1984; Levin, 1980; Shrigley, 1980; Thomas, Goodall, and Brown, 1983; Weber and Sloan, 1986). These disruptive behaviors, which are usually readily observable to an experienced teacher, are called surface behaviors because they usually are not a result of any deep-seated personal problem but are normal developmental behaviors of children.

Some teachers are able to manage appropriately, almost intuitively, surface behaviors. They have an almost instinctive grasp of the necessary classroom skills of "overlapping," that is, attending to two matters at the same time, and "with-it-ness," a subtle nonverbal communication to students that she is aware of all activities within the classroom (Kounin, 1970). Other teachers acquire these skills through hard work and experience. Teachers who do not have or do not develop these skills have to cope with abnormally high frequencies of surface behaviors, and in some instances, as in Case 7.1, the absence of these skills actually causes disruptive behavior.

Proactive Intervention Skills

Effective classroom managers are experts in the matter-of-fact use of not only overlapping and with-it-ness skills but also other more specific and narrower proactive intervention skills. Their expertise can be seen in the way they employ these skills with little if any disruption in the teaching/learning process. Developing expertise in the use of the following proactive skills should lessen the need for more intrusive management techniques.

1. *Changing the pace of classroom activities.* Rubbing eyes, yawning, stretching, and staring out the window are clear signs that a change of pace is needed. This is the time for the teacher to restructure the situation and involve students in games, stories, or other favorite activities that require active student participation and help to refocus student interests. To reduce the need for on-the-spot change-of-pace activities, lesson plans should provide for a variety of learning experiences that accommodate the attention spans and interests of the students both in time and in type.

2. *Removing seductive objects.* The skill may be used with little, if any, pause in the teaching act. However, there should be an agreement that the objects will be returned after class. Teachers who find themselves competing with toys, magazines, or combs may simply walk over to the student, collect the object, and quietly inform the student that it will be available after class.

3. *Interest boosting of a student who shows signs of off-task behavior.* Rather than using other, less-positive techniques, the teacher shows interest in the student's work, thereby bringing the student back on-task. Interest boosting is often called for when students are required to do individual or small group classwork. It is during these times that the potential for chatter, daydreaming, or other off-task behaviors is high. If the teacher observes a student engaging in activities other than the assigned math problems, for example, she can boost the interest of the student by walking over to the student and asking how the work is going or checking the answers of the completed problems. Asking the student to place correct problems on the board is also effective. Whatever technique is decided on, it must be employed in a matter-of-fact supportive manner to boost the student's interest in the learning activity.

4. *Redirecting the behavior of off-task students.* This skill helps to refocus the student's attention. Students who are passing notes, talking, or daydreaming may be asked to read, do a problem, or answer a question. When this technique is used, it is important to treat the student as if she were paying attention. For instance, if you call on the off-task student to answer a question and the student answers correctly, give positive feedback. If she doesn't answer or answers incorrectly, reformulate the question or call on someone else. A teacher who causes the student embarrassment or ridicule by stating, "You would know where we were if you were paying attention" invites further misbehavior. The "get back on-task" message the teacher is sending is clearly received by the off-task student whether or not she answers the question or finds the proper reading place and does not require any negative comments.

5. *Nonpunitive time out.* This skill should be used for students who show signs of encountering a provoking, painful, frustrating, or fatiguing situation. The teacher quietly asks the student if she would like to get a drink or invites her to run an errand or do a chore. The change in activity gives the student time to regain her control before reentering the learning environment. Teachers must be alert to the signs of frustration so they can act in a timely fashion to help students cope.

6. *Encouraging the appropriate behavior of other students.* A statement such as "I'm glad to see that Joan and Andrea have their books open" reminds off-task students of the behavior that is expected of them.

A teacher can redirect students to on-task behavior by the use of interest-boosting techniques.

7. *Providing cues for expected behaviors.* Cues can be quite effective in obtaining the desired behavior, but the teacher must be sure the cue is understood by all. For example, a teacher who expects students to be in their seats and prepared for class when the bell rings, must make sure that everyone understands that the bell signals the start of class. In schools without bells or other indicators, closing the door is an appropriate cue. Some teachers flick the lights to cue a class that the noise has reached unacceptable levels. Using the same cues consistently usually results in quick student response.

Remedial Intervention Skills

The masterful use of proactive skills diffuses many surface behaviors and causes minimal disruptions to the teaching act. However, there will always be classroom situations that induce misbehavior or students who continue to display disruptive behaviors.

These behaviors may range from mildly off-task to very disruptive. Mastering the delivery of the intervention skills discussed here and in Chapters 8 and 9 should help to produce an exceptional classroom in which misbehavior is minimized and teachers are free to teach and children are free to learn.

Before any intervention may be used, the teacher must have a basis on which to make decisions concerning common inappropriate behaviors in the classroom. To avoid inconsistency and arbitrariness, teachers must also have a systematic intervention plan of predetermined behaviors that clearly communicates disapproval to the student who calls out, throws paper, walks around, passes notes, or in any way interferes with the teaching or learning act (Canter, 1989; Lasley, 1989). This follows our definition of teaching presented in Chapter 1: *the conscious use of predetermined behaviors that increase the likelihood of changing student behaviors.*

The intervention decision-making approach is a sequence of hierarchically ordered teacher behaviors. Because we believe that students must learn to control their own behavior, the initial interventions are subtle, nonintrusive, and very student centered. Although these behaviors communicate disapproval, they are designed to provide students with the opportunity to control their own behavior. If the misbehaviors are not curbed, the interventions become increasingly more intrusive and teacher centered; that is, the teacher takes more responsibility for managing the students' behavior.

Because we also believe that management techniques should not in themselves disrupt the teaching and learning act (Brophy, 1988), early intervention behaviors are almost a private communication between the teacher and the off-task student. They alert the student to her inappropriate behavior but cause little if any noticeable disruption to either teaching or learning. If these nonverbal interventions, which make up the first tier of the decision-making hierarchy, are not successful, they are followed by the second and third tiers: teacher verbal behaviors and consequences. These tiers are increasingly more teacher centered, more intrusive, and may cause some interruption to the teaching/learning act. (These techniques are discussed in Chapters 8 and 9.)

The decision-making hierarchy described here and in the following two chapters is intended to be a dynamic model, not one that binds a teacher into a lockstep, sequential, cookbook intervention approach. Instead the model requires the teacher to make a decision as to which intervention in the hierarchy to employ first. The decision should depend on the type and frequency of the disruptive behavior and should be congruent with five implementation guidelines that follow. These guidelines should help to ensure that any beginning intervention, as well as those that may follow, meets the two foundational precepts of the hierarchy: increasing student self-control and decreasing disruptions to the teaching and learning environment.

1. The intervention provides a student with opportunities for the self-control of the disruptive behaviors. Self-control is not developed to its fullest in classrooms where teachers immediately intervene with teacher-centered techniques to manage student behavior. Because we believe individuals make conscious choices to behave in certain ways and that individuals cannot be forced to learn or exhibit appropriate behavior, early interventions should not force students but rather influence them to manage themselves. Students must be given responsibility in order to learn responsibility.

2. The intervention does not cause more disruption to the teaching and learning environment than the disruptive behavior itself. We have all witnessed teacher interventions that were more disruptive to the class than the off-task student behavior. This usually occurs when the teacher uses an intervention too far up the decision-making hierarchy. For example, the teacher chooses to use a public verbal technique when a private nonverbal intervention would be more effective and less disruptive. When this happens the teacher becomes more of a disruptive factor than the student.

3. The intervention lessens the probability that the student will become more disruptive or confrontational. Interventions should lessen and defuse confrontational situations. When teachers choose to employ public, aggressive, or humiliating techniques, they increase the likelihood of escalating confrontations and power struggles. Again, deciding where in the decision-making hierarchy to begin has a significant effect on whether a disruptive student will be brought back on task or will become confrontational.

4. The intervention protects students from physical and psychological harm and does not cause physical or psychological harm. When a teacher observes behaviors that could be harmful to any student, intervention should be swift and teacher-centered. In such situations, nonverbal techniques are usually bypassed for the assertive delivery of verbal interventions. In all cases we must be careful that the interventions are not in themselves a source of harm to students or to the teacher.

5. The choice of the specific intervention maximizes the number of alternatives left for the teacher to use if it becomes necessary. Every teacher knows that it often takes more than one intervention to manage student behavior. It is rare that disruptive behavior is noted, a teacher intervention occurs, and the student is back on task forever. It is the unwise teacher who sends a student out of the classroom for the first occurrence of a disruptive behavior. Such an intervention leaves few options available to the teacher if the student continues to misbehave when she returns. By using the decision-making hierarchy of intervention skills, the teacher reserves many alternative interventions.

It is important to remember that the teacher's goal in employing any remedial intervention skill is to redirect the student to appropriate behavior. Stopping the misbehavior may be the initial step in the process, but it is not sufficient. The teacher's goal is not reached until the student becomes reengaged in learning activities. Thus, whenever the teacher is introduced to a new technique for dealing with disruptive behavior, one of the questions she should ask in determining whether to employ the technique is, "Is this technique likely to redirect the student to appropriate behavior?"

The first tier of the hierarchy of remedial intervention skills, nonverbal skills, consists of four techniques: planned ignoring, signal interference, proximity interference, and touch interferencer. These body-language interventions were first identified by Redl and Wineman (1952). When they are used randomly, effective management of minor disruptions is not fully achieved. However, when they are consciously employed in a predetermined logical sequence, they serve to curb milder forms of off-task behavior (Shrigley, 1985).

Planned Ignoring

Planned ignoring is based on the reinforcement theory that if you ignore a behavior, it will lessen and eventually disappear. Although this sounds simple, it is difficult to ignore a behavior completely. That is why *planned* is stressed. When a student whistles, interrupts the teacher, or calls out, the teacher instinctively looks in the direction of the student, thereby giving the student attention and reinforcing the behavior. In contrast, planned ignoring intentionally and completely ignores the behavior. This takes practice.

There are limitations to this intervention. First, according to reinforcement theory, when a behavior has been reinforced previously, removal of the reinforcement causes a short-term increase in the behavior in the hope of again receiving reinforcement. Thus, when planned ignoring is first used, there probably will be an increase of the off-task behavior. Therefore, this technique should be used to manage only the behaviors that cause little interference to the teaching/learning act (Brophy, 1988). Second, the disruptive behavior often is being reinforced by the other students who attend to the misbehaving student. If it is, planned ignoring by the teacher has little effect.

The behaviors that usually are managed by planned ignoring are not having materials ready for the start of class, calling out answers rather than raising a hand, mild or infrequent whispering, interrupting the teacher, and daydreaming. Obviously the type of learning activity has much to do with the behaviors that can or cannot be ignored. If, after a reasonable period of time of ignoring the off-task behavior, the behavior does not decrease or the point is reached at which others are distracted by it, the teacher has to move quickly and confidently to the next step in the hierarchy, signal interference.

Signal Interference

Signal interference is any type of nonverbal behavior that communicates to the student without disturbing others that the behavior is not appropriate. Signal interventions must be clearly directed at the off-task student. There should be no doubt in the student's mind that the teacher is aware of what is going on and that the student is responsible for the behavior. The teacher's expression should be businesslike. It is ineffective for the teacher to make eye contact with a student and smile. Smiling sends a double message, which confuses students and may be interpreted as a lack of seriousness by the teacher.

Examples of signal interference behaviors are making eye contact with the student who is talking to a neighbor, pointing to a seat when a student is wandering around, head shaking to indicate "no" to a student who is about to throw a paper airplane, and holding up an open hand to stop a student's calling out. Like all coping skills, signal interference behaviors may be hierarchically ordered, depending on the type, duration, and frequency of off-task behavior. A simple hand motion may serve to manage calling out the first time, whereas direct eye contact with a disapproving look may be needed the next time the student calls out.

For disruptive behaviors that continue or for disturbances that more seriously affect others' learning, the teacher moves to the next intervention skill in the hierarchy, proximity interference.

Proximity Interference

Proximity interference is any movement toward the disruptive student. When signal interference doesn't work, or the teacher is unable to gain a student's attention long enough to send a signal because the student is so engrossed in the off-task behavior, proximity interference is warranted.

Often just walking toward the student while conducting the lesson is enough to bring the student back on task. If the student continues to be off task, the teacher may want to conduct the lesson in close proximity to the student's desk, which is usually quite effective. This technique works well during question-and-answer periods.

Proximity interference combined with signal interference results in a very effective nonverbal management technique. It's the rare student who is not brought back on task by a teacher who makes eye contact and begins walking toward her desk. Like signal interference, proximity interference techniques may be hierarchically ordered from nonchalant movement in the direction of the student to an obvious standing behind or next to the student during class. If proximity does not bring about the desired behavioral change, the teacher is in a position to implement the next step in the coping skill hierarchy, touch interference.

Touch Interference

When a teacher takes a child's hand and escorts the child back to her seat or when a teacher places a hand on a student's shoulder, she is using touch interference. Touch interference is a light, nonaggressive physical contact with the student. Without any verbal exchange, touch interference communicates to the student that the teacher disapproves of the disruptive behavior. When possible, the technique also ought to direct the student to the appropriate behavior, such as when a student is escorted to a seat or the student's hand is moved from a neighbor's desk and back to her own paper.

When using touch interference, it is important to be aware of its limitations and possible negative outcomes. Certain students construe any touch by the teacher as an

Touch is an effective intervention skill but one that can also produce student reactions.

aggressive act and react with aggressive behavior. On one occasion we saw a teacher calmly walk up to a student who was standing at her seat and place her hand on the student's shoulder. The student turned around and confronted the teacher, angrily yelling, "Don't you ever put your hands on me!" To lessen the chance of such an occurrence, teachers need to be sensitive to using touch interference when working with visibly angry or upset students and older students, especially those of the opposite sex. As with all management techniques, the teacher must be cognizant of the situational variables as well as the student characteristics.

Effectiveness of Nonverbal Intervention Skills

The use of these four remedial nonverbal intervention skills is considered successful if any one or any combination in the hierarchy leads the student to resume appropriate classroom behavior.

Notice how Mr. Rotman in Case 7.2 skillfully uses the four nonverbal remedial intervention techniques in combination with the proactive skills of removing seductive objects, interest boosting, and redirecting the behavior to manage the note passing between Jerry and Ben without noticeably disrupting the teaching/learning act. He is able to do this because the intervention skills are not randomly and haphazardly

---

CASE 7.2 • *Notes versus Math*

Mr. Rotman asks each student to write one math problem from the assignment on the board. As two students write their problems, he notices out of the corner of his eye, Jerry passing a note to Ben. Mr. Rotman decides to ignore the behavior, waiting to see if it is a matter of a single occurrence. When all the problems are on the board, Mr. Rotman asks questions about the solutions. During this questioning period, he notices Ben returning a note to Jerry. After a few attempts Mr. Rotman makes eye contact with Jerry while at the same time questioning Ben about one of the problems. This technique stops the note passing for the remainder of the questioning activity.

The next activity calls for the use of calculators, and he asks Jerry to please pass one calculator to each predetermined pair of students. Jerry and Ben are part-

ners, and Mr. Rotman monitors their behavior from a distance. As he circulates around the room helping students with the classwork, he makes sure that he stops to look over Jerry and Ben's work, encouraging them on its accuracy. Throughout the activity both boys are on task.

Following the group work, the students separate their desks, and Mr. Rotman begins to review the answers to the problems. He immediately notices that the two boys have begun to pass notes again. He quickly takes a position next to the boys, taps Jerry on the shoulder, and holds out his hand for the note. Jerry hands Mr. Rotman the note and he puts it in his pocket. Mr. Rotman stands near the boys for the rest of the period, asking questions of the class and reviewing the problems. Both Ben and Jerry volunteer and participate for the remainder of the class.

applied. Mr. Rotman has a mental flowchart of the hierarchical sequence so that movement from one behavior to the next is accomplished quickly, calmly, and confidently. This does not happen overnight. Teachers must preplan and practice proactive and remedial intervention techniques before having to implement them.

Shrigley (1985) studied the efficiency of nonverbal proactive and remedial intervention skills when used in a hierarchical sequence. He found that after a few hours of in-service training, 53 teachers were able to curb 40 percent of 523 off-task surface behaviors without having to utter a word or cause any interruption to either teaching or learning. Five percent of the behaviors were corrected by the use of planned ignoring. Signal interference was the most effective technique, rectifying 14 percent of the behaviors. Twelve percent and 9 percent were stopped by proximity and touch interference, respectively. To manage the remaining 60 percent of unresolved behavior problems, the teachers needed to implement verbal intervention, the group of intervention skills covered in the next chapter.

Remember, however, the hierarchy is a decision-making model. Depending on the type, frequency, and distracting potential of the behavior, the teacher may decide to bypass the initial intervention skills in favor of a later technique. There are certain behaviors that need immediate attention; they can neither be ignored nor allowed to continue. This is demonstrated in Case 7.3, in which Ms. Niaz decides to bypass planned ignoring and signal interference in favor of proximity interference to manage a disruption during a test.

No matter what technique eventually brings the student back on task, efforts need to be directed toward maintaining the appropriate behavior. This is most easily accomplished by the teacher who encourages and attends to the student's new behavior. The student must realize that she can obtain the same or even more attention and recognition for appropriate behavior than she did for disruptive behavior. The student who is ignored when calling out answers should be called on immediately when she raises her hand. The student who ceases walking around the room should be told at the end of the period that it was a pleasure having her in the class. These simple efforts of recognizing appropriate behavior are often overlooked by teachers, but they are a necessary supplement for the teacher who wants to maximize the effectiveness of proactive and remedial intervention skills.

CASE 7.3 • *Let Your Fingers Do the Walking*

Ms. Niaz explains the test-taking procedures to her class and then passes out the tests. She walks around the room, answering questions and keeping students aware of her presence. As she does, she notices that Danny is walking his fingers up Tonya's back. Tonya turns around and says, "Stop it!" As soon as she turns back to her test, Danny again bothers her. Ms. Niaz immediately walks toward Danny and spends the next ten minutes standing in close proximity to him.

Summary

This chapter begins by stressing the fact that teaching/learning is the joint responsibility of the teacher and the students. Students are more willing to accept their responsibilities when it is clear to them that the teacher is fulfilling her responsibilities. These responsibilities include being well prepared to teach by developing learning objectives and using effective teaching strategies, providing clear directions and explanations, ensuring that students understand evaluation criteria, communicating and consistently enforcing behavioral expectations, demonstrating enthusiasm and encouragement, and modeling expected behavior. These behaviors are minimum competencies that all teachers must possess and are considered prerequisites to effective classroom management.

Teachers proficient in classroom management are experts in the use of a variety of proactive intervention skills. Techniques such as changing the pace, removing seductive objects, interest boosting, redirecting behavior, nonpunitive time out, encouraging appropriate behavior, and providing cues are employed to bring students back on task while causing little if any disruption to the teaching/learning process.

A three-tiered, decision-making hierarchy of remedial intervention skills provides a means to manage the inappropriate surface behaviors that are not brought on task through proactive intervention skills. The structure of the hierarchy ranges from nonintrusive techniques that cause little disruption and provide students with the opportunity to control their own behavior to intrusive techniques that potentially disrupt teaching and learning. The first tier of nonverbal remedial intervention consists of four nonverbal behaviors: planned ignoring, signal interference, proximity interference, and touch interference. When systematically employed, these techniques have been shown to be effective in managing many surface behaviors.

References

Brophy, J. (1988). Educating teachers about managing classrooms and students. *Teaching and Teacher Education, 4,* 1, 1–18.

Canter, L. (1989). Assertive discipline—More than names on the board and marbles in a jar. *Phi Delta Kappan, 71,* 1, 57–61.

Huber, J. D. (1984). Discipline in the middle school—Parent, teacher, and principal concerns. *National Association of Secondary School Principals Bulletin, 68,* 471, 74–79.

Kounin, J. (1970). *Discipline and Group Management in Classrooms.* New York: Holt, Rinehart & Winston.

Lasley, T. J. (1989). A teacher development model for classroom management. *Phi Delta Kappan, 71,* 1, 36–38.

Levin, J. (1980). *Discipline and Classroom Management Survey: Comparison between a Suburban and Urban School.* Unpublished report, Pennsylvania State University, University Park.

Redl, F., and Wineman, D. (1952). *Controls from Within.* New York: Free Press.

Shrigley, R. L. (1980). *The Resolution of 523 Classroom Incidents by 54 Classroom Teachers Using the Six Step Intervention Model.* University Park: Pennsylvania State University, College of Education, Division of Curriculum and Instruction.

Shrigley, R. L. (1985). Curbing student disruption in the classroom—Teachers need intervention skills. *National Association of Secondary School Principals Bulletin, 69,* 479, 26–32.

Thomas, G. T., Goodall, R., and Brown, L. (1983). Discipline in the classroom: Perceptions of middle grade teachers. *The Clearinghouse, 57,* 3, 139–142.

Weber, T. R., and Sloan, C. A. (1986). How does high school discipline in 1984 compare to previous decades? *The Clearinghouse, 59,* 7, 326–329.

Exercises

1. Six teacher behaviors were listed as prerequisites to appropriate student behavior. Should these teacher behaviors be considered prerequisite? Why or why not?

2. Predict what type of student behavior may result if the teacher does not meet each of the six prerequisite teacher behaviors.

3. What, if any, deletions or additions would you make to the six prerequisite teacher behaviors? Explain any modification you suggest.

4. Suggest specific techniques a teacher could use that demonstrate each of the following proactive intervention skills:
   a. Changing the pace
   b. Interest boosting
   c. Redirecting behavior
   d. Encouraging appropriate behavior
   e. Providing cues

5. The hierarchy of remedial intervention skills is presented as a decision-making model, not as an action model. Explain why.

6. Two effective remedial intervention skills are signal interference and proximity interference. Suggest specific techniques a teacher could use that would demonstrate their use.

7. What types of student behaviors would cause you to decide to bypass initial remedial nonverbal intervention skills and enter the hierarchy at the proximity or touch-interference level?

8. Explain why you agree or disagree with the premise that management techniques should be employed in a manner that provides students with the greatest opportunity to control their own behavior.

9. Some teachers consider the hierarchial use of remedial intervention skills a waste of time. They say, "Why spend all this time and effort when you can just tell the student to stop messing around and get back to work." Explain why you agree or disagree with this point of view.

8

Managing Common Misbehavior Problems

Verbal Interventions and Use of Logical Consequences

The Basics

↓

Nature of the Discipline Problem

↓

Understanding Why Children Misbehave

↓

Philosophical Approaches to Classroom Management

↓

The Professional Teacher

↓

Structuring the Environment

↓

**Managing Common Misbehavior Problems:
Nonverbal Interventions**

↓

**Managing Common Misbehavior Problems:
Verbal Interventions and Use of Logical Consequences**
Verbal Intervention • Adjacent (Peer) Reinforcement • Calling on the
Student/Name-Dropping • Humor • Questioning Awareness of Effect • "I Message"
• Direct Appeal • Positive Phrasing • "Are Not For's" • Reminder of Rules
• Glasser's Triplets • Explicit Redirection • Canter's "Broken Record"
• Use of Logical Consequences

Principles of Classroom Management

1. When nonverbal teacher intervention does not lead to appropriate student behavior, the teacher should employ verbal intervention to deal with the misbehavior.
2. Some forms of verbal intervention defuse confrontation and reduce misbehavior; other forms of verbal intervention escalate misbehavior and confrontation.
3. When verbal intervention does not lead to appropriate student behavior, the teacher needs to apply logical consequences to the student's misconduct.

Introduction

Although it is true that John in Case 8.1 has caused many problems for Mr. Hensen and the other students in his class, what does Mr. Hensen accomplish by yelling at him? Although he does get his long-suppressed feelings off his chest, Mr. Hensen does more harm than good. He disrupts any learning that is taking place. He forces the other students to concentrate on John's behavior rather than on the content of the lesson, and he extends the off-task time by prolonging the reprimand. He reacts negatively and sarcastically to John, who already dislikes him and now is probably more determined than ever to "get Hensen's goat." Finally, by overreacting to a minor incident, Mr. Hensen has probably created some sympathy for John among the other students.

Although we know Mr. Hensen has overreacted, we also know that he is not alone. Many teachers find themselves in Mr. Hensen's position at one time or another. They allow many incidents of relatively minor misbehavior to build up until one day they just can't take it anymore, and they explode. In letting loose their pent-up feel-

---

CASE 8.1 • *Blowing His Stack*

"John, you are one of the most obnoxious students I have ever had the misfortune to deal with. How many times have I asked you not to call out answers? If you want to answer a question, raise your hand. It shouldn't tax your tiny brain too much to remember that. I'm sick and tired of your mistaken idea that the rules of this classroom apply to everyone but you. It's because of people like you that we need rules in the first place. They apply especially to you. I will not allow you to deprive other students of the chance to answer questions. Anyway, half of your answers are totally off the wall. I'm in charge here, not you. If you don't like it, you can tell your troubles to the principal. Now sit here and be quiet."

When Mr. Hensen finished his lecture and turned to walk to the front of the room, John discreetly flipped him the "bird" and laughed with his friends. John spent the rest of the period drawing pictures on the corner of his desk. The other students spent the remainder of the period in either uncomfortable silence or invisible laughter. Mr. Hensen spent the rest of the class trying to calm down and get his mind back on the lesson.

ings, these teachers make the situation worse rather than better. Teachers can avoid this by using the remedial intervention skills hierarchy first presented in Chapter 7 to contend with classroom behavior problems. This hierarchy consists of three major tiers of intervention: (1) nonverbal intervention skills, (2) verbal intervention, and (3) use of logical consequences. When teachers use this hierarchy to guide their thinking about classroom discipline problems, they are able to cope with misbehavior swiftly and effectively. This chapter presents the second and third tiers of the hierarchy.

Verbal intervention is one of the most powerful and versatile tools the teacher has for classroom management. When used effectively, verbal intervention makes classroom management relatively easy and less stressful. When used poorly and thoughtlessly, it may create new management problems, make existing problems worse, or turn temporary problems into chronic ones.

This chapter presents 12 verbal intervention techniques in a systematic, hierarchical format. As in the nonverbal intervention skills subhierarchy presented in Chapter 7, the verbal intervention subhierarchy begins with techniques designed to foster students' control over their own behavior and proceeds to those that foster greater teacher management over student behavior. Because, as we noted in Chapter 7, this is a decision-making hierarchy; the teacher must decide which particular verbal intervention technique to use with a student who is misbehaving after determining that nonverbal intervention is not appropriate or has not worked.

The final section of the chapter discusses the final tier of the management hierarchy, the use of logical consequences to manage student behavior.

Classroom Verbal Intervention

There are, as explained in Chapter 7, four advantages to using nonverbal intervention whenever possible: (1) disruption to the learning process is less likely to occur; (2) hostile confrontation with the student is less apt to happen; (3) the student is provided the opportunity to correct his own behavior before more teacher-centered, public interventions are employed; and (4) a maximum number of remaining alternative interventions is preserved. However, nonverbal intervention is not always possible. When misbehavior is potentially harmful to any student or potentially disruptive for a large number of students, it should be stopped quickly, and often verbal intervention is the quickest way to do so. Before discussing specific techniques, there are some guidelines teachers should keep in mind when using verbal intervention.

1. Whenever possible, use nonverbal interventions first.
2. Keep verbal intervention as private as possible. This minimizes the risk of having the student become defensive and hostile to avoid losing face in front of peers. Brophy (1988) suggests that this is one of the most important general principles for disciplinary intervention.
3. Make the verbal intervention as brief as possible. Your goal is to stop the misbehavior *and* redirect the student to appropriate behavior. Prolonging the ver-

bal interaction extends the disruption of learning and enhances the likelihood of a hostile confrontation.

4. As Haim Ginott (1972) suggests, speak to the situation, not the person. In other words, label the behavior as bad or inappropriate, not the person. If, for example, a student interrupts a teacher, "Interrupting others is rude" is a more appropriate response than "You interrupted me. You are rude." Labeling the behavior helps the student to see the distinction between himself and his behavior, which in turn helps him to understand that it is possible for the teacher to like him but not his behavior. If the student is labeled, he may feel compelled to defend himself. Furthermore, the student may accept the label as part of his self-concept and match the label with inappropriate behavior in the future. This is exactly what Jimmy Dolan decides to do in Case 8.2.

5. As Ginott has urged, set limits on behavior, not on feelings. For instance, tell the student, "It is O.K. to be angry, but it's not O.K. to show your anger by hitting." "It is O.K. to feel disappointed but it's not O.K. to show that disappointment by ripping your test paper up in front of this class and throwing it in the basket." Students need to recognize, trust, and understand their feelings. When teachers and parents tell students not to be angry or disappointed, they are telling them to distrust and deny their genuine and often justified feelings. The appropriate message for teachers and parents to communicate and understand is that there are appropriate and inappropriate ways for expressing feelings.

6. Avoid sarcasm and other verbal behaviors that belittle or demean the student. Using verbal reprimands to belittle students lowers self-esteem and creates sympathy among classmates.

CASE 8.2 • *Jimmy, the Little Sneak*

Jimmy Dolan is in the sixth grade at Shortfellow School. His teacher, Mr. Gramble, has had a long history of difficulty in dealing with classroom discipline. Jimmy is a fine student who rarely misbehaves. One day, as his back is partially turned to the class, Mr. Gramble notices Jimmy talking to a neighbor. In a flash, Mr. Gramble turns and pounces on Jimmy, who was only asking Craig Rutler for an eraser to correct a mistake in his homework. "So, you're the one who's been causing all the trouble," Mr. Gramble snaps. "You little sneak, and all the time I thought you were one of the few people who never caused trouble in here. Well, Buster, you can bet from now on I'll keep an eagle eye on you. You won't be getting away with any more sneaky behavior in here."

For a week or so, Jimmy goes back to his typical good behavior, but every time something goes wrong or someone misbehaves, Mr. Gramble blames Jimmy. After a week or so of unjust blame, Jimmy decides that he may as well start causing some trouble since he is going to get blamed for it anyway. In a very short time, Jimmy truly is a great sneak who causes all sorts of havoc and rarely gets caught in the act.

7. Begin by using a technique that fits the student and the problem and is as close as possible to the student-control end of the decision-making hierarchy.

8. If the first verbal intervention does not result in a return to appropriate behavior, use a second technique that is closer to the teacher-control end of the hierarchy.

9. If more than one verbal intervention technique has been used unsuccessfully, it is time to move to the next step of the management hierarchy—the use of logical consequences.

Equally as important as these guidelines on how to use verbal interventions is an awareness of commonly used ineffective verbal interventions. Many of these are instantaneous teacher reactions to disruptive students rather than systematic, pre-planned, professional decisions enhanced by the use and understanding of the hierarchy of remedial intervention skills. While there are many ineffective verbal interventions, they all share the common characteristics of not speaking directly to the disruptive behavior and not directing the student toward the appropriate behavior (Valentine, 1987).

Some ineffective verbal interventions encourage inappropriate behavior. For instance, "I dare you to do that again" actually increases the likelihood that a student will accept the dare and engage in further disruptions. Other verbal interventions focus on irrelevant behavior. "Aren't you sorry for what you did?" or "Why don't you just admit you have a problem?" address issues that are tangential to the real problem, the student's inappropriate behavior. Still other inappropriate interventions give abstract, meaningless directions or predictions, such as, "Grow up!" or "You'll never amount to anything." These do not address the disruptive behavior and are derogatory and humiliating. They increase the possibility of further confrontation when the student attempts to "save face."

With the guidelines in mind and a cognizance of ineffective verbal reactions, let's turn our attention to the hierarchy of effective verbal intervention. Remember that this is a hierarchy of decision making that begins with verbal interventions that foster student control over student behavior and gradually progresses to interventions that foster greater teacher management over student behavior. The teacher uses the hierarchy as a range of options to consider, not as a series of techniques to be tried in rapid succession. The teacher should begin the intervention at the point on the hierarchy that is likely to correct the misbehavior and still allow the student as much control and responsibility as possible. It is entirely appropriate to begin with a teacher-centered technique if the teacher believes that it is important to stop the misbehavior quickly and that only a teacher-centered intervention will do so. It is also important to remember that not all of these interventions are appropriate for all types of misbehavior or for all students. Lasley (1989) suggests that teacher-centered interventions are more appropriate for younger, developmentally immature children, and student-centered interventions are more appropriate for older, developmentally mature learners. Therefore, the effective use of this verbal intervention hierarchy requires the teacher to decide which particular intervention techniques are appropriate for both his students and the particular types of misbehavior that are occurring.

FIGURE 8.1 *Hierarchy of Classroom Verbal Intervention Techniques*

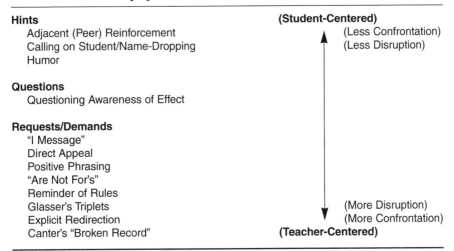

As Figure 8.1 indicates, the verbal intervention hierarchy has been broken into three major categories: hints, questions, and requests or demands. Hints are indirect means of letting the student know that his behavior is inappropriate. They do not directly address the behavior itself. Thus, of all the verbal interventions, they provide the greatest student control over behavior and are the least likely to result in further disruption or confrontation. Specific techniques that are classified as hints include adjacent or peer reinforcement, calling on students or name dropping, and humor.

Questions are used by the teacher to ask the student if he is aware of how he is behaving and how that behavior is affecting other people. They are more direct than hints but provide greater student control and less likelihood of confrontation than demands. The only questioning technique that is illustrated as such is questioning awareness of effect. However, almost any request or demand can be utilized as a question. For example, "pencils are not for drumming" can be rephrased as "what are pencils for?"

The third level of verbal intervention is labeled as requests/demands. These are teacher statements explicitly directed at a misbehavior that make clear that the teacher wants the inappropriate behavior stopped. Requests and demands exert greater teacher management over student behavior and have the potential to be disruptive and confrontational. Despite their disadvantages, it is sometimes necessary for teachers to use these interventions when lower level interventions have proved unsuccessful. The potential for confrontation can be minimized if the demands are delivered calmly, privately, and assertively rather than aggressively.

No matter which interventions a teacher employs, they must be used with full awareness of their limitations and of the implicit message about managing student behavior that each one conveys.

Adjacent (Peer) Reinforcement

This technique is based on the learning principle that behavior that is reinforced is more likely to be repeated. While usually reinforcement consists of reinforcing a student for his own behavior, Albert Bandura (1977) has demonstrated through his work on social learning theory that other students are likely to imitate an appropriate behavior when their peers have been reinforced for that behavior. The use of peer reinforcement as a verbal intervention technique focuses class attention on appropriate behavior rather than on inappropriate behavior. This intervention technique has been placed first in the hierarchy because it gives the student a chance to control his own behavior without any intervention on the part of the teacher that calls attention to the student or his behavior. As the reader will remember from Chapter 7, adjacent reinforcement not only can stop misbehavior but also can prevent other students from misbehaving.

To use this technique effectively, a teacher who notes a disruptive behavior finds another student who is behaving appropriately and commends that student publicly for the appropriate behavior. Recall from Case 8.1 Mr. Hensen's anger at John. Mr. Hensen could have handled the problem by saying, "Fred and Bob, I really appreciate your raising your hands to answer questions," or "I am really glad that most of us remember the rule that we must raise our hands before speaking."

This particular verbal intervention technique is more useful at the elementary level than at the secondary level. Younger students are usually more interested in pleasing the teacher than older students and often vie for the teacher's attention. Thus, public praise by the teacher is a powerful reinforcer of appropriate behavior. At the secondary level, peer approval is more highly valued than teacher approval; thus, public praise by the teacher is not a powerful reinforcer and indeed may not be a reinforcer at all. For these reasons, it is best to use public praise of individuals sparingly. Public reinforcement of the group as a whole, however, may be an appropriate intervention at the secondary level.

Calling on the Student/Name-Dropping

Using this technique, the teacher redirects the student to appropriate behavior by calling on the student to answer a question or by inserting the student's name in an example or in the middle of a lecture if asking a question is not appropriate. Rinne (1984) labels the technique of inserting the student's name within the content of a lecture "name-dropping." Hearing his name is a good reminder to a student that his attention should be focused on the lesson. This technique may be used to redirect students who are off task but are not disrupting the learning of others (see Chapter 7), as well as students who are overtly disrupting the learning process.

Calling on a student who is misbehaving is a subtle yet effective technique for recapturing the student's attention without interrupting the flow of the lesson or risking confrontation with the student. There are two possible formats for calling on disruptive students. Some teachers state the student's name first and then ask a question; others ask the question and then call on the student. The latter technique invariably results in the student being unable to answer the question because he did not hear it.

Often, the teacher who uses this technique follows the period of embarrassed silence with a comment on why the student can't answer and why it is important to pay attention. Although this procedure may satisfy the teacher's need to say, "I gotcha," it is preferable to call on the student first and then ask the question. Using the name first achieves the goal of redirecting the student's attention without embarrassing him.

In Case 8.1, calling on John to answer or saying John's name are not appropriate techniques for Mr. Hensen to use in dealing with the situation because they encourage John's calling out by giving him recognition. Although not appropriate in this particular case, calling on the student and name-dropping are appropriate in a wide range of situations with learners of all ages.

Humor

Humor that is directed at the teacher or at the situation rather than at the student can defuse tension in the classroom and redirect students to appropriate behavior. The use of humor tends to depersonalize situations and can help to establish positive relationships with students (Saphier and Gower, 1982).

If Mr. Hensen wished to use humor to handle John's calling out, he might say something like this: "I must be hallucinating or something. I'd swear I heard somebody say something if I didn't know for sure that I haven't called on anyone yet." In using this technique, teachers need to be very careful not to turn humor into sarcasm. There is a fine line between humor and sarcasm. Used as a verbal intervention, humor is directed at or makes fun of the teacher or the situation, whereas sarcasm is directed at or makes fun of the student. It is important to keep this distinction in mind to ensure that what is intended as humor does not turn into sarcasm.

Questioning Awareness of Effect

Sometimes students who disrupt learning are genuinely not aware of the effect their behavior has on other people. Our research (Levin, Nolan, and Hoffman, 1985) indicates that even students who are chronic discipline problems learn to control their behavior when they are forced to acknowledge both its positive and negative effects. Given this, making disruptive students aware of how their behavior affects other people can be a powerful technique for getting them to control their own behavior. Usually a teacher can make a student aware of the impact of his behavior through the use of a rhetorical question, which requires no response from the disruptive student. The teacher who wants to handle Mr. Hensen's problem by questioning the student's awareness of his behavior's effect might say something like this: "John, are you aware that your calling out answers without raising your hand robs other students of the chance to answer the question?" As soon as the question was asked, the teacher would continue with the lesson without giving John an opportunity to respond.

The informal question not only makes the student aware of the impact of his behavior but also communicates to other students the teacher's desire to protect their right to learn and may build peer support for appropriate behavior. In using this intervention, however, especially with students at the junior high level or above, the teacher must be prepared for the possibility that the student will respond to the question. If the student does respond and does so in a negative way, the teacher may choose to ignore the answer, thereby sending the message that he will not use class time to discuss the issue; or the teacher may respond, "John, your behavior is having a negative impact on other people, and so I will not permit you to continue calling out answers." This option sends the message that the teacher is in charge of the classroom and will not tolerate the misbehavior. In dealing with a possible negative response from the student, it is important to remember that the teacher's goal is to stop the misbehavior and redirect the student to appropriate behavior as quickly as possible. Prolonged confrontations frustrate that goal.

Sending an "I Message"

Thomas Gordon (1989), the author of *Teaching Children Self-Discipline at Home and in School,* has developed a useful technique for dealing with misbehavior verbally. He terms the intervention an "I message." The "I message" is a three-part message that is intended to help the disruptive student recognize the negative impact of his behavior on the teacher. The underlying assumption of the technique is the same as the assumption underlying the previously discussed "questioning awareness of effect": Once a student recognizes the negative impact of his behavior on others, he will be motivated to stop the misbehavior. The three parts of an "I message" are (1) a simple description of the disruptive behavior, (2) a description of its tangible effect on the teacher and/or other students, and (3) a description of the teacher's feelings about the effects of the misbehavior. Using "I messages" models for students the important behavior of taking responsibility for and owning one's behavior and feelings. There is one important caveat in the use of this technique. Just as the teacher expects students to respect the feelings that are expressed in an "I message," the teacher must respect feelings expressed by students.

To use an "I message" to stop John from calling out, Mr. Hensen might say, "John, when you call out answers without raising your hand (part 1), I can't call on any other student to answer the question (part 2). This disturbs me because I would like to give everyone a chance to answer the questions (part 3)." Teachers who enjoy a positive relationship with students, which gives them referent power (see Chapter 4), are usually successful in using "I messages." When students genuinely like the teacher, they are motivated to stop behavior that has a negative impact on the teacher. On the other hand, if the teacher has a poor relationship with students, he should avoid the use of "I messages." Allowing students who dislike you to know that a particular behavior is annoying or disturbing may result in an increase in that particular behavior.

Direct Appeal

Another technique that is useful for instances when a teacher enjoys a referent or expert power base is direct appeal. Direct appeal means courteously requesting that a student stop the disruptive behavior. For example, Mr. Hensen could say, "John, please stop calling out answers so that everyone will have a chance to answer." The direct appeal is not made in any sort of pleading or begging way.

Teachers must not use direct appeal in a classroom in which students seem to doubt the teacher's ability to be in charge. In this situation, the appeal may be perceived as a plea rather than as a straightforward request.

Positive Phrasing

Many times parents and teachers fall into the trap of emphasizing the negative outcomes of misbehavior more than the positive outcomes of appropriate behavior. We tell children and students far more frequently what will happen if they don't finish their homework than we tell them the good things that will occur if they do finish. Of course, it is often easier to identify the short-range negative outcomes of misbehavior than it is to predict the short-range positive impact of appropriate behavior. Still, when the positive outcomes of appropriate behavior are easily identifiable, simply stating what the positive outcomes are, can redirect students from disruptive to proper behavior. Shrigley (1985) has called this technique positive phrasing. It usually takes the form of "as soon as you do *X* (behave appropriately), we can do *Y* (a positive outcome)."

In using positive phrasing to correct John's calling out, Mr. Hensen might say, "John, you will be called on as soon as you raise your hand." The long-term advantage of using positive phrasing whenever possible is that students begin to believe that appropriate behavior leads to positive outcomes. As a result, they are more likely to develop internalized control over their behavior.

"Are Not For's"

Of all the verbal interventions discussed in this chapter, the phrase "are not for" (Shrigley, 1985) is the most limited in use. It is implemented primarily when elementary or preschool children misuse property or materials. For example, if a student is drumming on a desk with a pencil, the teacher may say, "Pencils *aren't for* drumming on desks; pencils *are for* writing." Although it is usually effective in redirecting behavior positively at the elementary or preschool level, most secondary students perceive this intervention as insulting. Using "are not for" is not an appropriate technique for Mr. Hensen since John is a secondary student and is not misusing property or material.

Reminder of the Rules

When a teacher has established clear guidelines or rules early in the year (see Chapter 6) and has received student commitment to them, merely reminding disruptive students of the rules may curb misbehavior. If past transgressions have been followed by a reminder and a negative logical consequence if the misbehavior continued, this approach is even more effective. Notice that at this point on the hierarchy, the teacher is no longer relying on the student's ability to control his own behavior but instead is using external rules to manage behavior.

In using this technique, Mr. Hensen might say, "John, the classroom rules state that students must raise their hands before speaking," or "John, calling out answers without raising your hand is against our classroom rules." The technique is particularly effective for elementary students and for junior high students. Although it may be used at the senior high level, at this level many students resent the feeling that they are being governed by too many rules. It is important to note that when a reminder of the rules does not redirect the misbehavior, the application of consequences must follow. If this does not occur, the effectiveness of rule reminders will be diminished because students will not see the link between breaking classroom rules and negative consequences.

Glasser's Triplets

In his system for establishing suitable student behavior, which is outlined in *Schools Without Failure* (1969), William Glasser proposed that teachers direct students to appropriate behavior through the use of three questions: (1) What are you doing? (2) Is it against the rules? (3) What should you be doing? The use of these questions, which are known as Glasser's triplets, obviously requires a classroom in which the rules have been firmly established in students' minds. To stop John from calling out answers, Mr. Hensen would simply ask Glasser's triplets. The expectation underlying Glasser's triplets is that the student will answer the questions honestly and will then return to the appropriate behavior. Unfortunately, not all students answer the triplets honestly, and therein lies the intervention's inherent weakness. Asking open-ended questions may result in student responses that are dishonest, improper, or unexpected.

If a student chooses to answer the questions dishonestly or not to reply at all, the teacher responds by saying (in John's case), "No, John, you were calling out answers. That is against our classroom rules. You must raise your hand to answer questions." To minimize the likelihood of an extended, negative confrontation ensuing from the use of Glasser's triplets, it is suggested that teachers use three statements instead of questions: "John, you are calling out. It is against the rules. You should raise your hand if you want to answer."

Explicit Redirection

Explicit redirection consists of an order to stop the misbehavior *and* return to acceptable behavior. The redirection is a teacher command and leaves no room for student rebuttal. If Mr. Hensen used explicit redirection with John, he might say, "John, stop calling out answers and raise your hand if you want to answer a question." Notice the contrast between this technique and those discussed in the earlier stages of the hierarchy in terms of the amount of responsibility the teacher assumes for managing student behavior.

The advantages of this technique are its simplicity, clarity, and closed format, which does not allow for student rebuttal. Its disadvantage lies in the fact that the teacher publicly confronts the student, who either behaves or defies the teacher in front of peers. Obviously, if the student chooses to defy the teacher's command, the teacher must be prepared to proceed to the next step in the hierarchy and enforce the command with appropriate consequences.

Canter's "Broken Record"

Lee Canter (1992) has developed a strategy for clearly communicating to the student that the teacher will not engage in verbal bantering and intends to make sure that the student resumes appropriate behavior. Canter has labeled his strategy "the broken record" because the teacher's behavior sounds like a broken record. The teacher begins by giving the student an explicit redirection statement. If the student doesn't comply or if the student tries to defend or explain his behavior, the teacher repeats the redirection. The teacher may repeat it two or three times if the student continues to argue or fails to comply. If the student tries to excuse or defend his behavior, some teachers add the phrase "that's not the point" at the beginning of the first and second repetitions. The following is an example of this technique as applied by Mr. Hensen.

> **HENSEN:** "John, stop calling out answers and raise your hand if you want to answer questions."
>
> **JOHN:** "But I really do know the answer."
>
> **HENSEN:** "That's not the point. Stop calling out answers and raise your hand if you want to answer questions."
>
> **JOHN:** "You let Mabel call out answers yesterday."
>
> **HENSEN:** "That's not the point. Stop calling out answers and raise your hand if you want to answer questions."

Return to lesson.

We have found the "broken record" technique to be very good for avoiding verbal battles with students. If, however, the statement has been repeated three times without any result, it is probably time to move to a stronger measure, such as the application of logical consequences.

Comply or Face the Logical Consequences: "You Have a Choice"

Although nonverbal and verbal interventions often stop misbehavior, sometimes the misbehavior remains unchecked. When this occurs, the teacher needs to use more overt techniques. The final tier on the decision-making management hierarchy is the use of logical consequences to manage student behavior.

As the reader will recall from Chapter 6, there are three types of consequences: natural, logical, and contrived (Dreikurs, Grundwald, and Pepper, 1998). Natural consequences result directly from student misbehavior without any intervention by the teacher although the teacher may point out the link between the behavior and the consequence. Using natural consequences is a management strategy because the teacher decides to let the natural consequences occur. That is, the teacher decides not to take any action to stop the consequence. Unlike natural consequences, logical consequences require teacher intervention and are related as closely as possible to the behavior; for example, a student who comes to class five minutes late is required to remain five minutes after school to make up the work, Contrived consequences are imposed on the student by the teacher and are either unrelated to student behavior or involve a penalty beyond that which is fitting for the misbehavior. Requiring a student who writes on his desk to write 1,000 times "I will not write on my desk," or sentencing a student who comes once to class five minutes late to two weeks of detention are contrived consequences. Since contrived consequences fail to help students see the connection between a behavior and its consequence and place the teacher in the role of punisher, we do not advocate their use. Consequently, contrived consequences are not part of the decision-making hierarchy.

When nonverbal and verbal interventions have not led to appropriate behavior, the teacher must take control of the situation and use logical consequences to manage student behavior. To do so, the teacher applies logical consequences calmly and thoughtfully in a forceful but not punitive manner.

Brophy (1988) suggests that the teacher who uses logical consequences should emphasize the student changing his behavior rather than retribution. When this is done, the teacher makes sure that the student understands the misbehavior must stop immediately or negative consequences will result. Often it is effective to give the student a choice of either complying with the request or facing the consequence. This technique is called "You Have a Choice." For example, if John continued to call out answers after Mr. Hensen had tried several nonverbal and verbal interventions, Mr. Hensen would say, "John, you have a choice. Stop calling out answers immediately and begin raising your hand to answer or move your seat to the back of the room and you and I will have a private discussion later. You decide." Phrasing the intervention in this way helps the student to realize that he is responsible for the positive as well as the negative consequences of his behavior and that the choice is his. It also places the teacher in a neutral rather than punitive role. Remember, students do, in fact, choose how to behave. Teachers can't control student behavior; they can only influence it.

Once the teacher moves to this final level of the hierarchy, the dialogue is over. Either the student returns to appropriate behavior or the teacher takes action. The manner in which the consequences are delivered is important and provides the teacher another opportunity to reinforce the idea that the student is in control of his behavior, that the choice to behave or misbehave is his to make, and that his choice has consequences. In Mr. Hensen's case, if John chose to continue to call out, Mr. Hensen would say, "John, you have chosen to move to the back of the room; please move." There are no excuses, no postponements. The teacher has stated his intentions clearly. Because consistency is crucial, it is imperative that the teacher not move to this final tier on the hierarchy unless he is ready to enforce the consequences that have been specified.

Obviously the exact consequence to be applied varies with the student misbehavior. However, one principle is always involved in the formulation of consequences: The consequence should be as directly related to the offense as possible. Consistent application of this principle helps students to recognize that their behavior has consequences and helps them learn to control their own behavior in the future by predicting its consequences beforehand.

Because it can be difficult to come up with directly related logical consequences on the spur of the moment (Canter, 1992), teachers should consider logical consequences for common types of misbehavior before the misbehaviors occur. Developing one or two logical consequences for each of the classroom rules developed in Chapter 6 is a good way to begin. When misbehavior occurs for which there is no preplanned logical consequence, a teacher should ask the following questions to help formulate a consequence directly related to the misbehavior:

1. What would be the logical result if this misbehavior went unchecked?
2. What are the direct effects of this behavior on the teacher, other students, and the misbehaving student?
3. What can be done to minimize these effects?

The answers to these three questions usually will help a teacher to identify a logical consequence. In Case 8.3, note how Ms. Ramonda used the first of the three questions to formulate the logical consequences for Doug's behavior.

It must be pointed out that Ms. Ramonda would have to speak to the school principal and obtain approval before allowing Doug to do nothing. Still, while most classroom behavior problems do not warrant the drastic measures that Ms. Ramonda took, the case does illustrate a successful use of logical consequences to deal with a difficult classroom situation. Ms. Ramonda's application of logical consequences in a firm but neutral manner helped to redirect Doug to more appropriate behavior and at the same time helped him to recognize the direct connection between his behavior and its consequences.

When "You Have a Choice" Doesn't Work

At this point almost all readers are probably thinking, what if "You have a choice" doesn't work? Some teachers confuse "not working" with a student choosing the negative consequences rather than changing his behavior. Remember teachers cannot force students to behave appropriately, but they can deliver the logical consequences when students choose them. Beyond this point, teachers can only hope that if they are consistent and follow the guidelines for verbal interventions, students will internalize the relationship between behavior and its consequences and choose to behave appropriately the next time.

Teachers can increase the likelihood of a student choosing appropriate behavior by using an assertive response style when employing "You have a choice." Assertiveness is

CASE 8.3 *"Doing Nothin'"*

Doug is a seventh-grade, learning disabled student who has serious reading problems and poses behavioral problems for many teachers. At the beginning of the year, he is assigned to Ms. Ramonda's seventh-period remedial reading class. Since Doug hates reading, he is determined to get out of the class and causes all sorts of problems for Ms. Ramonda and the other students. Ms. Ramonda's first reaction is to have Doug removed from her class to protect the other students; however, after talking to Doug's counselor and his resource room teacher, she comes to believe that it is important for Doug not to get his way and that he desperately needs to develop the reading skills that she can teach him.

Ms. Ramonda decides to try to use Doug's personal interests to motivate him. The next day she asks, "Doug, what would you like to do? " Doug answers, "Nothin', I don't want to do nothin' in here. Just leave me alone." For the next two days Doug sits in the back of the room and doodles as Ms. Ramonda tries to determine what the next step should be. Finally, Ms. Ramonda asks herself what the logical result of doing nothing is. She decides that the logical result is boredom and resolves to use that to motivate Doug.

On the following day, she announces to Doug that he will get his wish. From then on, he can do nothing as long as he wants to. She explains that he will no longer need books or papers or pencils since books are for reading, and papers and pencils are for writing, and doing nothing means doing none of those things. He will not be allowed to talk to her or to his friends, she explains, since that too would be doing something and he wants to do nothing. "From now on, Doug, you will be allowed to sit in the back corner of the room and do nothing, just as you wish."

For one full week, Doug sits in the back corner and does nothing. Finally, he asks Ms. Ramonda if he can do something. She replies that he can do some reading but nothing else. Doug agrees to try some reading. That breaks the ice. Ms. Ramonda carefully selects some low-difficulty, high-interest material for Doug and gradually pulls him into the regular classroom situation.

communicated to others by the congruent use of certain verbal and nonverbal behaviors. Do not confuse assertiveness with aggressiveness, which leads to unwanted student outcomes. An aggressive response is one in which a teacher communicates what is expected but in a manner that abuses the rights and feelings of the student. When this happens, students perceive the stated consequences as threats. An aggressive delivery of "You have a choice" would probably be viewed by students as "fighting words" and escalate both hostility and confrontation leading to further disruptive behaviors. When a teacher uses an assertive response style, the teacher clearly communicates what is expected in a manner that respects a student's rights and feelings. An assertive style tells the student that the teacher is prepared to back up the request for behavioral change with appropriately stated consequences but is not threatening. The authors like to describe assertiveness as a style that communicates to the student a *promise* of action if appropriate behavior is not

TABLE 8.1 *Comparison of Assertive and Aggressive Response Styles*

	Assertive	Aggressive
Audience	Private only to student	Public to entire class
How student is addressed	Student's name	"You, hey you"
Voice	Firm, neutral, soft, slow	Tense, loud, fast
Eyes	Eye contact only	Narrowed, frowning eyes
Stance	Close to student without violating personal space	Hands on hips, violating personal space
Hands	Gently touch student or student's desk	Sharp, abrupt gestures

forthcoming. Table 8.1 compares the verbal and nonverbal behaviors that differentiate assertive response styles from aggressive ones.

Of course there always will be some students who do not choose to behave. When the teacher assertively delivers the consequence, these students argue or openly refuse to accept and comply with the consequence. If this happens, the teacher must not be sidetracked by the student and enter into a public power struggle with the student. Instead, the teacher should integrate the use of Canter's "broken record" (Canter, 1992) and a final "You have a choice" in a calm, firm assertive manner. The following example between Mr. Hensen and John illustrates integration of these verbal interventions.

1. Mr. Hensen gives John a choice of raising his hand or moving to the back of the room. John calls out again. Mr. Hensen says, "John, you called out; therefore you have decided to move to the back of the class. Please move."
2. John begins to argue. At this point Mr. Hensen uses Canter's "broken record" and, if necessary, a final "You have a choice."

JOHN: "You know Tom calls out all the time and you never do anything to him."

HENSEN: "That's not the point. Please move to the back of the room."

JOHN: "I get the right answers."

HENSEN: "That's not the point. Please move to the back of the room."

JOHN: "This is really unfair."

HENSEN: "That's not the point. Move to the back of the room."

JOHN: "'I'm not moving and don't try to make me."

HENSEN: "John, you have a choice. Move to the back of the room now, or I will be in touch with your parents. You decide."

As this interaction illustrates, after two or three broken records, the teacher issues a final "You have a choice," and then disengages from the student. Some teachers will have the student removed from the classroom by an administrator as the consequence for the final "You have a choice." Whatever the consequence, the teacher must be willing and able to follow through. Thus, teachers must be sure the consequence can be carried out. Since interaction between a student and teacher at this level is likely to be of great interest to the other students in the class, it is imperative for the teacher to remain calm, firm, and assertive. This is a time for the teacher to show the rest of the class that he is in control of his behavior and that he means what he says. A teacher who remains in control, even if the student refuses to comply, will garner more respect from onlooking students than the teacher who becomes humiliating, harsh, or out of control.

Summary

This chapter has presented the final two tiers of the hierarchy introduced in Chapter 7: verbal intervention and use of logical consequences. The following guidelines for verbal intervention were developed: (1) use verbal intervention when nonverbal is inappropriate or ineffective; (2) keep verbal intervention private if possible; (3) make it as brief as possible; (4) speak to the situation, not the person; (5) set limits on behavior, not feelings; (6) avoid sarcasm; (7) begin with a verbal intervention close to the student-centered end of the hierarchy; (8) if necessary, move to a second verbal intervention technique closer to the teacher-centered end of the hierarchy; and (9) if two verbal interventions have been used unsuccessfully, move to the application of consequences.

In addition to the nine guidelines, three types of ineffective verbal communication patterns were reviewed. These are: (1) encouraging inappropriate behavior, (2) focusing on irrelevant behaviors, and (3) abstract, meaningless directions and predictions.

Twelve specific intervention techniques were presented in a hierarchical format ranging from techniques that foster greater student control over behavior to those that foster greater teacher management over student behavior. The verbal interventions were divided into three categories: hints, questions, and requests/demands. Hints include: (1) adjacent or peer reinforcement, (2) calling on the student or name-dropping, and (3) humor. The sole questioning intervention that was presented is (4) questioning awareness of effect. It was noted that many interventions could be used in a question format. The interventions classified as requests/demands include (5) "I message," (6) direct appeal, (7) positive phrasing, (8) "are not for's," (9) reminder of rules, (10) Glasser's triplets, (11) explicit redirection, and (12) Canter's "broken record."

The last section of the chapter discussed the final tier of the hierarchy: use of logical consequences. It was suggested this intervention should be phrased in terms of student choice and the consequences should be related as directly as possible to the misbehavior. Three questions were proposed to help teachers formulate logical consequences for those misbehaviors for which the teacher has not developed a conse-

FIGURE 8.2   *Hierarchy for Management Intervention*

Level 1: Nonverbal Intervention	**(Student-Centered)**
Planned Ignoring	(Less Confrontation)
Signal Interference	(Less Disruption)
Proximity Interference	
Touch Interference	
Level 2: Verbal Intervention	
Hints	
Adjacent (Peer) Reinforcement	
Calling on Student/Name-Dropping	
Humor	
Questions	
Questioning Awareness of Effect	
Requests/Demands	
"I Messages"	
Direct Appeal	
Positive Phrasing	
"Are Not For's"	
Reminder of Rules	
Glasser's Triplets	
Explicit Redirection	
Canter's "Broken Record"	(More Disruption)
	(More Confrontation)
Level 3: Use of Logical Consequences	**(Teacher-Centered)**
"You Have a Choice"	

quence hierarchy. The use of an assertive response style and the integration of "You have a choice" with Canter's "broken record" were presented as a means to increase the likelihood that a student chooses to behave appropriately.

When taken together with the information presented in Chapter 7, the ideas presented in this chapter constitute a complete hierarchy that teachers can use to guide their thinking and decision making concerning interventions to cope with classroom misbehavior. The hierarchy is presented in its complete format in Figure 8.2.

References

Bandura, A. (1977). *Social Learning Theory.* Englewood Cliffs, NJ: Prentice Hall.

Brophy, J. (1988). Educating teachers about managing classrooms and students. *Teaching and Teacher Education, 4,* 1, 1—8.

Canter, L. (1989). Assertive Discipline: More than names on the board and marbles in a jar. *Phi Delta Kappan, 71,* 1, 57–61.

Canter, L., and Canter, M. (1992). *Assertive Discipline: Positive Behavior Management for Today's Classrooms,* rev. ed., Santa Monica, CA: Canter Associates.

Dreikurs, R., Grundwald, B. B., and Pepper, F. C. (1998). *Maintaining Sanity in the Classroom: Classroom Management Techniques,* 2nd ed. New York: Taylor and Francis.

Ginott, H. (1972). *Between Teacher and Child.* New York: Peter H. Wyden.

Glasser, W. (1969). *Schools Without Failure.* New York: Harper & Row.

Gordon, T. (1989). *Teaching Children Self-Discipline at Home and in School.* New York: Random House.

Lasley, T. J. (1989). A teacher development model for classroom management. *Phi Delta Kappan, 71,* 1, 30–38.

Levin, J., Nolan, J., and Hoffman, N. (1985) A strategy for the classroom resolution of chronic discipline problems. *National Association of Secondary School Principals Bulletin, 69,* 7, 11–18.

Rinne, C. (1984). *Attention: The Fundamentals of Classroom Control.* Columbus OH: Merrill.

Saphier, J., and Gower, R. (1982). *The Skillful Teacher.* Carlisle, MA: Research for Better Teaching.

Shrigley, R. (1985). Curbing student disruption in the classroom—Teachers need intervention skills. *National Association of Secondary School Principals Bulletin, 69,* 7, 26–32.

Valentine, M. R. (1987). *How to Deal with Discipline Problems in the School: A Practical Guide for Educators.* Dubuque, IA: Kendall/Hunt.

Exercises

1. What types of student misbehavior might lead a teacher to use verbal intervention without first trying nonverbal techniques? Justify your answer.

2. Use each of the verbal intervention techniques presented in this chapter to help redirect the student to appropriate behavior in the following situations:
   a. Student won't get started on a seat work assignment.
   b. Student pushes his way to the front of the line.
   c. Student talks to a friend sitting on the other side of the room.
   d. Student lies about a forgotten homework assignment.

3. Choose any three sequential verbal intervention techniques from the hierarchy and justify their placement order in terms of providing students the greatest opportunity to control their own behavior.

4. Under what circumstances, if any, would it be appropriate for a teacher to move directly to the third tier of the hierarchy, use of logical consequences? Justify your answer.

5. Why is the use of logical consequences more teacher-centered in terms of control than explicit redirection or Canter's "broken record"?

6. Develop logical consequences, for each of the following misbehaviors:
   a. Student interrupts while teacher is talking to small group of students.
   b. Student steals money from another student's desk.
   c. Student copies a homework assignment from someone else.
   d. Student squirts a water pistol during class.
   e. Student throws spitballs at the blackboard.
   f. Student physically intimidates other students.
   g. Graffiti is found on the restroom wall.

7. List any classroom misbehaviors that do not have logical consequences. What can be done about these misbehaviors using the principles of the consequence model?

8. The use of "You have a choice," the last step in the hierarchy of verbal intervention techniques, is often very effective in obtaining a positive student behavioral change. Why is this technique often successful when previous techniques have not been?

9. List some common teacher verbal interventions that fall under the three types of ineffective verbal communication patterns.

10. Role play the assertive delivery of "You have a choice."

11. When a teacher uses an aggressive response style, what feelings and behaviors are commonly elicited from the student? What effect does an aggressive response style have on overall teacher effectiveness in both the academic and management domains?

12. When a teacher uses an assertive response style, what feelings and behaviors are commonly elicited from the student? What effect does an assertive response style have on overall teacher effectiveness in both the academic and management domains?

9

Classroom Interventions for Chronic Problems

> **The Basics**

> **Nature of the Discipline Problem**

> **Understanding Why Children Misbehave**

> **Philosophical Approaches to Classroom Management**

> **The Professional Teacher**

> **Structuring the Environment**

> **Managing Common Misbehavior Problems: Nonverbal Interventions**

> **Managing Common Misbehavior Problems: Verbal Interventions and Use of Logical Consequences**

> **Managing and Solving Chronic Behavior Problems in the Classroom**
> **Long-Term Problem-Solving Strategies**
> Relationship Building • Breaking the Cycle of Discouragement
> **Management Techniques**
> Self-Monitoring • Anecdotal Record Keeping • Behavior Contracting

Principles of Classroom Management

1. When dealing with students who pose chronic behavior problems, teachers should employ strategies to resolve the problems within the classroom before seeking outside assistance.

2. Finding positive qualities in students who have chronic behavior problems and building positive relationships with them increase the possibility that the problems can be resolved within the classroom.

3. Breaking the cycle of discouragement in which most students with chronic behavior problems are trapped increases the likelihood that the problems can be resolved within the classroom.

4. When teachers conduct private conferences and use effective communication skills with students who have chronic behavior problems, the likelihood that the problems can be resolved within the classroom increases.

5. Interventions that require students to recognize their inappropriate behavior and its impact on others increase the likelihood that the problems can be resolved within the classroom.

6. Interventions that require students with chronic behavior problems to be accountable for trying to control their behavior on a daily basis increase the likelihood that the problems can be resolved within the classroom.

7. Interventions that call for gradual but consistent improvement in behavior increase the likelihood that chronic problems can be resolved within the classroom.

Introduction

While research, as well as our own experience, indicates that the overwhelming majority of discipline problems (somewhere in the neighborhood of 97 percent) can be either prevented or redirected to positive behavior by the use of a preplanned hierarchy of nonverbal and verbal interventions (Shrigley, 1980), there are some students who pose classroom discipline problems of a more chronic nature. These students misbehave even after all preventive and intervention, verbal and nonverbal, techniques have been appropriately employed. They disrupt learning, interfere with the work of others, challenge teacher authority, and often try to entice others to misbehave on a fairly consistent basis. These are the students who prompt teachers to say, "If I could only get rid of that—Sammy, third period would be a pleasure to teach." "Every time I look at that smirk on Jodi's face, I'd like to wring her little neck." "If that—Greg weren't in this class, I would certainly have a lot more time to spend on helping the other students learn." The student described in Case 9.1 is a good example.

As Mr. Voman discovered when he talked to Ms. Kozin, Jodi had been a constant nuisance for the past month. The book-dropping incident was simply the straw that broke the camel's back. Jodi continually talked during lectures; forgot to bring pencils, books, and paper; refused to complete homework; didn't even attempt quizzes or tests; and reacted rudely whenever Ms. Kozin approached her. Ms. Kozin had tried nonverbal and verbal interventions, time out, detention, and notes to parents. By the time Jodi accidentally dropped her book, Ms. Kozin was totally fed up with her.

CASE 9.1 • *"I Just Dropped My Book"*

Jodi entered Mr. Voman's guidance office hesitatingly, sat down, and looked blankly at Mr. Voman.

MR. VOMAN: "Well, Jodi, What are you doing here?"

JODI: "Ms. Kozin sent me out of class and told me not to ever come back. She told me to come see you."

MR. VOMAN: "Why did she send you out of class?"

JODI: "I don't know. I just dropped my book on the floor accidentally!"

MR. VOMAN: "Now, come on, Jodi. Ms. Kozin wouldn't put you out of class just for that. Come on now. What did you do?"

JODI: "Honest, Mr. Voman, you can ask the other kids. All I did was drop my book."

MR. VOMAN: "Jodi, I'm going to go and talk to Ms. Kozin about this. Wait here until I get back."

JODI: "O.K., Mr. Voman, I'll wait here and you'll see that I'm not lying."

Many, though not all, students like Jodi have problems that extend beyond school. Some have poor home lives with few, if any, positive adult role models. Some have no one who really cares about them or expresses an interest in what they are doing. Some simply view themselves as losers who couldn't succeed in school even if they tried. As a result, they act out their frustrations in class and make life miserable for both their teachers and their peers.

No matter how understandable these students' problems may be, they must learn to control their behavior. If they do not, they are at risk of continued failure and unhappiness. Furthermore, although teachers are always concerned for the future of the disruptive student, they are also responsible for ensuring that misbehavior does not deprive the other students of their right to learn. Thus, chronic misbehavior must not be allowed to continue.

In attempting to deal with chronically disruptive students, classroom teachers often fall into a two-step trap. First, they frequently give in to that natural, fully understandable, human urge to "get even." They scream, punish, and retaliate. When retaliation fails, which it is apt to, because the chronically disruptive student often loves to see the teacher explode, the teacher feels helpless and seeks outside assistance; that is, she turns the student over to somebody else. Often, chronically disruptive students are sent to an administrator or counselor and sentenced to some form of in-school or out-of-school suspension.

Because outside referral removes the disruptive student from the class, the disruptive behavior does cease. However, this is usually a short-term solution because the student soon returns and after a brief period of improvement again disrupts the classroom. The severity and frequency of the misbehavior after a return to the classroom often increase. It has been hypothesized that misbehavior increases because the student views the referral either as a further punishment or as a victory over the teacher. When they view referrals as punishments, many disruptive students retaliate as soon as they return to the classroom. When they view referrals as victories, disruptive students often feel compelled to demonstrate even more forcefully their perceived power over the teacher.

Porter and Brophy (1988), in a research synthesis on effective teaching, strongly recommend dealing with chronic discipline problems within the classroom. "In a study of teachers' strategies for coping with students who presented sustained problems in personal adjustment or behavior, teachers who were identified as most effective in coping with such problems viewed them as something to be corrected rather than merely endured. Furthermore, although they might seek help from school administrators or mental health professionals, such teachers would build personal relationships and work with their problem students, relying on instruction, socialization, cognitive strategy training and other long-term solutions. In contrast, less effective teachers would try to turn over the responsibility to someone else (such as the principal, school social worker, or counselor)" (p. 78).

Contrary to popular belief, chronic behavior problems often can be managed successfully within the confines of the regular classroom and with a minimum of additional effort by the teacher. When they are, the disruptive student, the other students, and the teacher all benefit. The disruptive student learns to control her behavior without loss of instructional time and without developing the negative attitudes that are often evident in students who have been excluded from the classroom. The teacher gains a more tranquil classroom and additional confidence in her ability to handle all types of discipline problems successfully. Finally, the other students in the class are again able to concentrate their attention on the learning tasks before them.

This chapter will present two long-term strategies for solving chronic behavior problems and three specific management techniques that teachers can use to manage chronic behavior problems. The problem-solving strategies and management techniques are used simultaneously in the classroom; that is, as the teacher is managing the chronic misbehavior using the management techniques, she is also seeking ways to solve the long-term problems. The two long-term problem-solving strategies—relationship building and breaking the cycle of discouragement—are described first. This discussion is followed by a section on how to conduct effective private conferences with students. Effective private conferences are an important component of both the long-term problem-solving strategies and the management techniques. The final section introduces three specific management techniques: student self-monitoring, a student-directed management strategy; anecdotal record keeping, a collaborative management strategy; and behavior contracting, a teacher-directed management strategy.

Relationship Building

Without a doubt, the development of a positive relationship between the teacher and the student with a chronic behavior problem is one of the most effective strategies for helping such students. Usually these students do not have positive relationships with their teachers. Indeed, teachers often tend to avoid interaction with such students. This is quite understandable. Students who have chronic behavior problems are often difficult to deal with. They disrupt the carefully planned learning activities of the teacher. They sometimes intimidate other students and prevent their peers from engaging in classroom activities. They frequently challenge the teacher's authority and cause the teacher to doubt her own competence.

These doubts about competence arise from the misconception that the teacher can control a student's behavior. As we have noted continually in this text, the teacher can only influence a student's behavior and can react to that behavior. She cannot control anyone's behavior except her own. If a teacher has the mistaken notion that her job is to control a student's behavior, she will feel that she is not as competent as she should be every time the student acts inappropriately. Thus, one of the first steps a teacher should take in working with students who have chronic behavior problems is to recognize that her role is to help these students learn to control their own behavior. The teacher can only be held accountable for controlling her own behavior in such a way that it increases the likelihood that the students will learn and want to behave appropriately.

To accomplish this, the teacher must disregard any negative feelings she has toward the chronically disruptive student and work at building a positive relationship with that student. Understand that we are not suggesting that the teacher must like the student. This is not always possible. No teacher honestly likes every student whom she has ever encountered. However, a truly professional teacher does not act on or reveal those negative feelings.

Our experience has given us two important insights about working with students who have chronic behavior problems. First, teachers who look for and are able to find some positive qualities, no matter how small or how hidden, in chronically disruptive students are much more successful in helping those students learn to behave appropriately than those who do not. Second, the primary factor that motivated the vast majority of students who were at one time chronically disruptive to turn their behavior around was the development of a close, positive relationship with some caring adult. Case 9.2 illustrates the impact that a caring relationship can have on such an individual.

Of course, building positive relationships with students who have chronic behavior problems is not always an easy task. Many students with chronic behavior problems have a long history of unsuccessful relationships with adults. Because the adults in these relationships have ended up being abusive in one way or another, many of the students actively resist attempts to build positive relationships. Brendtro, Brokenleg, and Van Bockern (1990) suggest that the teacher who works with students with chronic behavior problems should think of the student's natural desire to form attachments with significant others as if it were a piece of masking tape and the significant others were walls. Each time the student begins to form a relationship with an adult, the masking tape sticks to the wall. Each time the relationship ends in a negative or hurtful way, the masking tape is ripped off the wall. This process of attachment and hurt is repeated several times. Eventually, the masking tape stops sticking. In other words, the desire to form attachments and relationships with adults is lost. In

CASE 9.2 • *Darnell*

Darnell, who was born to a single mother in a rundown, crime-ridden neighborhood, was raised by his grandmother, the one kind, caring, and protective figure in his early life. Despite her efforts to shield him, Darnell was exposed to drugs, street violence, and a variety of illegal activity while he was still in elementary school. In middle school, Darnell, who describes himself at that age as full of anger and energy, became involved in petty theft and violent attacks on other adolescents and adults. As a result, he was sent to a juvenile detention facility and, after his release, assigned to Barbara, a juvenile probation officer.

Barbara was a streetwise veteran in her fifties who had worked with many troubled adolescents. As Darnell has said, "She did not take any crap." Barbara insisted that Darnell stop his aggressive behavior. She made it clear to him that she saw him as an intelligent young man who had the potential to be successful if he changed his behavior. Over the six-year period Darnell and Barbara worked together, Darnell changed dramatically.

In Darnell's words, "Barbara taught me how to take my anger and my aggression and turn them into positive forces, first on the basketball court and then later, much later in the classroom." As a result of the close, positive relationship Barbara built, Darnell earned passing grades in school, stayed out of trouble, and became a good enough point guard to earn a scholarship to a small state college. He became a special education teacher and returned to his home to teach, hoping to make a difference in the lives of kids like him.

After returning, he saw the need to change the educational system itself but felt powerless to do so. After a few frustrating years, he left teaching and went on to earn a master's degree in counseling, a Ph.D. in curriculum, and a principal's certificate. Today, Darnell is a middle-school principal in the inner city where he was raised. He lives in the city with his wife and young son and spends his time helping inner city kids turn their energy and anger to useful purposes in much the same way as Barbara helped him.

the eyes of the student, it becomes safer not to build any relationships at all than to risk another relationship that will result in hurt and disappointment.

Thus, teachers who want to build relationships with such students must be persistent, consistent, and predictable in their own behavior toward the student. They must search for positive qualities in the students and work at building the relationship without much initial encouragement or response from the student. As Brendtro, Brokenleg, and Van Bockern note, the desire to build a relationship does not have to spring from a feeling of liking or attraction. The teacher simply has to choose to act toward the student in caring and giving ways. Over time, positive feelings of liking and attraction develop. Notice how Carol, the student teacher in Case 9.3, slowly builds a relationship with Cindy. Although such dramatic results do not always or even typically occur, the efforts can be rewarding.

CASE 9.3 • *Relating to Cindy*

Carol, a student teacher in chemistry, decided to make Cindy "her project." Cindy was an overweight, physically unattractive junior who did not seem to have any friends at all. She spoke to no one, did not participate in class activities, and had failed every test and quiz from September to late January when Carol took over the class.

Every day in the four minutes before class began, Carol walked back to Cindy's desk and tried to chat with her. For two full weeks Carol got absolutely no response, not even eye contact. Cindy completely ignored her. Although upset and disappointed, Carol decided to persist. One day during the third week without a response, Carol noticed Cindy reading the college newspaper during class. Instead of viewing this as a discipline problem, Carol decided to use it as the foundation for a relationship. She had Cindy stay after class and told her that she had seen the

newspaper. She asked if Cindy was interested in newspapers. Cindy replied that she wanted to be a journalist. Carol told Cindy she would be happy to bring her a copy of the college newspaper every day as long as Cindy would read it after class. For the first time Cindy replied, saying, "That would be great."

Everyday for the next ten weeks, Carol drove fifteen minutes out of her way to pick up a newspaper for Cindy. The impact on Cindy was remarkable. She began coming to class early and staying after class each day to speak with Carol. She attended class activities and even participated verbally about once a week or so. Remarkably, she passed every test and quiz from that point until Carol's student teaching experience ended. Given the cumulative nature of the content of chemistry, this academic turnaround astounded Carol, her supervisor (one of the authors), and her cooperating teacher.

Bob Strachota (1996) calls attempts to build positive relationships with students who have chronic behavior problems "getting on their side." He notes that teachers need to view themselves as allies rather than opponents of these students and has suggested several steps to help teachers do so. The first step is "wondering why." Strachota points out that many teachers become so preoccupied with techniques for stopping the misbehavior that they forget to ask such fundamental questions as (1) why is the student behaving in this way? and (2) what purpose does it serve or what need does it fulfill? Strachota's underlying assumption is that behavior is purposeful rather than random and directed at meeting some need even if the goal of the behavior is faulty or mistaken (see Chapter 3). If the teacher can identify the need, it is often possible to substitute a positive behavior that will result in fulfillment of the need.

The second step is to develop a sense of empathy and intimacy with the student. Have you ever found yourself in a situation in which you wanted to stop a behavior but couldn't get control of it? Have you ever yelled at your children using the same words as your parents despite your promise to yourself that would never happen? Have you ever eaten too much or had too much to drink although you vowed that you wouldn't? If you have, then you have a great opportunity to develop a sense of empathy with these students. If you can view yourself and the student in similar terms—wanting to stop a behavior but not being able to—you are much more likely to be able to work successfully with the student.

The third step is to stay alert for cues and behaviors that reveal other aspects of the student's personality. Sometimes teachers become so riveted on the misbehavior that they do not look at other aspects of the student's behavior and personality. Students who pose chronic behavior problems have other aspects to their beings as well, but it takes self-control and persistence to focus on them. When a teacher is controlled and focused enough to see the student's personality and behavior in its entirety, she is often able to find positive and attractive aspects that can be used as a foundation for building a positive relationship.

Strachota's fourth and final step is for the teacher to monitor carefully her own behavior in interacting with the student. Strachota points out, "What's going on for me leaks out in the way I talk. I know what I sound like when I am happy, relaxed, curious, flexible, enthusiastic, etc. I know the difference when I feel tense, short, angry, controlling, hurried, sarcastic, or harsh" (1996, p. 75). Sometimes teachers unintentionally communicate negative feelings toward disruptive and low-achieving students (see Chapter 5). If a teacher listens closely to what she is saying and observes how she is behaving, she can avoid negative messages and instead offer positive, caring ones.

Our experience reinforces Strachota's belief that the teacher's mindset is critical. In most chronic behavior situations, the teacher sees the student as an opponent in the conflict. Teachers who are successful in resolving chronic behavior problems see themselves on the student's side, working together to overcome the problem.

Breaking the Cycle of Discouragement

Many students with chronic behavior problems suffer from low self-esteem and have a low success-to-failure ratio (see Chapters 3 and 10). Their need for a sense of significance or belonging, a sense of competence or mastery, a sense of power or independence, and a sense of virtue or generosity have not been fulfilled. As explained in Chapter 3, when these needs are not fulfilled, individuals take action to fulfill them. Unfortunately, the student with chronic behavior problems often takes actions that are inappropriate and negative. These negative behaviors are met with negative teacher responses, punishments, and consequences that further reduce the student's self-esteem and lead to further misbehavior, negative responses, punishments, and consequences. This cycle of discouragement, which is depicted in Figure 9.1, will continue until a teacher takes action to break it.

Although it is entirely appropriate for these students to receive negative messages about their inappropriate behavior and to experience the negative consequences of such actions, if that is all that occurs, the cycle of discouragement is simply reinforced. Suppose after reading this chapter, you walked into your kitchen and saw

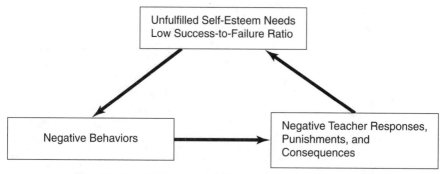

FIGURE 9.1 *The Cycle of Discouragement*

water pouring from underneath your kitchen sink. What would you do? While you might prefer to close the kitchen door, pretend you never saw it, and go golfing, that would not be the appropriate adult response. The appropriate response would be to shut off the water and then fix the leak. Shutting off the water is like applying punishment or consequences. It stops the water (the inappropriate behavior), but it does not fix the leak (the unfulfilled self-esteem needs). While it is necessary to stop the misbehavior, the teacher must also find ways to meet those unfulfilled needs and break the cycle of discouragement.

Just as there are students who are caught in the cycle of discouragement, there are students who are caught in the cycle of encouragement. These students have a high success-to-failure ratio and are having their needs for feelings of significance, competence, power, and virtue met. As a result, they behave in positive and caring ways toward teachers and peers. These positive behaviors are reciprocated, and students are given the message that they are attractive, competent and virtuous, resulting in the cycle of encouragement depicted in Figure 9.2. We believe that the appropriate way to solve chronic behavior problems is to break the cycle of discouragement by stopping the inappropriate behavior through management techniques *and,* at the same time, engaging in behaviors that will help to meet the student's needs for feelings of significance, competence, power, and virtue. Together, these two actions result in the disruption of the cycle of discouragement as shown in Figure 9.3.

To accomplish this, teachers who are dealing with students with chronic behavior problems should ask themselves four questions:

1. What can I do to help meet this student's need for significance or belonging?
2. What can I do to help meet this student's need for competence or mastery?
3. What can I do to help meet this student's need for power or independence?
4. What can I do to help meet this student's need for virtue or generosity?

Obviously, suggestions that follow are not the only possibilities. We know that teachers will use their own creativity to build upon and enhance these ideas.

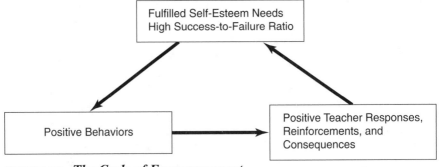

FIGURE 9.2 *The Cycle of Encouragement*

Clearly, behavior on the part of the teacher that aims to build a positive student-teacher relationship is one powerful tool for meeting a student's need for significance. The previous section of this chapter has provided a variety of guidelines and suggestions for building such relationships. Cooperative learning strategies (see Chapters 5 and 6) and other forms of group work help to meet the student's need for feelings of

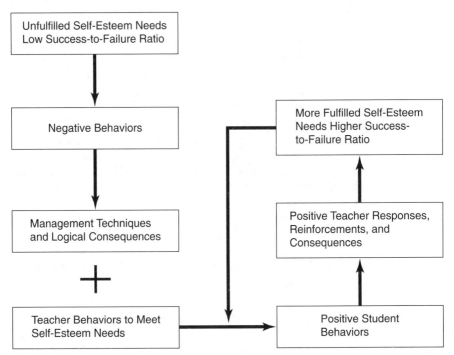

FIGURE 9.3 *Disrupting the Cycle of Discouragement*

belonging. Student teams that work together productively over time also can help the student to develop a sense of group identity and belonging. Often students who are chronically disruptive are not well liked by their peers. Thus, putting them in a student-selected group does not usually work and may result in the disruption of the group. The likelihood of positive group interaction can be increased greatly by the teacher's careful selection of the appropriate group for the student. Typically the optimum group includes students who are good at controlling their own behavior, are sensitive to the needs of others, and can tolerate some initial conflict. It is also helpful if the teacher uses cooperative learning activities to teach students productive social skills (see Chapter 6).

At the elementary level, it is sometimes effective to place the student with chronic behavior problems in a responsible role, for example, message carrier. This often enhances the student's sense of belonging. In middle school and high school finding clubs, intramurals, or other extracurricular activities or out-of-school activities (sometimes a job) in which the student has some interest and talent and then supporting the student's participation in this activity helps to enhance the student's sense of belonging. At all levels, the teacher should make it a point to give the student attention and positive feedback when she engages in appropriate behavior.

The need for a sense of competence can be met by the use of encouragement as described in Chapter 3. Often students with chronic behavior problems and their parents receive only negative messages. Showing an interest in those things that the student values and making sure that you, as the teacher, recognize those strengths will help to increase the student's sense of competence. Sometimes setting short-term goals with the student and then helping the student to keep track of his progress in meeting the goals helps the student to feel more competent.

At all times, feedback to the student with chronic behavior problems should emphasize what the student can do as opposed to what the student cannot do. Suppose, for example, that a student with chronic behavior problems takes a valid test of the material the student was supposed to learn, makes a concerted effort to do well, and receives a 67 on the test. In most classrooms, the only message that the student would receive, would be one of failure, which would reinforce the student's own feelings of incompetence. If we examine the situation more objectively, however, we can see that the student knows twice as much as she does not know. This does not mean that 67 is good or acceptable, but rather than communicating that the student is a failure, the teacher can point out that the student has indeed learned and then use that limited success to encourage the student to continue to make the effort to learn. Using encouraging communication, engaging the student in short-term goal setting, stressing effort and improvement, and focusing on the positive aspects of the student's behavior and performance can increase the student's sense of competence.

A student's need for a sense of power revolves around the need to feel that she is not simply a pawn on a chess board. We all need to feel that we have control over the important aspects of our lives. When students are deprived of the opportunity to be self-directing and to make responsible choices, they often become bullies or totally dependent on others, unable to control their own lives. A teacher can enhance the student's sense of power by providing opportunities to make choices and by allowing the student to experience the consequences of those choices. As noted in Chapter 4, there is a wide range of classroom decisions in which, depending on the teacher's philosophy, the student can have a voice. When students are deprived of the opportunity to make choices, especially students with chronic behavior problems, they often become resentful and challenging of the teacher's authority. It is very important for the teacher not to engage in power contests with these students. Thus the best course of action for the teacher is to find appropriate opportunities for these students to make responsible choices.

The need for a sense of virtue or generosity revolves around the need to feel that we are givers as well as takers. When we have a fulfilled sense of virtue, we realize that we are able to give to and nurture others. Elementary teachers often use "book buddies" and cross-grade tutoring opportunities to develop a sense of virtue among their students. Many secondary students have their sense of virtue fulfilled by participating in food drives, marathons and walkathons for charities, and other types of community service projects. Some of the most successful rehabilitation programs for juvenile offenders engage these adolescents in activities that are beneficial to others in the community (Brendtro, Brokenleg, and Van Bockern, 1990). Although it is sometimes difficult to arrange classroom activities that tap into the need for a sense of virtue, peer tutoring and other opportunities to share talents can enhance a student's sense of virtue or generosity.

Before turning to techniques for managing chronic behavior problems, it should be emphasized that relationship building and breaking the cycle of discouragement require commitment, persistence, patience, and self-control on the part of the teacher. These strategies will not turn things around over night. Sometimes they do not result in any tangible benefits for several weeks or months. Persisting with them and ignoring the natural desire to get even or give up constitute the ultimate in professional behavior. It is extremely hard to do, but it is often the only thing that makes a real difference to students with chronic behavior problems in the long run.

Private Conferences

Holding private conferences with students who have chronic behavior problems is the *sine qua non* of the strategies that are intended to manage or solve these behavior problems. Until the teacher takes the time to sit down with the student to discuss the student's behavior and to attempt to find ways to help the student behave in more productive ways, the teacher has not begun to attempt to manage or solve the problem. A private conference or a series of conferences with the student accomplishes several important tasks. First, it makes sure that the student is aware that her behavior is a problem that must be dealt with. Second, sometimes it is one of the basic steps toward building a positive relationship with the student. Thus, it can be an important step toward helping the student to take ownership of the behavior and find ways to bring it under control.

Receiving Skills

During private conferences, the teacher needs to be aware of the student's perception of the problem and point of view in order to be sure that the intervention focuses on the actual problem. Suppose, for example, the student's chronic misbehavior is motivated by the student's belief that she doesn't have the ability to do the assigned work. Solutions that ignore the student's underlying feeling of incompetence are not likely to be successful in the long run. Therefore, it is important to be sure you receive the message that the student is sending. The following receiving skills will help to ensure that you receive the student's message.

1. *Use silence and nonverbal attending cues.* Allow the student sufficient time to express her ideas and feelings and employ nonverbal cues such as eye contact, facial expressions, head nodding, and body posture (for example, leaning toward the student) to show that you are interested in and listening to what she is saying. Most important, make sure these cues are sincere; that is, that you really are listening carefully to the student.

2. *Probe.* Ask relevant and pertinent questions to elicit extended information about a given topic, for clarification of ideas, and for justification of a given idea. Questions such as "Can you tell me more about the problem with Jerry?" "What makes you say that I don't like you?" "I'm not sure I understand what you mean by hitting on you; can you explain what that means?" show that you are listening and want more information.

3. *Check perceptions.* Paraphrase or summarize what the student has said using slightly different words. This acts as a check on whether you have understood the student correctly. This is not a simple verbatim repetition of what the student has said. It is an attempt by the teacher to capture the student's message as accurately as possible in the teacher's words. Usually a perception check ends by giving the student an opportunity to affirm or negate the teacher's perception; for example, "So, as I understand it, you think that I'm picking on you when I give you detention for not completing your homework; is that right?" or "You're saying that you never really wanted to be in the gifted program anyway, and so you don't care whether you are removed from the program. Do I have that right?"

4. *Check feelings.* Feeling checks refer to attempts to reach student emotions through questions and statements. In formulating the questions and statements, use nonverbal cues (for example, facial expression) and paralingual cues (voice volume, rate, and pitch) to go beyond the student's statements and understand the emotions behind the words. For instance, "It sounds as if you are really proud of what you're doing in basketball, aren't you?" or "You look really angry when you talk about being placed in the lower section. Are you angry?"

Sending Skills

Individual conferences not only allow the teacher to be sure she understands the problem from the student's vantage point, but also allow the teacher to be sure the student understands the problem from the teacher's point of view. Using sending skills to communicate the teacher's thoughts and ideas clearly is a first step toward helping the student gain that insight. Ginott (1972) and Jones (1980) offer the following guidelines for sending accurate messages:

1. *Deal in the here and now.* Don't dwell on past problems and situations. Communicate your thoughts about the present situation and the immediate future. Although it is appropriate to talk about the past behavior that has created the need for the private conference, there is nothing to be gained by reciting a litany of past transgressions.

2. *Make eye contact and use congruent nonverbal behaviors.* Avoiding eye contact when confronting a student about misbehavior gives the student the impression that you are uncomfortable about the confrontation. In contrast, maintaining eye contact helps to let the student know that you are confident and comfortable in dealing with problems. Because research indicates that students believe the nonverbal message when verbal and nonverbal behavior are not congruent (Woolfolk and Brooks, 1983), be sure nonverbal cues match the verbal messages. Smiling as you tell the student how disappointed you are in her behavior is clearly inappropriate.

3. *Make statements rather than ask questions.* Asking questions is appropriate for eliciting information from the student. However, when the teacher has specific information or behaviors to discuss, the teacher should lay the specific facts out on the table rather than try to elicit them from the student by playing "guess what's on my mind."

4. *Use "I"—take responsibility for your feelings.* You have a right to your feelings. It can be appropriate to be annoyed at students, and it can be appropriate to be proud of students. Sometimes teachers try to disown their feelings and act as if they were robots. Students must know that teachers are people who have legitimate feelings and that their feelings must be considered in determining the effects of the student's behavior on others.

5. *Be brief.* Get to the point quickly. Let the student know what the problem is as you see it and what you propose to do about it. Once you have done this, stop. Don't belabor the issue with unnecessary lectures and harangues.

6. *Talk directly to the student, not about her.* Even if other people are present, talk to the student rather than to parents or counselors. Use "you" and specifically describe the problem to the student. This behavior sends the student the powerful message that she, not her parents or anyone else, is directly responsible for her own behavior.

7. *Give directions to help the students correct the problem.* Don't stop at identifying the problem behavior. Be specific in setting forth exactly what behaviors must be replaced and in identifying appropriate behaviors to replace them.

8. *Check student understanding of your message.* Once you have communicated clearly what the specific problem is and what steps you suggest for solving it, ask a question to be sure the student has received the message correctly. Often it is a good idea to ask the student to summarize the discussion. If the student's summary indicates that she has missed the message, the teacher has an opportunity to restate or rephrase the main idea in a way that the student can understand.

With these guidelines for effective communication in mind, we can now consider three specific techniques for managing students with chronic behavior problems. There are five assumptions underlying these techniques:

1. The number of students in any one class who should be classified as having chronic behavior problems is small, usually fewer than five. If there are more than five, it is a good indication that the teacher has not done all that could be done to prevent the problems from occurring.
2. The teacher is well prepared for each class, engages the students in interesting learning activities, and employs a variety of effective teaching strategies (see Chapter 5).
3. The expectations for behavior are clearly understood by students and enforced on a consistent basis (see Chapter 6).
4. The teacher manages commonplace disruptions with a preplanned hierarchy of nonverbal and verbal interventions and logical consequences.
5. The teacher attempts to build positive relationships with students who have chronic behavior problems and attempts to break the cycle of discouragement by helping them to meet their self-esteem needs.

The teacher who is not aware of these assumptions may use the management techniques that follow ineffectively or inappropriately in a given situation.

When there are several students who exhibit chronic behavior problems, they usually fall into one of two categories—those who have the greatest potential for improving their behavior quickly and those whose behavior causes the greatest disruption. When there are several students with chronic behavior problems in one class, the teacher may have to choose to work with one category over another. There are pitfalls in either choice. Usually those with the greatest odds for quick improvement are the students with the least severe behavioral problems. Thus, even if the teacher succeeds in helping them, the general level of disruption in the classroom may remain quite high. On the other hand, those students who have the most severe and most disruptive behavior usually require the longest period of time to improve but their improvement tends to have a more dramatic impact on the classroom.

There are no clear guidelines as to which category of students teachers should choose. It is really a matter of personal preference. If the teacher is the type of individual who needs to see results quickly in order to persist, she is probably better off choosing those students with the greatest likelihood for quick improvement. If, however, the more serious behavior is threatening to any individuals, the teacher must begin intervention with those students.

It must be noted that self-monitoring, anecdotal record keeping, or behavior contracting probably will not be effective in managing chronic behavior problems if the five assumptions underlying these techniques have not been met. If these assumptions have been met, then the teacher has done all that she can do to prevent behavior problems from occurring, and the following three management techniques have a reasonably high chance of success.

Management Techniques

Self-Monitoring

Some students who exhibit chronic disruptive behaviors perceive a well-managed private conference as a sign of a teacher's caring and support. Some students leave the conference with a new understanding that their behaviors are interfering with the rights of others and will no longer be tolerated in the classroom. Given the nature and background of chronic behavioral problems, however, most students will need more intensive and frequent intervention techniques. The challenge is to design techniques that are congruent with the belief that students must be given opportunities to learn how to control their own behavior.

Self-monitoring of behavior is a student-directed approach that is often effective with students who are really trying to behave appropriately but seem to need assistance to do so. The technique is usually more appropriate for elementary students who have extremely short attention spans or who are easily distracted by the everyday events of a busy classroom. While self-monitoring can be effective with some older students, the teacher must consider the age appropriateness of the self-monitoring instrument that the student will use.

For self-monitoring to be effective, the instrument must clearly delineate the behaviors to be monitored and must be easy for a student to use. The student must also clearly understand the duration of the self-monitoring and the frequency of behavioral checks. Unfortunately, teachers occasionally design an instrument that is too cumbersome to use or is too time consuming. Thus, using the instrument actually interferes with on-task behavior.

In the beginning, the student may require teacher cues to indicate when it is time to check behavior and record it on the self-monitoring instrument. These cues may be private, nonverbal signals agreed upon by the teacher and the student. In the beginning, it is a good idea for the teacher to co-monitor the student's behavior using the same instrument. When this is done, the teacher and the student can compare their monitoring consistency and discuss the proper use of the instrument as well as the progress that is being made.

The effectiveness of self-monitoring relies heavily on how the use of the instrument is explained to the student. If self-monitoring is presented as a technique that students can use to help themselves with the teacher's assistance, support, and encouragement, the likelihood of improved behavior is high. When teachers have successfully communicated the purpose of the technique and stressed the possible positive outcomes, students have actually thanked them for the opportunity and means to demonstrate on-task behavior. On the other hand, if the intervention is introduced as a form of punishment, the likelihood of positive behavioral change is diminished.

While other examples of more comprehensive self-monitoring instruments may be found in Chapter 6, Figure 9.4 is an example of a simple self-monitoring instrument for a wide range of behaviors. When a teacher uses this instrument, it is imperative that she and the student clearly understand what behaviors are defined as on task, and therefore coded "1," and what behaviors are off task and coded "0." In addi-

Yes = 1							No = 0				
1	2	3	4	5	6	7	8	9	10	11	12

Score = sum of the cells = _____

FIGURE 9.4 *Am I on Task?*

tion, a workable coding period needs to be established so that each block represents a predetermined period of time.

As with any intervention that focuses on the improvement of chronic behavior, progress may be slow. Two steps forward and one step backward may be the best a student can do in the beginning. We must remember that chronic misbehavior does not develop in a day, and it will not be replaced with more appropriate behavior in a day. It is difficult to learn new behaviors to replace behaviors that have become ingrained and habitual. Therefore, the teacher must be patient and focus on improvements. It is usually best to work on one behavior at a time. For example, if a student continually talks to neighbors and calls out, the teacher and student should decide on which behavior to work on first. If the student is successful in managing the selected behavior, experience has shown that subsequent behaviors are more readily corrected.

As behavior improves, the teacher should begin to wean the student from self-monitoring. As a first step, once the teacher is convinced that the student is reliably monitoring her own behavior, the teacher stops co-monitoring and relies solely on the student's report. Next, as behaviors begin to improve, the teacher lengthens the period of time between self-checks. Finally, the teacher removes the student completely from self-monitoring. When this happens, the teacher uses the event to build self-esteem and self-control by making the student aware that she has changed her behavior on her own and should be quite proud of her accomplishments. Any corresponding improvements in academics or peer interactions should also be noted and tied to the student's improved behavior.

Figure 9.5 is a checklist that teachers can use to evaluate the self-monitoring procedures and instruments that they design.

Anecdotal Record Keeping

If the teacher either has tried self-monitoring or has decided not to try this technique because of philosophical objections or the student's refusal to make the required commitments, there is a second option, called anecdotal record keeping, for remediating chronic behavioral problems. This method, which is a collaborative approach to managing classroom behaviors (see Chapter 4), has been used successfully by student teachers and veteran teachers alike to handle a variety of chronic discipline problems at a variety of grade levels (Levin, Nolan, and Hoffman, 1985). It is based on the principles of Adlerian psychology, which state that changes in behavior can be facilitated

FIGURE 9.5   *Self-Monitoring Checklist*

1.	Do the teacher and student clearly understand and agree on the behaviors to be monitored?	____ Yes	____No
2	Is the time period for self-checks clearly specified?	____ Yes	____No
3.	Does the student understand how to use the instrument?	____ Yes	____No
4.	Have the teacher and student agreed on a meeting time to discuss the self-monitoring?	____ Yes	____No
5.	Is the instrument designed so that small increments of improved behavior will be noted?	____ Yes	____No
6.	Is the instrument designed to focus on one behavior?	____ Yes	____No

by making people aware of their behavior and its consequences for themselves and others (Sweeney, 1981).

Anecdotal record keeping is usually most appropriate for middle and secondary students because students at these levels have better developed self-regulation. To employ the technique, the teacher merely records the classroom behavior, both positive and negative, of a chronically disruptive student over a period of a few weeks. Although it is preferable to have the student's cooperation, anecdotal record keeping can be employed without it.

The record the teacher has made of the student's behavior and the measures that have been taken to improve that behavior form the basis for a private conference with the student. There are nine guidelines that should be followed in conducting this initial conference:

1. The teacher should begin on a positive note.
2. The teacher should help the student to recognize the past behavior and its negative impact, showing the student the record of past behaviors and discussing it if necessary.
3. The teacher should explain that this behavior is unacceptable and must change.
4. The teacher should tell the student that she will keep a record of the student's positive and negative behavior on a daily basis and that the student will be required to sign the record at the end of class each day.
5. The teacher should record the student's home phone number on the top of the record and indicate that she will contact the parents to inform them of continued unacceptable behavior. (This option may not be useful for senior high students because parents are often not as influential at this age.)
6. The teacher should be positive and emphasize expectations of improvement.
7. The conference should be recorded on the anecdotal record.
8. A verbal commitment for improved behavior from the student should be sought. This commitment, or the refusal to give it, should be noted on the anecdotal record.

9. The student should sign the anecdotal record at the end of the conference. If the student refuses to sign, the refusal should be recorded.

After the initial conference, the teacher continues the anecdotal record, each day highlighting positive behaviors, documenting negative behaviors, and noting any corrective measures taken. Keeping this systematic record enables the teacher to focus on the behavior (the deed) rather than on the student (the doer) (Ginott, 1972). The teacher reinforces the student for improved behaviors and, if possible, clarifies the connection between improved behaviors and academic achievement. Thus, the teacher "catches the student being good" (Canter, 1989; Jones, 1980) and demonstrates the concept of encouragement (Dreikurs, Grundwald, and Pepper, 1998). To illustrate the concept of student accountability, the teacher must be consistent in recording behaviors, sharing the record with the student, and obtaining the student's signature on a daily basis (Brophy, 1988). If the student refuses to sign the record on any day, the teacher simply records this fact on the record. Figure 9.6 is the anecdotal record used with one tenth-grade student over a three-week period. The technique succeeded after the management hierarchy had been utilized with little improvement in the student's behavior. Note that the teacher highlighted positive behaviors to "catch the student being good."

While teachers may think that this technique will consume a lot of instructional time, it does not. If the documentation occurs in the last few minutes of class, perhaps when students are doing homework or getting ready for the next class, the two or three minutes required for it compare favorably to the enormous amount of time wasted by unresolved chronic discipline problems. Thus, this technique actually helps to conserve time by making more efficient use of classroom time.

In studying the use of anecdotal record keeping, Levin, Nolan, and Hoffman (1985) requested teachers to log their views on the effectiveness of the procedure. Here are three representative logs by secondary teachers.

Teacher's Log—Eleventh-Grade English

About a week and a half ago, I implemented the anecdotal record in one of my classes. Two male students were the subjects. The improvement shown by one of these students is very impressive.

On the first day that I held a conference with the student, I explained the procedure, showed him my records for the day, and asked for his signature. He scribbled his name and looked at me as if to say, "What a joke." On the second day, his behavior in class was negative again. This time, when I spoke to him and told him that one more day of disruptive behavior would result in a phone call to his parents, he looked at me as if to say, "This joke isn't so funny anymore." From that moment on, there was a marked improvement in his behavior. He was quiet and attentive in class. After class, he would come up to me and ask me where he was supposed to sign his name for the day. And he "beamed" from my remarks about how well behaved he was that day. Only one time after that did I have to speak to him for negative behavior. I caught him throwing a piece of paper. As soon as he saw me looking at him, he said, "Are you going to write that down in your report?" Then, after class, he came up to me with a worried expression on his face and asked, "Are you going to call my parents?" I didn't because of the previous days of model behavior.

FIGURE 9.6 *Anecdotal Record*

Student's Name _____

Home Phone _____

Date	Student Behavior	Teacher Action	Student Signature
4/14	Talking with Van Out of seat 3 times Refused to answer question	Verbal reprimand Told her to get back Went on	
4/16	Had private conference Rhonda agreed to improve	Explained anecdotal record Was supportive	
4/17	Stayed on task in lab	Positive feedback	
4/20	Late for class Worked quietly	Verbal reminder Positive feedback	
4/21	Worked quietly Wrestling with Jill	Positive feedback Verbal reprimand	
4/22	No disruptions Volunteered to answer	Positive feedback Called on her 3 times	
4/23	Late for class Left without signing	Detention after school Recorded it on record	
4/24	Missed detention	Two days' detention	
4/27	Stayed on task all class	Positive feedback	
4/28	Listened attentively to film	Positive feedback	
4/29	Worked at assignment well	Positive feedback	
4/30	Participated in class No disruptions Left without signing	Called on her twice Positive feedback Recorded it	
5/1	Conference to discontinue anecdotal records		

I must say that I was skeptical about beginning this type of record on the students. It seemed like such a lengthy and time-consuming process. But I'll say what I'm feeling now. If the anecdotal record can give positive results more times than not, I'll keep on using it. If you can get one student under control, who is to say you can't get five or ten students under control? It truly is a worthwhile procedure to consider.

Teacher's Log—Tenth-Grade Science

Day 1
As a third or fourth alternative, I used an anecdotal record to help control the discipline problems incurred [*sic*] in my second-period class. Previously, I had used direct requests or statements (for example, "What are you doing? What should you be doing?" "Your talking is interfering with other students' right to learn," etcetera). The anecdotal record involved having one-to-one conferences with the four students. The conferences were aimed at reviewing the students' classroom behaviors and securing commitments from them for improved behavior. It was fairly successful, as I received a commitment from the four involved; and they, in turn, let the rest of the class in on the deal. In choosing the four students, I tried to pick a student from each trouble pair. Hopefully, this will eliminate misbehavior for both.

Day 2
The progress in my class with the anecdotal records was excellent today, as I expected. The four students were exceptionally well behaved. I will be sure to keep extra-close tabs on their progress the next few days to prevent them from reverting back [*sic*] to old ways.

Day 3
My second-period class was again very well behaved. I did, however, need to put a few negative remarks (for example, talking during film) on the anecdotal records. I will continue to keep close tabs on the situation.

Day 4
My second-period class (anecdotal records) is quickly becoming one of my best. We are covering more material, getting more class participation, and having less extraneous talking. I did need to make a couple of negative remarks on the record; but on seeing them, the students should, hopefully, maintain a positive attitude and appropriate behavior.

Teacher's Log—Eighth-Grade Science

Day 1
I discovered a method with which to deal with some major discipline problems in one of my classes. It uses an anecdotal record, which is a record of student actions and student behaviors. I think it will probably work because it holds the student accountable for her behaviors. If something must be done, the student has nobody to blame but herself.

Day 2
Today, I set up private conferences with anecdotal record students. I wonder if they'll show up—and if they do, how will they respond?

Day 3

Two students (of three) showed up for their anecdotal record conferences. The third is absent. Both students were very cooperative and made a commitment to better behavior. One student even made the comment that she thought this idea was a good one for her. The way things look, this will work out fairly well. We'll see . . .

Day 8

One of the students on anecdotal record has improved in behavior so much that I informed her that if her good behavior kept improving, I'd take her off the record next Wednesday. I think it will be interesting to see how her behavior will be; will it keep improving or will it backtrack again?

Implementing any new strategy may be difficult, and anecdotal record keeping is no exception. The teacher must expect that some students will be quite hostile when the procedure is introduced. Some may adamantly refuse to sign the record; others may scribble an unrecognizable signature. The teacher must remain calm and positive and simply record these behaviors. This action communicates to the student that she is solely responsible for her behavior and that the teacher is only an impartial recorder of the behavior. Student behavior will usually improve, given time. Since improved behavior becomes a part of the record, the anecdotal record reinforces the improvement and becomes the basis for a cycle of improvement.

When the student's behavior has improved to an acceptable level, the teacher informs that it will no longer be necessary to keep the anecdotal record because of the improvement in her behavior. It is important, as suggested earlier, to connect the improved behavior to academic success and improved grades if possible. It must also be made clear to the student that her fine behavior is expected to continue. Because continued attention is a key link in the chain of behaviors that turn disruptive students into students who behave appropriately, the teacher must continue to give the student attention when she behaves appropriately. If the student's behavior shows no improvement, it may be time to discontinue the process.

It can be quite difficult to decide when to stop recording behavior. There are no hard-and-fast rules, but there are some helpful guidelines. If the student has displayed acceptable behavior for a few days to a week, the record may be discontinued. If the student's behavior remains disruptive continuously for a week, the record keeping should be discontinued and the student told why. If the misbehavior is somewhat reduced, it may be advisable to have a second conference with the student to determine whether to continue record keeping.

Behavior Contracting

The third technique is behavior contracting. Behavior contracting is a teacher-directed strategy (see Chapter 4). This technique is grounded in the principles of operant conditioning, which state that a behavior that is reinforced is likely to be repeated and that a behavior that is not reinforced will disappear.

This technique involves the use of a a written agreement, known as a behavior contract, between the teacher and student that commits the student to behave appropriately and offers a specified reward when the commitment is met. The contract details the expected behavior, a time period during which this behavior must be exhibited, and the reward that will be provided. The purposes of the contract are to manage behavior that is not managed by normal classroom procedures, to encourage self-discipline, and to foster the student's sense of commitment to appropriate classroom behavior. Although behavior contracting can be used with students at any grade level, it often is more appropriate and effective with elementary and middle school students since older students often resent the obvious attempt to manipulate their behavior. This technique is frequently and effectively used in special education classes.

Because an integral part of behavior contracting is the use of rewards, often extrinsic, concrete rewards, some teachers may be philosophically opposed to the technique. These teachers often overcome their philosophical objections by replacing concrete, extrinsic rewards with those more focused on learning activities, such as additional computer time, library passes, or assignment of special classroom duties and responsibilities. Teachers who feel that students should not be rewarded for behavior that is normally expected should keep in mind the fact that this technique has been shown to be effective and is one of the last possible strategies that can be used within the classroom. However, if there are strong philosophical objections to the technique, the teacher should not use it because the likelihood of its successful use is diminished if its philosophical underpinnings are in contradiction to the teacher's (see Chapter 4).

Teachers who decide to use behavior contracting should remember that it is unlikely that one contract will turn a chronically disruptive student into the epitome of model behavior. Usually the teacher must use a series of short-term behavior contracts that result in steady, gradual improvement in the student's behavior. A series of short-term behavior contracts allow the student to see the behavior changes as manageable and to receive small rewards after short intervals of improvement. In other words, a series of contracts provides the student with the opportunity to be successful. Manageable changes in behavior, shorter time intervals, and frequent opportunities for success make it more likely that the student will remain motivated.

In designing the series of contracts, the teacher should keep three principles in mind. First, design the contracts to require specific, gradual improvements in behavior. For example, if a student normally disrupts learning six times a period, set the initial goal at four disruptions or fewer per day. Over time increase the goal until it is set at zero disruptions per day. Second, gradually lengthen the time period during which the contract must be observed in order to gain the reward. For instance, the set time is one day for the first contract, a few days for the second contract, a week for the third contract, and so on. Third, move little by little from more tangible, extrinsic rewards to less tangible, more intrinsic rewards. Thus, a pencil or other supplies are the rewards under the first few contracts, and free time for pleasure reading is the reward under a later contract. Using these three principles takes advantage of a behavior modification technique called behavior shaping and gradually shifts management over the student's behavior from the teacher to the student, where it rightfully belongs.

Before writing the contract, the teacher should make a record of the student's past misbehaviors and the techniques that were used to try to ameliorate these misbehaviors. The teacher should use all available evidence, including documents and personal recollections, and try to be as accurate and neutral as possible. This record will help the teacher to decide which specific behaviors must be changed and how much change seems manageable for the student at one time. It also ensures that all appropriate management techniques have been used before the implementation of the behavior contract process. Once the record is compiled, the teacher holds a private conference with the student. It is best to begin the conference on a positive note. The teacher should communicate to the student that she has the potential to do well and to succeed if she can learn to behave appropriately. In doing this, the teacher is employing the concept of encouragement (Dreikurs, Grundwald, and Pepper, 1998). The teacher should then attempt to get the student to acknowledge that her behavior has been inappropriate and to recognize its negative impact on everyone in the classroom. Stressing the effect of the student's behavior on others promotes the development of higher moral reasoning (Tanner, 1978). To help the student recognize that her behavior has been unacceptable, the teacher may want to use questions similar to these: "What have you been doing in class?" "How is that affecting your chances of success?" "How would you like it if other students treated you like that?" "How would you like it if you were in a class you really liked but never got a chance to learn because other students were always causing trouble?" Thereafter, the teacher should tell the student that her behavior, no matter what the explanation for it, is unacceptable and must change. This is followed by a statement such as "I'd like to work out a plan with you that will help you to behave more appropriately in class."

The teacher must clearly state how the plan works. Because a contract is an agreement between two people, if the student refuses to make a commitment to the contract, the technique cannot be used. If, however, the student commits herself to improvements in classroom behavior for a specified period of time some positive consequences or rewards result. The reward may be free time for activities of special interest; a letter, note, or phone call to parents describing the improvements in behavior; or supplies, such as posters, pencils, and stickers, from the school bookstore. The most important consideration in deciding what particular reward to use is whether or not it is perceived as motivating by the student. For that reason, it is often a good idea to allow the student to suggest possible rewards or to discuss rewards with the student. If the student's parents are cooperative, it is sometimes possible to ask them to provide a reward at home that is meaningful to the student. At this point, the teacher should draw up the contract, setting forth the specific improvements in behavior, the time period, and the reward. The contract should then be signed by both the teacher and student and each should receive a copy. In the case of young students, it is often a good idea to send a copy of the contract home to parents as well. The conference should end as it began, on a positive note. The teacher, for example, might tell the student that she is looking forward to positive changes in the student's behavior.

Figure 9.7 is an example of a behavior contract and a behavior contract checklist that may be used by teachers to evaluate the quality of contracts that they draw up. The

FIGURE 9.7 *Third Contract between Jessica and Ms. Jones*

1. *Expected Behavior*
   Jessica remains in her seat for the first 30 minutes of each social studies period.

2. *Time Period*
   Monday, February 27, to Friday, March 3.

3. *Reward*
   If Jessica remains in her seat for the first 30 minutes of each social studies period,

   a. she can choose the class's outdoor game on Friday afternoon, March 3.

   b. Ms. Jones will telephone her parents to tell them of the improvement in Jessica's behavior on Friday afternoon, March 3.

4. *Evaluation*

   a. After each social studies period, Ms. Jones records whether Jessica did or did not get out of her seat during the first 30 minutes.

   b. Jessica and Ms. Jones will meet on Friday, March 3, at 12:30 PM to determine whether the contract has been performed and write next week's fourth contract.

   Student _____

   Teacher _____

   Date _____

Behavior Contract Checklist

1. Is the expected behavior described specifically? _____ Yes _____No

2. Is the time period specified clearly? _____ Yes _____No

3. Has the reward been specified clearly? _____ Yes _____No

4. Is the reward motivating to the student? _____ Yes _____No

5. Is the evaluation procedure specified? _____ Yes _____No

6. Has a date been set to meet to review the contract? _____ Yes _____No

7. Has the student understood, agreed to, and signed the contract? _____ Yes _____No

8. Has the teacher signed the contract? _____ Yes _____No

9. Do both the teacher and student have copies? _____ Yes _____No

10. Did the student's parents get a copy of the contract? _____ Yes _____No

---

sample contract was the third in a series between Jessica and her fifth-grade teacher, Ms. Jones. Before the behavior contract intervention, Jessica spent the vast majority of each day's 40-minute social studies period wandering around the room. The first two contracts resulted in her being able to remain seated for about half the period.

Once the contract is made, the teacher should record the behavior of the student each day in regard to the terms specified in the contract. At the end of the contract period, the teacher can use this record to conduct a conference with the student. If the student has kept her commitment, the teacher should provide the reward. If the student's behavior needs further improvement, the teacher can draw up a new contract that specifies increased improvement over a longer time period. If at the end of the contract, the student's behavior has improved sufficiently to conform to final expectations, the teacher can inform the student that a behavior contract is no longer needed. If possible, the teacher should point out to the student the direct relationship between the improved behavior and the student's academic success in the classroom. The teacher also should make clear that she expects acceptable behavior and success to continue. Of course, the teacher must continue to give the student attention after the contract has ended. This consistent attention helps the student to recognize that positive behavior results in positive consequences and usually helps to maintain appropriate behavior over a long period of time.

If at the end of the contract period the student has not kept the commitment, the teacher should accept no excuses. During the conference, the teacher should assume a neutral role, explaining that the reward cannot be given because the student's behavior did not live up to the behavior specified in the contract. The teacher should point out to the student that the lack of reward is simply a logical consequence of the behavior. This helps the student to see the cause-and-effect relationship between behavior and its consequences. If the student learns only this, she has learned an extremely valuable lesson.

At this point, the teacher must decide whether or not it is worth trying a new contract with the student. If the teacher believes that the student tried to live up to the contract, a new contract that calls for a little less drastic improvement or calls for improvement over a slightly shorter time frame may be worthwhile.

If the student has not made a sincere effort to improve, obviously the contracting is not working. It is time to try another option. Nothing has been lost in the attempt except a little bit of time, and the teacher has accumulated additional documentation, which will be helpful if it is necessary to seek outside assistance.

There is one final technique for the teacher to try when these classroom management techniques do not work. This is the exclusion of the student from the classroom until she makes a written commitment to improve her behavior.

Prior to exclusion, the teacher tells the student that she is no longer welcome in the class because of her disruptive behavior, which is interfering with the teacher's right to teach and the students' right to learn. The teacher then tells the student to report to a specified location in the school where appropriate classroom assignments involving reading and writing will be given. The student is also told that she will be held accountable for the completion of all assignments in an acceptable and timely manner, the same as required in the regular classroom. The teacher stresses that the student may return to the classroom at any time by giving a written commitment to improve her behavior. This written commitment must be in the student's own words and must specify the changed behavior that will be evident when the student returns to the classroom. Of course, exclusion presupposes that the administration is supportive of such a technique and has made appropriate arrangements for the setting.

Our experience has shown that those few students who have been excluded from the classroom and have then made the written commitment and returned have remained in the classroom with acceptable behavior. Exclusion finally demonstrates to the student that her behavior will no longer be tolerated and that the entire responsibility for the student's behavior is on the student and only the student.

If a student does not make the written commitment within a reasonable period of time, usually no more than a few days, outside assistance (in the form of parents, counselor, principal, or outside agency) must be sought (see Chapter 10). If it is necessary to seek outside assistance, the teacher's use of self-monitoring, anecdotal record keeping, or behavior contracting will provide the documented evidence needed to make an appropriate referral.

Summary

This chapter has discussed the strategies that can be used in working with students who have chronic behavior problems. Two long-term strategies for resolving chronic problems, building positive relationships, and breaking the cycle of discouragement were described. In addition, three techniques for managing students with chronic behavior problems were introduced: self-monitoring, anecdotal record keeping, and behavior contracting. Of the three techniques, self-monitoring is most compatible with the student-directed philosophy; anecdotal record keeping is most compatible with the collaborative philosophy; and behavioral contracting is most compatible with the teacher-directed philosophy. This chapter also discussed when, how, and with which students to employ these strategies and techniques. The communication skills needed for a private conference, an essential component of any strategy for working with students who have chronic behavior problems, were divided into receiving skills and sending skills. Finally, the technique of exclusion from the classroom, the final step between in-class teacher management and outside referral, was presented.

References

Brendtro, L., Brokenleg, M., and Van Bockern, S. (1990). *Reclaiming Youth at Risk: Our Hope for the Future.* Bloomington, IN: National Educational Services.

Brophy, J. (1988). Educating teachers about managing classrooms and students. *Teaching and Teacher Education, 4,* 1, 1–18.

Canter, L. (1989). Assertive discipline: More than a few names on the board and marbles in a jar. *Phi Delta Kappan, 71,* 1, 57–61.

Dreikurs, R., Grundwald, B. B., and Pepper, F. C. (1998). *Maintaining Sanity in the Classroom: Classroom Management Techniques,* 2nd ed. New York: Harper & Row.

Ginott, H. G. (1972). *Teacher and Child.* New York: Macmillan.

Glasser, W. (1969). *Schools Without Failure.* New York: Harper & Row.

Jones, V. F. (1980). *Adolescents with Behavior Problems.* Boston: Allyn and Bacon.

Levin, J., Nolan, J., and Hoffman, N. (1985). A strategy for the classroom resolution of chronic discipline problems. *National Association of Secondary School Principals Bulletin, 69,* 479, 11–18.

Porter, A. C., and Brophy, J. (1988). Synthesis of research on good teaching: Insights from the work of the IRT. *Educational Leadership, 45,* 8, 74–83.

Shrigley, R. L. (1980). *The Resolution of 523 Classroom Incidents by 54 Classroom Teachers Using the Six Step Intervention Model.* University Park: Pennsylvania State University, College of Education, Division of Curriculum and Instruction.

Strachota, R. (1996). *On Their Side: Helping Children Take Charge of Their Learning.* Greenfield, MA: Northeast Foundation for Children.

Sweeney, T. J. (1981). *Adlerian Counseling: Proven Concepts and Strategies.* Muncie, IN: Accelerated Development.

Tanner, L. N. (1978). *Classroom Discipline for Effective Teaching and Learning.* New York: Holt, Rinehart & Winston.

Woolfolk, A., and Brooks, D. (1983). Nonverbal communication in teaching. In E. W. Gordon (Ed.), *Review of Research in Education, 10.* Washington, DC: American Educational Research Association.

Exercises

1. Think of the teachers you had in school who were most successful in building positive relationships with students. What qualities did these teachers possess? How was their behavior toward students different than the behavior of teachers who were not good at building relationships? What implications do these differences have for building positive relationships with students who have chronic behavior problems?

2. This chapter suggests that teachers should attempt to empathize with students who have chronic behavior problems. Does this mean that disruptive behavior should be excused or condoned?

3. This chapter presents several ideas for breaking the cycle of discouragement by helping to meet students' self-esteem needs. In each of the following four categories of self-esteem needs, suggest additional behaviors that a teacher might use to enhance student self-esteem: (a) the need for significance, (b) the need for competence, (c) the need for power, (d) the need for virtue.

4. Form a triad with two other classmates. Designate a letter (A, B, or C) for each of you. Role play three conferences between a teacher and a chronically disruptive student. In each role play, the individual playing the teacher will create the scenario that has led to the conference. During each conference, the person who plays the role of teacher should practice using effective receiving and sending skills. The process observer will give feedback to the teacher on his or her use of effective communication. Divide the roles for the three conferences according to the following format:

	Person A	Person B	Person C
Conference 1	Teacher	Student	Process observer
Conference 2	Process observer	Teacher	Student
Conference 3	Student	Process observer	Teacher

5. Design a self-monitoring instrument that is appropriate for elementary children and monitors (a) calling out, (b) talking to neighbors, and (c) staying focused on seat work.

6. This chapter classified self-monitoring as a student-directed approach to the management of chronic behavior problems. Do you agree? If so, what makes it a student-directed approach? If not, how should it be classified? If not, is it possible to have a student-directed technique to manage chronic behavior problems?

7. Should chronically disruptive students receive special rewards for behaviors that are typically expected of other students? Justify your answer.

8. Make a list of rewards under the regular classroom teacher's control that could be used in behavior contracts for students at each of the following levels: (a) elementary, (b) middle or junior high, (c) senior high.

9. Develop a list of learning-focused positive consequences that could be substituted for the use of concrete, extrinsic rewards in behavior contracts.

10. Design an initial behavior contract for the following situation: Jonathan, a sixth-grade, middle school student who loves sports, has refused to do homework for the last three weeks, has started fights on three different occasions during the past three weeks, and has disrupted class two or three times each day during the past three weeks.

11. We classify anecdotal record keeping as a collaborative approach to classroom management. Do you agree? If so, what makes it a collaborative approach? If not, how should it be classified?

12. Examine the sample anecdotal record in Figure 9.6. Explain whether you concur with the following decisions made by the teacher: (a) to continue the intervention after 4/23 and 4/24; (b) to stop the record after 4/30. Justify your statements.

13. What types of misbehavior constitute sufficient grounds for exclusion from the classroom? Justify your answers.

10

Seeking Outside Assistance

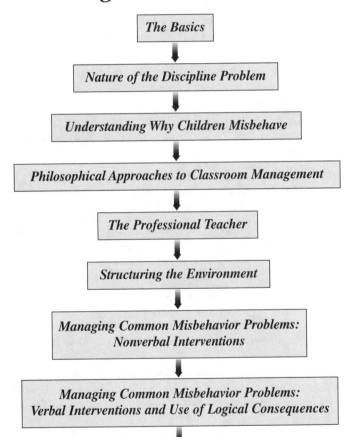

The Basics

Nature of the Discipline Problem

Understanding Why Children Misbehave

Philosophical Approaches to Classroom Management

The Professional Teacher

Structuring the Environment

Managing Common Misbehavior Problems: Nonverbal Interventions

Managing Common Misbehavior Problems: Verbal Interventions and Use of Logical Consequences

Managing and Solving Chronic Behavior Problems in the Classroom

Seeking Outside Assistance
Understanding the Nature of Persisting Misbehavior • Recognizing When Outside Assistance Is Needed • Making Referrals
• Counselors • Administrators • School Psychologists
• Working with Parents • Protecting Students' Rights

Principles of Classroom Management

1. Professional teachers recognize that some chronic misbehavior problems are not responsive to treatment within the classroom or are beyond their expertise and necessitate specialized outside assistance.
2. When outside assistance must be sought to manage a chronic misbehavior problem adequately and appropriately, the use of a multidisciplinary team is the most effective approach.
3. Parental support and cooperation with the school is critical when attempting to manage a student who chronically misbehaves. Careful planning and skilled conferencing techniques are essential in developing a positive home–school working relationship.

Introduction

Even when teachers employ all of the strategies suggested in this text to prevent, manage, and solve discipline problems, there are some students who simply cannot behave appropriately without some type of specialized outside assistance or intervention. These students are a continual source of frustration to the teacher and the other students in the classroom. Indeed, students with unmanageable behavior problems can so overshadow the positive educational climate of the classroom that a teacher can begin to question his professional competence. Thus, it is very important for teachers to acknowledge that there are certain circumstances under which they should and must seek outside support and expertise. In fact, the mark of a skilled professional is to recognize the limits of his expertise and to make the necessary and appropriate consultations and referrals without any sense of professional inadequacy.

Sometimes the first referral the teacher makes is to contact the student's parents. This may be done through written correspondence or a phone conversation. Teachers should make this contact when (1) the misbehavior is a minor surface behavior that continues after the teacher has employed the strategies discussed in this text and (2) the teacher is confident that parental input is all that is needed to assist in managing the misbehavior. The contact should be made only after the student has been given a choice of improving his behavior or having his parents be informed of his behavior. The teacher should point out the primary responsibility for controlling his behavior rests with the student, not his parents. Often this in itself will bring the desired change. If not, parental contact is made and usually results in consequences at home that are enough to motivate a change in school behavior.

At other times the behavior is such that the teacher decides parental contact will not be sufficient to remedy the problem and that he needs outside expertise to understand and cope with the student. In these cases, parental contact comes after consultation with other professional staff members. Consultation ensures that the student's parents will have an adequate description of the problem, an explanation of the intervention strategies attempted, and a comprehensive proposed plan of action.

Whether parental contact is the first step or a later step in seeking outside assistance, it is critical that the contact sets the stage for a cooperative home–school relationship. For this to occur, often it is necessary to overcome negative, defensive parental perceptions and attitudes toward the school and/or the teacher. Thus, any parental contact must be preceded by careful planning and preparation. In addition to the student's parents, the teacher may consult with the school's counselors, administrators, psychologists, learning specialists, and social workers. By doing this, specialized expertise is brought to bear on understanding and working with both the student who is displaying unremitting misbehavior and his family. In some cases referrals outside the school may be necessary.

This chapter discusses the nature of persisting misbehavior, the point at which a teacher needs to seek outside assistance, preparing for and conducting parent conferences, and the roles of other school staff members. The final section details behaviors that may not be disruptive but that teachers must be aware of because they may be symptomatic of other serious problems that require outside referrals.

The Nature of Persisting Misbehavior

Chapter 3, which dealt exclusively with why children misbehave, noted that much of the daily disruptive behavior observed in children is characteristic of the developmental stages that all children go through and a normal reaction to society and recent societal changes. Obviously some children display disruptive behavior more frequently or more deviantly than others, but again, most of this behavior is within the range of normal child and adolescent behavior and usually can be managed through the techniques and strategies suggested in this text. However, there are some students who display behaviors that resist all attempts at modification.

These students often are reacting to negative influences within their environment. These influences may be quite obvious and identifiable, or they may be rather subtle. When a teacher is trying to understand a long-term pattern of misbehavior, environmental influences must be viewed in a summative manner. Long-term behavior is not understood by examining one or two snapshots of specific environmental influences. A history of influences must be considered.

One concept that is especially helpful in understanding historical influences is the success/failure ratio. This is a ratio of the amount of success a student experiences in his daily life to the amount of failure he experiences. Most students exhibit adaptive, productive behavior and feel good about themselves when they are successful. Students who do not meet with a reasonable degree of success become frustrated and discouraged, and their behavior becomes maladaptive and destructive (Glasser, 1969). Although students with chronic behavior difficulties may appear hard and defiant, they are often very damaged and vulnerable. Frequently they are encased in a negative and failure-oriented system of experiences, beliefs, and expectations that are highly resistant to normal classroom influences. These experiences have left them unresponsive to the normal classroom reinforcements intended to increase the success/failure ratio. What are the influences that cause students to have a low success/failure ratio?

Failure in the Classroom Environment

Some students simply are not or cannot find a way to be successful at school in academic, social, and/or extracurricular activities. For these students, school is a daily source of failure that significantly reduces their overall success/failure ratio. Success in school and behavior are so interrelated that it has been concluded that "most misbehaving students do not feel successful in school" (Wolfgang and Glickman, 1980, p. 112).

In some cases, careful observation and evaluation will uncover a learning or behavioral disability. The disability may have gone undiagnosed because it did not become apparent until the child moved toward higher grade levels, where behavioral expectations and the conceptual demands of the curriculum increased. These students are not involved or interested in what they learn. Their misbehavior serves as a protection from further hurt and feelings of inadequacy (Wolfgang and Glickman, 1980). In other cases, students may possess personality traits that cause classmates to pick on or ignore them. The behavioral difficulties that these students display may be understood as an expression of their frustration and discouragement, which many times escalate into the observable behaviors of anger and retaliation. For these students, reward and gratification stem more from their success at focusing attention on themselves than from meeting appropriate behavioral and instructional objectives.

Failure Outside the Classroom Environment

Some students exhibit extreme behaviors that seem to have little to do with the day-to-day realities of the class environment. Extreme apprehension, distrust, disappointment, hurt, anger, or outrage are triggered in them under the most benign circumstances or with the slightest provocation. A teacher may find such a student reacting to him as if he were an abusive or rejecting parent, other adult, or peer.

These distorted emotional responses are reactions that often have been shaped outside the classroom and reflect problems that exist within the home and family or long-standing problems with peers. Some studies have concluded that 50 percent of children who experience behavior problems at school also experience them at home (Johnson, Bolstad, and Lobitz, 1976; Patterson, 1974). Some students with long-standing interpersonal relationship difficulties find the normal social pressures of the classroom too much to tolerate. Just as failure within the classroom lowers a student's perceived success/failure ratio, so does failure outside the classroom.

In some instances, initial failure outside the classroom actually lowers the student's perceived success/failure ratio more than initial failure within the classroom. This occurs because the student's difficulties outside the classroom result in distorted, inappropriate classroom behaviors that cause additional experiences of failure within the classroom.

Failure as a Result of Primary Mode of Conduct

For some students, misbehavior seems to be the natural state of affairs. Their behavior seems to be an expression of their own internal tension, restlessness, and discomfort rather than a reaction to any apparent environmental influence. These students' difficulties emerge during the preschool and kindergarten years. Their teachers view them as immature, emotionally volatile, inattentive, demanding, overly aggressive, and self-centered. They are usually quick to react with anger to any sort of stress or frustration. Unfortunately, their behavior is too often explained simplistically as the natural expression of the "difficult child" temperament. For some, there is a significant improvement with age; for others, the problems intensify as negative reactions to home and school further reduce the success/failure ratio. Many of these children are eventually diagnosed with attention-deficit hyperactivity disorder (ADHD) or oppositional defiant disorder (ODD).

When Outside Assistance Is Needed

How does a teacher decide when to seek outside consultation or referral? Although there are no rules, two general guidelines can assist with the decision. First, referral is warranted when a teacher recognizes that a developing problem is beyond his professional expertise. When a true professional recognizes this, he acts to identify and contact specialized professional assistance. Second, the more deviant, disruptive, or frequent the behavior, the more imperative it is to make referrals. In other words, referral is necessary when

1. a misbehaving student does not improve after the hierarchical interventions described in this text have been exhausted or
2. the hierarchical approach has resulted in improvement, but the student continues to manifest problems that disrupt either teaching or learning.

There are some students who are not discipline problems but show signs that may be symptoms of serious problems that require the attention of professionals with specialized training. Symptoms of social difficulty, illness, anxiety, depression, learning difficulty, abuse, substance abuse, suicide, and family discord become apparent to the knowledgeable and sensitive teacher. A more detailed discussion of these symptoms is included in a later section of this chapter.

The Referral Process

When outside assistance is warranted, the teacher must have access to a network of school support personnel who are trained to cope with children with unremitting problematic classroom behavior. Most often the first referral is to a counselor and/or an administrator (typically a principal in elementary school and an assistant principal at the secondary level). Contact with the counselor and/or the appropriate administrator helps to ensure that parents are not called in before the school has explored all the possible interventions at its disposal. Except for serious problems, parents should be contacted only when it is apparent that the school has no other alternatives (Jones and Jones, 1995).

Parents are apt to be responsive and cooperative if they can see a history of teacher and school interventions. Working closely with the parents of students with chronic behavior problems is so critical that it will be discussed in depth later in this chapter. First, what role does the administrator or counselor play?

The Role of the Counselor

In schools where there is a counselor on the professional staff, the teacher contacts the student's counselor as soon as the decision has been made to seek outside assistance. The teacher should be prepared to present documented data on the student's misbehavior and all approaches the teacher has used in the attempt to manage the disruptive behavior. Anecdotal records and behavior contracts (see Chapter 9) are excellent sources for this information.

In difficult situations, a teacher may become stuck, repetitively applying strategies that do not work. As an outside observer, the counselor is quite useful. He is a neutral onlooker with a fresh view who may be able to suggest modifications in the strategies or techniques the teacher has tried. The counselor may want to explore further the student's behavior, the teacher's style, the nature of the teacher–student interaction, and the learning environment by visiting the classroom or by scheduling further conferences with the student and/or teacher, either alone or together. Once this has been done, the counselor may be able to provide objective feedback and offer suggestions for new approaches and/or work closely with the student to develop more acceptable behaviors.

The counselor also can help to improve the strained teacher–student relationship by assisting the teacher and the student simultaneously. He can offer support to the teacher who must cope with the stress of managing a chronically disruptive child and he can discuss with the student classroom problems that arise from behavior, academics, or social interactions. Because the counselor has a thorough understanding of the viewpoints of both the teacher and student, he is able to act as an intermediary.

Often problems are adequately handled at the counselor level. However, in those cases in which this is not sufficient, additional consultants are called on. Typically they include an administrator, parents, or a school psychologist.

The Role of the Administrator

In many cases of chronic misbehavior, certain in-school strategies or decisions require the authoritative and administrative power of the principal or assistant principal. For example, decisions to remove a student from a classroom for an extended period of time, to change a student's teacher, and to institute in-school or out-of-school suspensions must be approved and supported by an administrator. An administrator's approval often is needed to refer a student to a learning specialist or the school psychologist.

Very deviant behavior may require action at the school district level. In cases of expulsion or recommendations for placement in specialized educational settings outside the school, the administrator will be expected to provide testimony at any hearings that may be held and thus must be thoroughly familiar with the student's history.

The Role of the School Psychologist

If there are indications that a student's problems are rooted in deeper and more pervasive personality disturbances or family problems, the clinical resources of the school psychologist should be sought. The initial role of the school psychologist is one of evaluation and diagnostic study. Although the school psychologist will apply independent observational, interview, and testing techniques, these are really an extension of the day-to-day data that have already been accumulated by the classroom teacher, counselor, and administrator. The results of the school psychologist's evaluative studies may lead to recommendations for further study, specialized programming, or referral to outside resources.

The Consultation Team

Once the counselor, an administrator, and possibly a learning specialist or school psychologist are involved, a consultative team has been created. Although a team approach is not formalized in many schools, it can be quite effective in delineating responsibilities and keeping the lines of communication open and clearly defined. The team approach facilitates group problem solving, offers a multidisciplinary perspective, and reduces the possibility that any one individual will become overburdened with a sense of responsibility for "the problem." As with any team, a leader is needed to coordinate the team's efforts. The counselor may be a good coordinator because he is thoroughly familiar with the student and has quick access to all members of the team.

Recently many school districts have come to realize that teachers cannot be expected to possess the expertise necessary to deal effectively with all the learning and behavior problems found in today's classrooms. To provide support in modifying these problems, school-based consultation teams that follow systematic models of assistance and/or intervention have been implemented. These teams are often referred to as Intervention Assistance Teams, Motivational Resource Teams, and so on. In Pennsylvania, for example, all elementary schools are required to have "Instructional Support Teams." These teams, made up of classroom teachers, instructional support specialists, principals, parents, and others, work together to modify the regular classroom environment to increase student achievement and improve behavior before a student can be referred for testing for possible placement in special education. At the secondary level, there are "Student Assistance Teams" made up of teachers, counselors, principals, and others who provide assistance to students who are having serious difficulties either personally, behaviorally, or academically.

Working with Parents

When it is apparent that the teacher and school have explored all the interventions at their disposal, the student's parents should be contacted. It is essential to have the support and cooperation of parents in working effectively with a chronically misbehaving student. Unfortunately, parental contacts often are characterized by negative reactions and defensiveness on the part of parents and the teacher. It is imperative to minimize negativity and maximize positive support and cooperation. This takes careful planning and a great deal of skill in interpersonal interaction and conferencing techniques on the part of the consultative team members (Canter, 1989).

When Parents Should Be Contacted

Parents should be contacted under the following conditions:

1. When the student displays unremitting misbehavior after the teacher and the school have employed all available interventions.
2. When the consultative team decides that the student needs a change in teacher or schedule.
3. When the consultative team decides that the student should be removed from a class for an extended period of time or from school for even one day.
4. When the consultative team decides that the student needs to be tested for learning, emotional, or physical difficulties.
5. When the consultative team decides that outside specialists such as psychiatrists, physicians, and social workers are required.

The Importance of Working with Parents

When the school has exhausted its alternatives in attempting to manage a chronically misbehaving student, it is essential for the student's parents to be contacted and made members of the consulting team. After all, whether a student is disruptive or not, all parents have the right to be informed of their child's behavioral and academic progress. Furthermore, parental support of the school has a major impact on a child's positive attitude toward school (Jones, 1980). When a student's parents feel good about the teacher and school, the student usually receives encouragement and reinforcement for appropriate school behavior (Jones and Jones, 1995). Thus, parents can be one of the teacher's strongest allies, which is particularly helpful when the student has chronic behavior problems (Brookover and Gigliotti, 1988). Thus, parental support and cooperation must be cultivated by the teacher and other school staff members. To this end, schoolwide programs such as parent visitation, back-to-school nights, parent–teacher organizations, parent advisory boards, and volunteer programs have been instituted. Individual teachers complement these efforts by communicating positive aspects of children's schooling to their parents through notes and phone calls, inviting parents to call when they have any questions, and requiring students to take home graded assignments and tests.

Frequently these children, especially when they are adolescents, are not motivated or responsive to the encouragements a school can provide. Their parents, on the other hand, can provide a wider variety of more attractive encouragements. Indeed, a system of home consequences contingent on school behavior can be an effective means for modifying classroom behavior (Ayllon, Garber, and Pisor, 1975). Such a system is illustrated in Case 10.1. Thus, because with few exceptions, parents care greatly about their children, they represent an interested party that can provide an inexpensive, continuous treatment resource to augment school efforts. The school's positive working relationship with parents often is the most critical component for effectively managing a disruptive student.

CASE 10.1 • *In Order to Drive, You Must Speak Spanish*

Dawn is 15 years old. Her grades have gone from Bs to Ds in Spanish and social studies. The decline in academic performance results from inattentiveness and poor study habits. After the teacher and counselor speak to Dawn without any noticeable improvement, her parents are called.

During a conference, Dawn explains that she doesn't like Spanish or social studies and doesn't see why she needs these subjects anyway. Her teachers try to explain why these subjects are important, especially in today's world, but have little success. Finally her parents intervene and point out to Dawn that she has scheduled driver's education for the spring semester. If she expects to be able to drive, they say, she must demonstrate responsibility and discipline and one way to do so is to do well in all school subjects. They finally give Dawn a choice, either her grades improve or she will not be allowed to take driver's education or obtain her learner's permit.

Her teachers and parents keep in contact, and by the end of the fall semester Dawn's grades are again Bs.

Understanding Parents

For all the positive help parents may be able to offer, many teachers and other school personnel feel uncomfortable contacting them, and many parents harbor negative feelings toward their child's teachers and school. School personnel often complain that parent contacts necessitate using time, usually before or after school, that could be put to better use. Teachers also complain that they often feel intimidated by parents who think that teachers should be able to maintain control of their child without parental help. Also because education is funded by tax dollars, they sometimes appear to believe they should be able to judge and monitor teacher performance. However, as professionals, teachers and other school staff must not allow these feelings to jeopardize the opportunity to gain the support and cooperation of parents.

If parental contacts result in distrust, apprehension, and dissatisfaction for both parents and teachers, efforts to assist the disruptive student probably will fail. In time, the parents' sense of alienation from the school will be passed onto the child, further lessening the possibility of the school working with the parents to find a means to redirect the student toward acceptable behavior. Therefore, the members of the consultative team must create an atmosphere that facilitates a change of negative parental perceptions and assumptions into positive ones. This is more easily accomplished when team members understand the parents' perspectives.

Many children who chronically misbehave in school display similar behaviors at home. Often, their parents have been frustrated by their own failures in managing their child. Since parents consider their children extensions of themselves and products of their parenting, they are not anxious to be reminded of how inadequate they have been. Sometimes there has been a long history of negative feedback from teachers, counselors, and administrators that has created a feeling of powerlessness and humiliation. Because these parents feel everyone is blaming them for their child's misbehavior, they are quite wary of any sort of school contact and react by withdrawing, resisting, or angrily counterattacking and blaming the school for the problems. This does not have to happen. Through careful planning and the use of proper conferencing skills, the school consultative team can gain the needed support and cooperation from parents.

Conducting Parent Conferences

When the consultative team determines that conditions warrant parental involvement, the counselor, who is the coordinator, usually makes the first contact. The tone of this initial contact is extremely important in developing a cooperative working relationship. The counselor should expect some degree of defensiveness on the part of the parent, especially if the student has had a history of school misbehavior. This attitude should be understood and not taken personally. The cause of the school's concern should be stated clearly and honestly. The climate of the conversation should be "How can we work as a team to best meet your child's needs?" rather than "Here we go again!" or "We've done everything we can; now it's up to you."

Once a conference has been scheduled, the team must decide who will attend the conference. Should all the members of the consultative team be in attendance? Should the student be at the conference? The answers depend on the particular problem, the amount of expertise needed to explain the situation and the approaches that have been tried, and who will need to be available to answer any questions that may arise. In addition, it must be kept in mind that the conference must be conducted in a positive manner that is least threatening to the parents. This often means the fewer people present, the less threatening the conference appears to parents. In most circumstances, the initial conference is conducted by the counselor or administrator and the teacher. Unless the problem includes discussing behavior or other signs that indicate serious health, emotional, or legal problems, the student is usually present.

The counselor should begin the conference by introducing all in attendance, thanking the parents for their willingness to attend, and outlining the goal of the conference. Throughout the conference, the counselor ensures that everyone has an equal chance to express his or her viewpoint. The counselor also looks for any signs that indicate that the conference is deteriorating into a debate or blaming session and acts rapidly to defuse the situation by directing the conference back to the major purpose of how best to meet the student's needs.

Obviously appropriate interpersonal and conferencing skills must be familiar to and practiced by all professionals in attendance. Some of these skills are to be friendly, to be supportive, and to use active listening, which includes paraphrasing to ensure proper understanding by all included (see Chapter 9). The teacher should be prepared to have some positive things to say about the student. Information should be elicited through the use of questions rather than directive statements aimed at the student or parents. Neither the child nor the parents should be attacked, disparaged, or blamed. However, sometimes parents and the student attack, disparage, and blame the teacher or other school officials. If this occurs, it is important to remember that one does not defend one's professional competence with words, but with behavior.

One of the best means to demonstrate professional competence is through the use of previously collected data that illustrate and demonstrate the concerns of the school and the need for the conference. The data should include a history of objective and specific information about the student's behaviors and the actions taken by the teacher and the school to manage them. Anecdotal records are an excellent source for this data (see Chapter 9). The use of these data reduces the likelihood of the conference turning into a debate, illustrates that the problem is not exaggerated, and defuses any attempt by the parent to suggest that the school did not take appropriate and necessary actions.

Throughout the conference the parents' and student's feelings, viewpoints, and suggestions should be actively solicited. The outcome of the conference, it is hoped, will be an agreed-upon course of action or the decision that the counselor will contact the parents in the near future with a suggested course of action. The meeting ends on an optimistic note with a summary, a show of appreciation, and an encouraging statement that with both the home and school working as a team, a successful outcome is likely.

With some students, it may be decided to try additional school and/or classroom strategies with little additional parental involvement. This decision is usually a result of new information that allows the school to design additional appropriate strategies

CASE 10.2 • *"Won't Be Much Help"*

Sharon is in eighth grade. Her behavior is perfect. She is of average intelligence, rarely absent, well dressed, and has some friends. She seems like the typical, happy eighth-grader. However, she always asks one of her teachers if she can stay late to help with anything. If there is nothing for her to do, she just sits and talks. As the end of the first report period approaches, it appears that Sharon will receive all Ds and Fs.

Most of her teachers have spoken with her, and she has also been referred to the counselor. Throughout all of these sessions she maintains that she is happy and nothing is wrong. Extra academic help is given but results in no improvement.

Before report cards are issued, a con-ference is scheduled with Sharon, her mother, the counselor, and her teachers. Sharon's mother arrives; she is well dressed, well spoken, and seems somewhat concerned. She listens attentively to each teacher explain Sharon's poor academic performance. When they have finished, she states, "Sharon's dad left five years ago. I'm busy. I need to look after myself and get my life moving in the right direction. I have a career and I date a lot. Truthfully, besides buying her clothes and making sure she eats properly, I haven't much time for Sharon. I would truly appreciate anything you can do to help Sharon because I know I won't be much help. Is there anything else?"

or because the parents, like Sharon's mother in Case 10.2, clearly demonstrate their disinterest. Sharon's mother is atypical, not because she is disinterested but because she openly and honestly admits it. Sometimes when parents are disinterested, there is a tendency on the part of the school personnel to give up and adopt an attitude that "if they don't care, then we've done what we can." However, children should never be denied access to potentially effective school intervention programs because their parents are disinterested, uncooperative, or unsupportive (Walker, 1979).

When it is apparent that parental involvement will probably improve the child's behavior significantly or there is evidence of a deficiency in parenting skills, increased parental involvement will be requested. Many school districts now provide classes or employ parent educators to work with parents of children experiencing behavior problems in school.

Symptoms of Serious Problems

Some students display symptoms of serious problems that may or may not be accompanied by disruptive and/or academic difficulties. These problems may be related to physical or emotional health or associated with an abusive home or with substance abuse. All of these areas may fall outside the expertise and domain of the school. An aware teacher often recognizes these symptoms and notifies the appropriate school official, usually the counselor, who then decides the proper step.

Some of the signs that may be significant include the following:

1. *Changes in physical appearance.* Often students reveal their underlying problems through sudden changes in their physical appearance. Posture, dress, and grooming habits are reflections of underlying mood and self-image, and a student's deterioration in these habits should be noted with concern. More striking changes such as rapid weight loss or gain, particularly in light of the dramatic increase in eating disorders among high-school students, should be investigated. While unusual soreness, bruises, cuts, or scarring are signs of possible neglect or abuse, they may also indicate self-mutilation or other self-destructive tendencies.

2. *Changes in activity level.* Teachers need to be aware of the significance of changes in activity level. Excessive tardiness, lethargy, absenteeism, and a tendency to fall asleep in class may result from a variety of problems, including depression and substance abuse. Hyperactivity, impulsivity, lowered frustration and tolerance levels, and overaggressiveness also may represent the student's effort to deal with emotional unrest and discomfort.

3. *Changes in personality.* Emotional disturbances in children and adolescents are sometimes reflected in very direct forms of expression and behavior. The seemingly well-adjusted child who is suddenly sad, easily agitated, or has angry outbursts not characteristic of his prior behavior should be closely observed and monitored.

4. *Changes in achievement status.* A decline in a student's ability to focus on his work, persist at his studies, or produce or complete work successfully is often an indication of the draining effects of emotional turmoil or significant changes in the home environment.

5. *Changes in health or physical abilities.* Complaints of not being able to see or hear, when it appears the student is paying attention, should be referred to the nurse for followup. Complaints of frequent headaches, stomachaches, dizziness, unhealing sores, skin rashes, and frequent bathroom use lead to concern for the student's health.

6. *Changes in socialization.* Children who spend most of the time by themselves, seem to have no friends, and are socially withdrawn are not often identified as problem students because their symptoms do not have a disturbing impact on the classroom. These students may drift from one grade to another without appropriate attention and concern. However, they often leave a sign of their underlying misery in their behavior, artwork, and creative writing samples.

In most cases of serious problems, schools are able to arrange for or make referrals to a host of specialized professionals, including psychologists, psychiatrists, nutritionists, medical doctors, social workers, and legal authorities. However, appropriate intervention rests with the aware and concerned teacher who must make the initial observations and referral.

Legal Aspects of Seeking Outside Assistance

There are some legal issues that must be considered to protect children's and parents' rights when seeking outside assistance. Most school districts are aware of these laws and have developed appropriate procedures to abide by them.

The Individuals with Disabilities Education Act (IDEA) and Public Law 94-142 require parental consent before conducting any evaluation that might change the educational classification, evaluation, or placement of a child. Evaluation is defined as any selective procedure not used with all children in a school, class, or grade.

The release of student files is regulated by the Buckley Amendment (PL 93-380, as amended by PL 93-568). Briefly, schools may not release a student's records to outside sources without written consent from the parents. This release must state the reasons for the release, the specific records to be released, and who will receive the records.

Many states also have laws that require teachers to report any signs of child abuse. Many of these have provisions that impose fines on school personnel who fail to meet this responsibility.

Students have specific rights in many areas, including freedom of expression, dress and grooming, corporal punishment, and student activities. Unfortunately, many of these rights are infringed upon by certain disciplinary actions taken by teachers and school administrators. These infringements usually go unnoticed or unchallenged. However, "when the infraction is of a very serious nature involving possible suspension or expulsion of the student, the legal rights of the student become of paramount importance" (Melnick and Grosse, 1984, p. 147). School officials must be aware of these rights and ensure that they are protected.

Summary

Some students simply do not experience the degree of success in the classroom that supports the development and maintenance of appropriate behavior. Their conduct problems remain unremitting despite the application of appropriate hierarchical strategies, or they show other signs and symptoms indicative of serious underlying disturbances. In these cases, some type of specialized or out-of-school assistance may be required.

A team approach, which may include the student, parents, teacher, counselor, administrator, and outside specialists, is an effective means for expanded evaluation and for the development of specialized interventions that may extend beyond the normal classroom. The counselor typically plays the crucial role of team coordinator in communicating with and integrating the efforts of parents and in-school and out-of-school consultants. The support and cooperation of parents is critical to increase the likelihood of successful intervention. Any negative parental attitudes must be defused. This is best accomplished through careful planning and the skilled use of conferencing techniques when working with parents. Protecting students' rights throughout any process focused on managing misbehavior is paramount.

References

Ayllon, T., Garber, S., and Pisor, K. (1975). The elimination of discipline problems through a combined school–home motivation system. *Behavior Therapy, 6,* 616–626.

Brookover, W. B., and Gigliotti, R. J. (1988). *Parental Involvement in the Public Schools.* Alexandria, VA: National School Boards Association.

Canter, L. (1989). Assertive discipline—More than names on the board and marbles in a jar. *Phi Delta Kappan, 71,* 1, 57–61.

Glasser, W. (1969). *Schools Without Failure.* New York: Harper & Row.

Johnson, S. M., Bolstad, O. D., and Lobitz, G. K. (1976). Generalization and contrast phenomena in behavior modification with children. In E. J. Marsh, L. A. Hamerlynck, and L. C. Handy (Eds.), *Behavior Modification and Families.* New York: Brunner/Mazell.

Jones, V. F. (1980). *Adolescents with Behavior Problems.* Boston: Allyn and Bacon.

Jones, V. F. and Jones, L. S. (1995). *Comprehensive Classroom Management: Creating Positive Learning Environments for all Students,* 4th ed. Boston: Allyn and Bacon.

Melnick, N., and Grosse, W. J. (1984, summer). Rights of students: A review. *Educational Horizons,* pp. 145–149.

Patterson, G. R. (1974). Intervention for boys with conduct problems: Multiple settings, treatments and criteria. *Journal of Consulting and Clinical Psychology, 42,* 471–481.

Walker, H. M. (1979). *The Acting-Out-Child: Coping with Classroom Disruption.* Boston: Allyn and Bacon.

Wolfgang, G. H., and Glickman, C. D. (1980). *Solving Discipline Problems: Strategies for Classroom Teachers.* Boston: Allyn and Bacon.

Exercises

1. The student's success/failure ratio is an extremely important variable that influences student behavior. There are many areas in which students experience success and failure, including academic, social, and extracurricular areas. List several specific areas in a school setting in which students can experience success or failure.

2. The importance of success in specific areas depends on the student's age. Using the list of specific areas for success developed in question 1, rate each area's importance for students in elementary, middle, junior high, and senior high school.

3. Some students do not experience much academic success. What can a teacher do to provide successful school experiences for them?

4. Develop a list of symptoms that could be added to the list of potentially serious problems that may warrant outside assistance. Be able to justify why each symptom should be included on the list.

5. Are there any dangers associated with using a list similar to the one developed in question 4? Before answering, consider such areas as contextual setting, duration and severity of behavior, and so on. If there are dangers, what can a teacher do to minimize them?

6. Even when students are not exhibiting behavioral problems, it is important for teachers to gain the support of parents. In what ways can teachers develop such support?

7. Sometimes teachers may decide to contact the parents before consulting a student's counselor. When should parents be contacted before the counselor?

8. In consultation with your instructor, contact a school (use your own school if you are presently teaching) and identify all the resources available to assist teachers with seriously misbehaving students.

9. Children with attention deficit hyperactivity disorder and oppositional defiant disorder are in mainstreamed classrooms. Research the behaviors these children exhibit and suggest or research strategies that are effective in managing these children.

10. It has been said that if a teacher is a good teacher for difficult children, he will be an excellent teacher for all the children in his class. Explain what this means.

Appendix

The Discipline Problem Analysis Inventory (DPAI)

The discipline problem analysis inventory is a tool the classroom teacher can use to reflect on inappropriate student behavior and its prevention, causes, and solutions. The inventory presents questions teachers can ask themselves regarding the development of hierarchical management plans or a particular student misbehavior. Part I of the inventory contains questions regarding the prevention of misbehavior. Part II contains questions regarding the resolution of misbehavior.

Part I: Have I Done All I Can to Prevent Misbehavior?

Chapter 1: The Basics

1. Do I consider how my behavior affects student behavior?
2. Am I familiar with the principles of classroom management as presented in this book?
3. Do I employ a professional decision-making approach to classroom management?

Chapter 2: Nature of the Discipline Problem

1. Do the behaviors I am trying to correct constitute discipline problems as defined in the text? Do they interfere with teaching or the rights of others to learn? Are they psychologically or physically unsafe? Do they destroy property?
2. Do my behaviors contribute to any discipline problems?
3. Do my behaviors maximize the time students spend on learning?
4. Do I deal with nondiscipline behavior problems after the rest of the class is involved in the learning activities?

Chapter 3: Understanding Why Children Misbehave

1. Is the misbehavior a result of unmet physiological needs (for example, nourishment, rest, temperature, ventilation, noise, lighting)?

2. Is the misbehavior a result of unmet safety and security needs (for example, fear of other students, teachers, staff members, parents, other adults; insecurity about rules and expectations)?

3. Is the misbehavior a result of unmet needs for belonging and affection?

4. Do I provide opportunities for students to feel significant, competent, powerful, and have a sense of virtue?

5. Is the misbehavior a result of a mismatch between the student's cognitive developmental level and instructional goals, tasks, or methods?

6. Is the misbehavior a result of a mismatch between the student's moral developmental level and my management plan?

7. Is the misbehavior a result of striving to meet the faulty goals of attention, power, revenge, or inadequacy?

8. Am I trying not to personalize students' misbehaviors?

Chapter 4: Philosophical Approaches to Classroom Management

1. Have I analyzed which power bases(s) I employ to manage classroom behavior?

2. Have I asked myself the nine basic questions to analyze which theory of classroom management is consistent with my beliefs about teaching and learning?

3. Do I employ the power base(s) that is consistent with my beliefs about teaching and learning?

4. Are my management behaviors consistent with the power base(s) and theory of management I want to employ?

Chapter 5: The Professional Teacher

1. Do I plan my lessons to include findings from effective teaching research by including:

   An introduction?

   Clearly presenting the content?

   Checking for student understanding?

   Providing for coached and solitary practice?

   Providing for closure and summarization?

   Conducting periodic reviews?

2. Do I increase student motivation to learn by considering student interests, student needs, instruction novelty and variety, student success, student attributions, tension, feeling tone, feedback, and encouragement?

3. Do I communicate high expectations for learning and behavior by equalizing response opportunities, providing prompt and constructive feedback, and treating each student with personal regard?

4. Do I use questioning to involve students actively in the learning process by asking questions at different cognitive levels and using probing questions, wait time, a variety of techniques to elicit response, and a variety of positive reinforcements?

5. Do I maximize both allocated and engaged time in learning?

6. Do I teach for deep understanding, emphasizing topics that are important, at the appropriate developmental level, and related to students' lives and interests outside of school?

7. Do I use the five components of authentic instruction?

8. Do I use all five of the teaching frameworks described in "Dimensions of Learning"?

9. Do I use cooperative learning activities that contain all three essential elements of cooperative learning?

10. Do I teach in ways that allow students to demonstrate their knowledge using all seven types of human intelligence?

11. Do I use personal goal setting and appropriate attributions for student success and failure to increase student motivation and promote positive feelings of self-efficacy?

Chapter 6: Structuring the Environment

1. Do I make my room physically comfortable by considering lighting, ventilation, and noise reduction?

2. Do I design seating arrangements to accommodate the various learning activities?

3. Does the seating arrangement ensure that each student can see the instructional activities, the teacher has close proximity to each student, and seats are not placed in high traffic areas or close to distractions?

4. Do I use my bulletin boards to recognize students and provide students with active participation?

5. Do I develop and teach procedures for everyday routines?

6. Do I analyze the classroom environment to determine the rules needed to protect teaching, learning, safety, and property?

7. Do I clearly communicate the rules and their rationales to students?

8. Do I attempt to obtain student commitments to abide by the rules?

9. Do I teach and evaluate student understanding of the rules?

10. Do I develop and enforce each rule with a natural or logical consequence?

11. Do I consider my students' cultural values, norms, and behavioral expectations in setting classroom rules and guidelines and in interpreting student behavior?

12. Do I use cooperative learning activities and teach social skills to my students in order to create group norms that will promote prosocial behavior and engagement in learning activities?

Part II: Am I Effectively Resolving Misbehavior?

Chapter 7: Managing Common Misbehavior Problems: Nonverbal Interventions

1. Do I meet the six prerequisites to appropriate student behavior?

   Am I well prepared to teach?

   Do I provide clear directions and expectations?

   Do I ensure student understanding of evaluation criteria?

   Do I clearly communicate, rationalize, and consistently enforce behavioral expectations?

   Do I demonstrate enthusiasm and encouragement and model expected behavior?

   Do I establish positive relationships with students?

2. Do I effectively employ proactive coping skills by changing the pace of instructions, removing seductive objects, boosting interest, redirecting behavior through nonpunitive time out, reinforcing appropriate behavior, and providing cues?

3. Do I consider the five intervention guidelines when deciding which coping skill to employ?

   Does the intervention provide students with opportunities for self-control?

   Is the intervention less disruptive than the students' behavior?

   Does the intervention lessen the probability that students will become confrontational?

   Does the intervention protect students and the teacher from physical or psychological harm?

   Does the intervention maximize the number of management alternatives available to the teacher?

4. Do I effectively use the remedial coping skills (planned ignoring, signal interference, proximity interference, and touch interference) in a hierarchical order?

Chapter 8: Managing Common Misbehavior Problems: Verbal Interventions and Use of Logical Consequences

1. Do I follow the guidelines for using verbal interventions?

Do I keep them as private as possible?

Do I make them brief?

Do I speak to the situation, not the person?

Do I set limits on behaviors, not feelings?

Do I avoid sarcasm and belittlement?

2. Do I monitor my verbal interventions for ineffective communication patterns?

3. Do I employ verbal interventions in a hierarchical manner (adjacent reinforcement, calling on student, humor, awareness questioning, direct appeal, "I message," positive phrasing, "are not for's," rule reminders, triplets, explicit redirection, "broken record")?

4. Do I employ natural and/or logical consequences using "You have a choice"?

5. When I use consequences, do I consistently follow through or do I use them as threats?

Chapter 9: Classroom Interventions for Chronic Problems

1. Do I build positive relationships with students who exhibit chronic behavior problems?

2. Do I attempt to disrupt the cycle of discouragement and replace it with a cycle of encouragement?

3. Do I effectively use appropriate receiving skills during private conferences with students?

Do I use nonverbal attending cues?

Do I use probing questions?

Do I check perceptions?

Do I check feelings?

4. Do I effectively use appropriate sending skills during private conferences with students?

Do I deal in the present?

Do I make eye contact?

Do I make statements rather than ask questions?

Do I use "I" to relate my feelings?

Am I brief?

Do I talk directly to the students?

Do I give the student directions on how to correct the problem?

Do I check for understanding?

5. Have I reviewed the self-monitoring checklist to ensure that I have developed and employed an effective self-monitoring technique?

Do teacher and student understand/agree on behaviors?

Is the time period specified?

Does the student understand the instrument's use?

Have the teacher and student agreed on a meeting/discussion time?

Will the instrument facilitate the noting of small increments of progress?

Does the instrument focus on one behavior?

6. Have I reviewed the guidelines for initiating and employing anecdotal record keeping to ensure that I have effectively implemented the procedure?

Am I positive?

Do I help the student recognize the past behavior and its negative impact?

Do I explain that the behavior is unacceptable?

Do I explain the anecdotal record-keeping procedure?

Do I communicate an expectation for improvement?

Do I attempt to obtain the student's commitment for improved behavior?

Do I record the conference and obtain the student's signature?

7. Have I reviewed the behavior contract checklist to ensure that I have effectively developed and employed the behavior contract?

Do I specify the behavior, time period, reward, and evaluation?

Do I provide a motivating reward?

Do I ensure that the student understood, agreed to, and signed the contract?

Do I sign the contract?

Do I, the student, and the student's parents get copies?

8. Do I exclude the student from the classroom and require a written statement of better behavior before allowing the student to return to class?

Chapter 10: Seeking Outside Assistance

1. Do I provide many opportunities for the student to be successful in the classroom?

2. Does the behavior warrant outside consultation?

3. Do I consult with a counselor or an administrator about the chronically misbehaving student?

4. Should parents be contacted?

   Does the student display unremitting misbehavior?

   Has the consultative team decided that the student needs a change of schedule or teacher; should be removed from class or school for a period of time; should be tested for learning, emotional, or physical difficulties; should be referred to outside specialists?

5. Do I employ the behaviors that allow me to work positively with parents and gain their support and cooperation?

6. Does the student show any behaviors or signs that may be symptomatic of other serious problems?

   Has the student undergone changes in physical appearance, activity level, personality, achievement states, health or physical abilities, or socialization?

7. Do I protect student rights?

Index

Numbers followed by the letter *f* indicate figures; numbers followed by the letter *t* indicate tables.